Certificate in Business Accounting

BA1: Fundamentals of Business Economics

For exams from January 2024

Exam Practice Kit

In this edition

- Banks of objective test questions across the whole syllabus
- Answers with detailed feedback
- Advice on exam technique

BPP
LEARNING
MEDIA

Eighth edition 2023

ISBN 9781 0355 0785 6
Previous ISBN 9781 0355 0272 1
eISBN 9781 0355 0817 4

British Library Cataloguing-in-Publication Data
A catalogue record for this book is available from the British Library

Published by

BPP Learning Media Ltd
BPP House, Aldine Place
142-144 Uxbridge Road
London W12 8AA

learningmedia.bpp.com

Printed in the United Kingdom

Your learning materials, published by BPP Learning Media Ltd, are printed on paper obtained from traceable sustainable sources.

AICPA & CIMA
Registered Tuition Provider

BPP
LEARNING
MEDIA

Contents

Question and Answer index

Using your BPP Exam Practice Kit

One of the key criteria for achieving exam success is question practice. There is generally a direct correlation between candidates who study all topics and practise exam questions and those who are successful in their exams. This Kit gives you ample opportunity for such practice throughout your preparations for your OT exam.

All questions in your exam are compulsory and all the component learning outcomes will be examined so you must **study the whole syllabus**. Selective studying will limit the number of questions you can answer and hence reduce your chances of passing.

Practising as many exam-style questions as possible will be the key to passing this exam. You must do questions under **timed conditions** as part of your preparations.

Breadth of question coverage

Questions will cover the whole of the syllabus so you must study all the topics in the syllabus.

The weightings in the table below indicate the approximate proportion of study time you should spend on each topic, and is related to the number of questions per syllabus area in the exam.

BA1: Fundamentals of Business Economics	
Syllabus topics	Weighting
A Macroeconomic and Institutional Context of Business	25%
B Microeconomic and Organisational Context of Business	30%
C Informational Context of Business	20%
D Financial Context of Business	25%

Errata

BPP Learning Media do everything possible to ensure the material is accurate and up to date when sending to print. In the event that any errors are found after the print date, they are uploaded to the following website:

www,bpp,com/learningmedia/Errata

The Exam

The exam is a computer based assessment, which is available on demand at assessment centres all year round.

The exams at Certificate Level can be taken in any order, but candidates must pass or be exempt from them all before they can move on to the Operational Level.

Each exam lasts for two hours and will contain 60 questions.

The exam will be made up of different types of questions, as shown below:

Question Type	Explanation
Multiple choice	Standard multiple choice items provide four options. One option is correct and the other three are incorrect. Incorrect options will be plausible, so you should expect to have to use detailed, syllabus-specific knowledge to identify the correct answer rather than relying on common sense.
Multiple response	A multiple response item is the same as a multiple choice question, except more than one response is required. You will be told how many options you need to select.
Number entry	Number entry (or 'fill in the blank') questions require you to type a short numerical response. You should carefully follow the instructions in the question in terms of how to type your answer – eg the correct number of decimal places.
Drag and drop	Drag and drop questions require you to drag a 'token' onto a pre-defined area. These tokens can be images or text. This type of question is effective at testing the order of events, labelling a diagram or linking events to outcomes.
Hot spot	These questions require you to identify an area or location on an image by clicking on it. This is commonly used to identify a specific point on a graph or diagram.
Item set	2–4 questions all relating to the same short scenario. Each question will be 'standalone', such that your ability to answer subsequent questions in the set does not rely on getting the first one correct.

Passing the Exam

- Read, and **re-read the question** to ensure you fully understand what is being asked.

- When starting to read a question, especially one with a lengthy scenario, **read the requirement first**. You will then find yourself considering the requirement as you read the data in the scenario, helping you to focus on exactly what you have to do.

- **Do not spend too much time on one question** – remember you should spend two minutes, on average, per question.

- If you cannot decide between two answers – look carefully and decide whether for one of the options you are making an unnecessary assumption – **do not be afraid of trusting your gut instinct.**

- **Do not keep changing your mind** – research has shown that the first answer that appeals to you is often the correct one.

- Remember that marks are awarded for correct answers, and marks will not be deducted for incorrect answers. Therefore **answer every single question**, even ones you are unsure of.

- Always submit an answer for a given question even if you do not know the answer – **never leave any answers blank.**

- **Pace yourself** – you will need to work through the exam at the right speed. Too fast and your accuracy may suffer, too slow and you may run out of time. Use this Kit to practise your time keeping and approach to answering each question.

- If you are unsure about anything, remember to **ask the test administrator** before the test begins.

- Remember to **keep moving on!** You may be presented with a question which you simply cannot answer due to difficulty or if the wording is too vague. If you find yourself spending five minutes determining the answer for a question then your time management skills are poor and you are wasting valuable time.

- If you finish the exam with time to spare, use the rest of the time to **review your answers** and to make sure that you answered every question.

Mathematical formulae

Internal Rate of Return (IRR)

$$R_1 + (R_2 - R_1) \times \frac{NPV_1}{NPV_1 - NPV_2}$$

Least-squares Regression

The linear regression equation of y on x is given by:

$$Y = a + bX \quad \text{or} \quad Y - \bar{Y} = b(X - \bar{X})$$

where $\quad b = \dfrac{\text{Covariance}(XY)}{\text{Variance}(X)} = \dfrac{n\sum XY - (\sum X)(\sum Y)}{n\sum X^2 - (\sum X)^2}$

and $\qquad a = \bar{Y} - b\bar{X}$

Or solve $\qquad \sum Y = na + b\sum X$

$$\sum XY = a\sum X + b\sum X^2$$

Coefficient of Correlation

$$r = \frac{\text{Covariance}(XY)}{\sqrt{\text{Var}(X).\text{Var}(Y)}} = \frac{n\sum XY - (\sum X)(\sum Y)}{\sqrt{(n\sum X^2 - (\sum X)^2)(n\sum Y^2 - (\sum Y)^2)}}$$

$$R(\text{rank}) = 1 - \frac{6\sum d^2}{n(n^2 - 1)}$$

Present value table

PRESENT VALUE TABLE

Present value of $1, that is $(1+r)^{-n}$ where r = interest rate; n = number of periods until payment or receipt.

Periods (n)	Interest rates (r)									
	1%	2%	3%	4%	5%	6%	7%	8%	9%	10%
1	0.990	0.980	0.971	0.962	0.952	0.943	0.935	0.926	0.917	0.909
2	0.980	0.961	0.943	0.925	0.907	0.890	0.873	0.857	0.842	0.826
3	0.971	0.942	0.915	0.889	0.864	0.840	0.816	0.794	0.772	0.751
4	0.961	0.924	0.888	0.855	0.823	0.792	0.763	0.735	0.708	0.683
5	0.951	0.906	0.863	0.822	0.784	0.747	0.713	0.681	0.650	0.621
6	0.942	0.888	0.837	0.790	0.746	0705	0.666	0.630	0.596	0.564
7	0.933	0.871	0.813	0.760	0.711	0.665	0.623	0.583	0.547	0.513
8	0.923	0.853	0.789	0.731	0.677	0.627	0.582	0.540	0.502	0.467
9	0.914	0.837	0.766	0.703	0.645	0.592	0.544	0.500	0.460	0.424
10	0.905	0.820	0.744	0.676	0.614	0.558	0.508	0.463	0.422	0.386
11	0.896	0.804	0.722	0.650	0.585	0.527	0.475	0.429	0.388	0.350
12	0.887	0.788	0.701	0.625	0.557	0.497	0.444	0.397	0.356	0.319
13	0.879	0.773	0.681	0.601	0.530	0.469	0.415	0.368	0.326	0.290
14	0.870	0.758	0.661	0.577	0.505	0.442	0.388	0.340	0.299	0.263
15	0.861	0.743	0.642	0.555	0.481	0.417	0.362	0.315	0.275	0.239
16	0.853	0.728	0.623	0.534	0.458	0.394	0.339	0.292	0.252	0.218
17	0.844	0.714	0.605	0.513	0.436	0.371	0.317	0.270	0.231	0.198
18	0.836	0.700	0.587	0.494	0.416	0.350	0.296	0.250	0.212	0.180
19	0.828	0.686	0.570	0.475	0.396	0.331	0.277	0.232	0.194	0.164
20	0.820	0.673	0.554	0.456	0.377	0.312	0.258	0.215	0.178	0.149

Periods (n)	Interest rates (r)									
	11%	12%	13%	14%	15%	16%	17%	18%	19%	20%
1	0.901	0.893	0.885	0.877	0.870	0.862	0.855	0.847	0.840	0.833
2	0.812	0.797	0.783	0.769	0.756	0.743	0.731	0.718	0.706	0.694
3	0.731	0.712	0.693	0.675	0.658	0.641	0.624	0.609	0.593	0.579
4	0.659	0.636	0.613	0.592	0.572	0.552	0.534	0.516	0.499	0.482
5	0.593	0.567	0.543	0.519	0.497	0.476	0.456	0.437	0.419	0.402
6	0.535	0.507	0.480	0.456	0.432	0.410	0.390	0.370	0.352	0.335
7	0.482	0.452	0.425	0.400	0.376	0.354	0.333	0.314	0.296	0.279
8	0.434	0.404	0.376	0.351	0.327	0.305	0.285	0.266	0.249	0.233
9	0.391	0.361	0.333	0.308	0.284	0.263	0.243	0.225	0.209	0.194
10	0.352	0.322	0.295	0.270	0.247	0.227	0.208	0.191	0.176	0.162
11	0.317	0.287	0.261	0.237	0.215	0.195	0.178	0.162	0.148	0.135
12	0.286	0.257	0.231	0.208	0.187	0.168	0.152	0.137	0.124	0.112
13	0.258	0.229	0.204	0.182	0.163	0.145	0.130	0.116	0.104	0.093
14	0.232	0.205	0.181	0.160	0.141	0.125	0.111	0.099	0.088	0.078
15	0.209	0.183	0.160	0.140	0.123	0.108	0.095	0.084	0.074	0.065
16	0.188	0.163	0.141	0.123	0.107	0.093	0.081	0.071	0.062	0.054
17	0.170	0.146	0.125	0.108	0.093	0.080	0.069	0.060	0.052	0.045
18	0.153	0.130	0.111	0.095	0.081	0.069	0.059	0.051	0.044	0.038
19	0.138	0.116	0.098	0.083	0.070	0.060	0.051	0.043	0.037	0.031
20	0.124	0.104	0.087	0.073	0.061	0.051	0.043	0.037	0.031	0.026

Cumulative present value table

CUMULATIVE PRESENT VALUE TABLE

Cumulative present value of $1 per annum, Receivable or Payable at the end of each year for n years $\frac{1-(1+r)^{-n}}{r}$

Periods (n)	Interest rates (r)									
	1%	2%	3%	4%	5%	6%	7%	8%	9%	10%
1	0.990	0.980	0.971	0.962	0.952	0.943	0.935	0.926	0.917	0.909
2	1.970	1.942	1.913	1.886	1.859	1.833	1.808	1.783	1.759	1.736
3	2.941	2.884	2.829	2.775	2.723	2.673	2.624	2.577	2.531	2.487
4	3.902	3.808	3.717	3.630	3.546	3.465	3.387	3.312	3.240	3.170
5	4.853	4.713	4.580	4.452	4.329	4.212	4.100	3.993	3.890	3.791
6	5.795	5.601	5.417	5.242	5.076	4.917	4.767	4.623	4.486	4.355
7	6.728	6.472	6.230	6.002	5.786	5.582	5.389	5.206	5.033	4.868
8	7.652	7.325	7.020	6.733	6.463	6.210	5.971	5.747	5.535	5.335
9	8.566	8.162	7.786	7.435	7.108	6.802	6.515	6.247	5.995	5.759
10	9.471	8.983	8.530	8.111	7.722	7.360	7.024	6.710	6.418	6.145
11	10.368	9.787	9.253	8.760	8.306	7.887	7.499	7.139	6.805	6.495
12	11.255	10.575	9.954	9.385	8.863	8.384	7.943	7.536	7.161	6.814
13	12.134	11.348	10.635	9.986	9.394	8.853	8.358	7.904	7.487	7.103
14	13.004	12.106	11.296	10.563	9.899	9.295	8.745	8.244	7.786	7.367
15	13.865	12.849	11.938	11.118	10.380	9.712	9.108	8.559	8.061	7.606
16	14.718	13.578	12.561	11.652	10.838	10.106	9.447	8.851	8.313	7.824
17	15.562	14.292	13.166	12.166	11.274	10.477	9.763	9.122	8.544	8.022
18	16.398	14.992	13.754	12.659	11.690	10.828	10.059	9.372	8.756	8.201
19	17.226	15.679	14.324	13.134	12.085	11.158	10.336	9.604	8.950	8.365
20	18.046	16.351	14.878	13.590	12.462	11.470	10.594	9.818	9.129	8.514

Periods (n)	Interest rates (r)									
	11%	12%	13%	14%	15%	16%	17%	18%	19%	20%
1	0.901	0.893	0.885	0.877	0.870	0.862	0.855	0.847	0.840	0.833
2	1.713	1.690	1.668	1.647	1.626	1.605	1.585	1.566	1.547	1.528
3	2.444	2.402	2.361	2.322	2.283	2.246	2.210	2.174	2.140	2.106
4	3.102	3.037	2.974	2.914	2.855	2.798	2.743	2.690	2.639	2.589
5	3.696	3.605	3.517	3.433	3.352	3.274	3.199	3.127	3.058	2.991
6	4.231	4.111	3.998	3.889	3.784	3.685	3.589	3.498	3.410	3.326
7	4.712	4.564	4.423	4.288	4.160	4.039	3.922	3.812	3.706	3.605
8	5.146	4.968	4.799	4.639	4.487	4.344	4.207	4.078	3.954	3.837
9	5.537	5.328	5.132	4.946	4.772	4.607	4.451	4.303	4.163	4.031
10	5.889	5.650	5.426	5.216	5.019	4.833	4.659	4.494	4.339	4.192
11	6.207	5.938	5.687	5.453	5.234	5.029	4.836	4.656	4.486	4.327
12	6.492	6.194	5.918	5.660	5.421	5.197	4.988	4.793	4.611	4.439
13	6.750	6.424	6.122	5.842	5.583	5.342	5.118	4.910	4.715	4.533
14	6.982	6.628	6.302	6.002	5.724	5.468	5.229	5.008	4.802	4.611
15	7.191	6.811	6.462	6.142	5.847	5.575	5.324	5.092	4.876	4.675
16	7.379	6.974	6.604	6.265	5.954	5.668	5.405	5.162	4.938	4.730
17	7.549	7.120	6.729	6.373	6.047	5.749	5.475	5.222	4.990	4.775
18	7.702	7.250	6.840	6.467	6.128	5.818	5.534	5.273	5.033	4.812
19	7.839	7.366	6.938	6.550	6.198	5.877	5.584	5.316	5.070	4.843
20	7.963	7.469	7.025	6.623	6.259	5.929	5.628	5.353	5.101	4.870

Questions

1 Organisations and stakeholders

1   Which of the following statements best describes the principal-agent problem?

   ○   A company's shareholders monitor the performance of senior managers by attending the company's annual general meetings.

   ○   The owners of a firm cannot be sure that managers will pursue the strategy which is most appropriate to achieving the owners' goals.

   ○   The ownership of a company is distributed between a large number of shareholders.

   ○   Managers' rewards are linked to a company's performance, with performance being measured against long-term targets as well as short-term ones.

2   Which of the following is/are a key stakeholder group(s) for a charity?

   Select all that apply

   ☐   Employees and volunteers
   ☐   Shareholders
   ☐   Donors
   ☐   Beneficiaries

3   What is the principal difference between a public limited company and a private limited company?

   ○   A private limited company is much smaller than a public limited company.
   ○   A public limited company is state-owned.
   ○   Shares in a private limited company have to be sold privately.
   ○   A private limited company does not have to file its accounts where the public can read them.

4   Which of the following are types of public sector organisations?

   1   Public limited company
   2   Charity
   3   Producer co-operative
   4   QUANGO

   ○   1 and 4
   ○   1, 2, 3
   ○   2, 3 and 4
   ○   4 only

5   The senior managers of a company have used Mendelow's matrix to help them identify how to manage different stakeholder groups, and have recognised that the company's shareholders need to be 'kept satisfied' by the goals and objectives set for the company.

   What level of power and interest does this indicate that the shareholders have in the company?

   ○   High power; High interest
   ○   High power; Low interest
   ○   Low power; High interest
   ○   Low power; Low interest

6   Which of the following issues are true in relation to objectives in not-for-profit and public sector organisations?

    1   The wide range of stakeholders, with differing interests, makes it difficult to set objectives.

    2   It is difficult to translate objectives into performance measures.

    3   The broad strategic objectives of not-for-profit organisations will tend to change frequently over time.

    ○   1 and 2 only

    ○   1 and 3 only

    ○   2 and 3 only

    ○   1, 2 and 3

7   Which of the following are features of not-for-profit organisations?

    1   Resources are used in a way which keeps costs as low as possible while delivering the required level of quality.

    2   Their primary aim is to maximise the wealth they generate for their shareholders.

    3   They aim to generate the maximum output possible from the resources they use.

    ○   1 and 2 only

    ○   1 and 3 only

    ○   2 and 3 only

    ○   1, 2 and 3

8   Which THREE of the following are agents of DEF Co's shareholders?

    ☐   The Chief Executive of DEF Co

    ☐   A bank that has lent money to DEF Co

    ☐   DEF Co's suppliers

    ☐   DEF Co's non-executive directors

    ☐   DEF Co's customers

    ☐   The Chairman of DEF Co

9   ADB is a business which is owned by its workers. The workers share the profits and they each have a vote on how the business is run.

    Which TWO of the following best describe ADB?

    ☐   Public sector

    ☐   Private sector

    ☐   Not-for-profit

    ☐   Co-operative

10 Which TWO of the following organisations rely most heavily on value for money indicators and efficiency for assessing performance, rather than information about financial performance and profitability?

☐ A private accountancy college
☐ A local authority hospital
☐ A small retailer
☐ A public limited company
☐ A school run by the local educational authority

11 The directors of a company want to increase the prices for all of their products, following a rise in the cost of key raw materials used in the manufacture of the products.

Which of the following stakeholder groups is most likely to object to this change?

○ Employees
○ Shareholders
○ Customers
○ Suppliers

12 Two of Sunshine Co's stakeholder groups are putting the company under pressure to improve its return on investment.

Which TWO of the following groups is this most likely to be?

☐ Shareholders
☐ Customers
☐ Bankers
☐ Suppliers
☐ Employees

The following information relates to Questions 13–15.

Kim has recently joined the accounts department of PPW, a public relations and marketing business. Historically, PPW has operated as a single division, but the CEO has now decided that its clients should be separated into two divisions: one dealing with profit-seeking organisations, the other with not-for-profit organisations.

13 Kim has been given press cuttings about three of PPW's clients and asked to add them to the client's files. However, she isn't sure which division they are in.

From the headlines below, identify whether the clients are profit-seeking or not-for-profit organisations:

Client 1 – 'Shareholders vote against directors' remuneration at AGM'   ▼

Client 2 – 'Dividends increased despite slight fall in sales'   ▼

Client 3 – 'Hospital forced to cut staff in face of government funding cuts'   ▼

Pull down list:

Not-for-profit
Profit-seeking

14   After talking to her boss, Kim has got quite confused because, as well as talking about profit-seeking and not-for-profit organisations, her boss was talking about organisations being public sector, private sector or mutually owned. Kim has asked you to help her categorise some different organisations.

Identify whether the following are best described as public sector, private sector or mutually owned organisations.

A company whose shares are bought and sold on a stock market ▾

A police force ▾

A football club controlled by its supporters ▾

Pull down list:

Mutually owned
Private sector
Public sector

---

15   Kim has admitted to you she is finding it difficult to know how to distinguish between different types of organisation. She has been looking at aims and objectives of some of PPW's clients, but cannot identify whether they are profit-seeking or not-for-profit organisations.

Identify whether each of the following aims or objectives are characteristic of profit-seeking or not-for-profit organisations.

Organisation 1 – Prevent crime and protect local communities, and bring to justice those people who commit offences ▾

Organisation 2 – Maintain recent growth rates in order to increase market share ▾

Organisation 3 – Achieve favourable pay, benefits and safe working conditions for members ▾

Pull down list:

Profit-seeking
Not-for-profit

---

16   Perway Co is a large, manufacturing company. Identify whether each of the following stakeholder groups are internal, connected or external stakeholders for Perway.

Stakeholder group	Type of stakeholder
Perway's customers	▾
Perway's staff	▾
Trade unions representing Perway's staff	▾
Perway's bank	▾
Environmental pressure groups complaining about pollution from Perway's factories	▾
Perway's suppliers	▾

Pull down list:

Internal
Connected
External

17   Which TWO of the following are NOT general characteristics of an organisation?

    ○   Organisational goals that are aligned with the individual goals of the managers.

    ○   Formal control systems such as budgets.

    ○   Division of responsibilities between employees.

    ○   Sharing of knowledge.

    ○   People working together towards a common objective.

18   Which of the following statements about directors' pay in a public limited company is / are correct?

    (1)   A share option scheme will help to align the objectives of directors with the objectives of shareholders.

    (2)   Linking directors' bonuses to profits made in the year may discourage capital investment.

    (3)   Directors pay should be determined by the Managing Director.

    ○   1 only.

    ○   2 and 3 only.

    ○   1 and 2 only.

    ○   1,2 and 3.

2 Measuring returns to shareholders

1   You have the following information about a company.

	$
PBIT	4,000,000
Interest expenses	400,000
Taxes	170,000
Capital expenditure	600,000

Calculate the free cash flow to the firm.

$ [   ]

2   In the last financial year, a company made $200 million profit from operations, before deducting interest charges of $10 million and tax liabilities of $55 million. Its capital employed was $800 million, consisting of debt of $80 million and equity of $720 million.

What was the company's return on capital employed (ROCE) for the last financial year?

    ○   16.9%

    ○   18.1%

    ○   23.8%

    ○   25.0%

3   The figures below have been taken from a company's financial statements for the years ending 31 December 20X8 and 20X9.

	20X9	20X8
	$	$
Operating profit	210,000	200,000
Interest payable	18,000	18,000
Profit before tax	192,000	182,000
Tax charges	38,400	36,400
Profit after tax	153,600	145,600
Capital employed	560,000	535,500

What is the company's return on capital employed (ROCE) for 20X9?

(Give your answer to 1 decimal place.)

| | %

---

4   XYZ Co's shareholders require a constant dividend payment of $2 per share.

If the required rate of return has increased from 8% to 10%, how much has the value of the shares fallen by?

- ○   5%
- ○   10%
- ○   15%
- ○   20%

---

5   You have the following information on a company.

	$
Operating profit (PBIT)	4,000,000
Interest expenses	400,000
Taxes	170,000
Preferred dividends	500,000
Number of equity shares issued	10,000,000

What are the company's earnings per share (EPS), to 2 decimal places?

- ○ $0.29
- ○ $0.34
- ○ $0.36
- ○ $0.40

---

6   Which of the following will lead to a rise in the required rate of return (ie the minimum return the investor would want in return for investing in a firm's shares)?

- ○   A reduction in a company's gearing ratio
- ○   Poorer outlook for business in general
- ○   A fall in the general level of interest rates
- ○   The firm adopts less risky business strategies

---

7   Which of the following is most likely to lead to a rise in the price of a firm's shares?

    ○   A fall in the level of interest rates in the country
    ○   The bankruptcy of one or more of its rivals due to tough times in the industry
    ○   Increased borrowing by the firm
    ○   A fall in the firm's EPS

---

8   A company is considering a new investment project, and has calculated that the present value of the cash inflows from the project are less than the present value of the cash outflows, ie there is a negative net present value (NPV).

What does this negative NPV imply?

    ○   The time period used as the basis for assessing future cash flows in the NPV calculation should be increased.

    ○   The investment should not be undertaken as it will lead to a fall in the share price of the company.

    ○   The investment should only be undertaken if the firm has no better use for the capital.

    ○   The firm should increase its cost of capital before making future investment decisions.

---

9   Which of the following are taken into account by the discount factor applied by shareholders to future earnings when calculating shareholder value?

1   The rate of inflation
2   The amount of earnings that will be lost as taxation
3   The level of risk attached to future income streams

    ○   1 and 2 only
    ○   1 and 3 only
    ○   2 and 3 only
    ○   1, 2 and 3

---

10   Which of the following is the most appropriate for indicating long-term shareholder wealth?

    ○   Share price
    ○   Rate of return on capital
    ○   Earnings per share
    ○   Profit

---

11   Which of the following are most likely to increase the price of the shares in XYZ plc?

Select all that apply.

    ☐   A fall in interest rates
    ☐   Increasing demand for some of XYZ's key products
    ☐   News of better economic stability in XYZ's home country
    ☐   Falling ROCE at XYZ plc
    ☐   Increasing levels of borrowing at XYZ plc

12   The following information has been extracted from a company's financial statements.

	$
Operating profit (PBIT)	2,800,000
Interest expenses	240,000
Taxes	480,000
Share capital (50 cent shares):	4,000,000

Calculate the company's earnings per share, giving your answer to 2 decimal places.

$ [   ]

The following information relates to Questions 13–15.

The following information relates to a company's results and performance for the year ended 31 December 20X1.

	$m
Profit before interest and tax	29.0
Interest charges	3.0
Taxation	8.0
Preference dividends	2.0
Share capital ($0.5 shares)	7.5
Retained profits	49.5
Non-current liabilities	30.0

13   What is the company's return on capital employed (ROCE) for the year ended 31 December 20X1?

(Give your answer to 2 decimal places.)

[   ] %

---

14   What is the company's earnings per share (EPS) figure?

(Give your answer to 2 decimal places.)

$ [   ]

---

15   The company's equity shareholders expect a return of at least 15%.

By how much do the company's current profits exceed the minimum level of profit it needs to generate in order to satisfy its shareholders?

○ $7.45 million
○ $9.45 million
○ $14.875 million
○ $16.875 million

---

16   In the past year, the price of Sun Co's shares has increased from $2.75 to $3.10 per share. Sun Co has also paid a dividend of $0.25 per share.

What was the rate of return earned by investors in Sun Co during the past year?

○   9.1%
○   12.7%
○   19.4%
○   21.8%

---

17   Alpha Co has recently reported its results for the last financial year, and it earned a profit after tax of $3.4 million in the year. Alpha Co has announced it will pay a dividend of $0.1 per share.

Alpha Co's issued share capital is $2 million, made up of 2 million shares of $1 each. The market price of Alpha Co's shares is currently $2.80.

What is the dividend yield on Alpha Co's shares?

○   3.6%
○   5.9%
○   8.2%
○   10.0%

3 Demand, supply and price

1   In the diagram shown below, point X represents equilibrium. Two things now happen:

(i)   A technological innovation in production equipment reduces the average unit cost of manufacturing the commodity.

(ii)   Household incomes increase in real terms.

Identify the point on the diagram which will represent the new equilibrium following these changes.

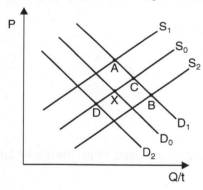

○   Point A
○   Point B
○   Point C
○   Point D

2   Consider the market for DVD discs. Due to new developments in production technology, the cost of producing DVD discs has become substantially lower.

Which of the following will be most likely to happen as a result?

○   The supply curve for DVD discs will shift to the right. The price of the discs will fall and more discs will be supplied.

○   The supply curve for DVD discs will shift to the right. The price of the discs will fall and fewer discs will be supplied at this price.

○   There will be a movement to the left along the supply curve and fewer discs will be supplied at a lower price.

○   The supply curve for DVD discs will shift to the left. The price of discs will rise, but fewer discs will be supplied at this price.

3   Which of the following will be expected to lead to a shift in the demand curve for foreign holidays?

    1   An advertising campaign for foreign holidays
    2   A fall in the disposable incomes of consumers
    3   A rise in the price of domestic holidays
    4   A rise in the price of foreign holidays

    O   1 and 2
    O   1 and 3
    O   3 and 4
    O   1, 2 and 3

4   Which of the following will cause the demand curve for a product to shift to the left?

    O   A rise in household income
    O   The product becomes more fashionable
    O   A fall in the price of a substitute
    O   A fall in the price of a complement

5   Which of the following will be expected to cause a supply curve to shift to the right?

    1   An increase in the cost of factors of production, such as wage costs
    2   The introduction of a government subsidy
    3   The introduction of an indirect tax on the good being supplied
    4   New technology which makes production quicker and cheaper

    O   2 and 4
    O   1 and 4
    O   1 and 3
    O   1, 2 and 4

6   The raw material, Q, is one of the key resources used in the production of a good, Finto. The market for Q is currently in equilibrium.

The supply of Finto has recently increased.

What impact will this change have on Q's market equilibrium?

    O   Demand for Q will fall, leading to a surplus of Q and causing the price of Q to fall.
    O   Supply of Q will increase, leading to a surplus of Q and causing the price of Q to fall.
    O   Demand for Q will increase, leading to a shortage of Q and causing the price of Q to rise.
    O   Demand for Q will increase, leading to shortages of both Q and Finto.

7   FFF is one of the key raw materials used in the production of Zebops.

Until recently, the markets for FFF and Zebops were both in equilibrium. However, additional supplies of FFF have just been discovered.

Identify whether this discovery will increase or decrease the following:

Supply of Zebops [▼]

Price of Zebops [▼]

Pull down list:

Increase
Decrease

---

8   A company produces two products: the A1 and the B2.

Which of the following will be expected to shift the supply curve for A1 to the right?

Select all that apply.

☐   A government subsidy for A1
☐   An increase in the price of A1
☐   An increase in the price of B2
☐   Technological advances which reduce the costs of producing B2
☐   A reduction in the cost of raw materials used to make A1

---

9   Which of the following will result in a leftward shift in the supply curve of professional scientists?

1   A reduction in government spending on science training
2   A fall in the real wage levels of professional scientists
3   An increase in salaries being paid to science graduates in non-scientific jobs in commerce

O   1 and 2 only
O   1 and 3 only
O   2 and 3 only
O   1, 2 and 3

---

10   Which of the following scenarios will be expected to occur if improvements in technology mean that the costs of producing a good are reduced?

O   The supply curve for the good will shift to the right, prices will rise and demand will contract.
O   The supply curve for the good will shift to the right, prices will fall and demand will increase.
O   The supply curve for the good will shift to the left, prices will rise and demand will increase.
O   The supply curve for the good will shift to the left, prices will fall and demand will contract.

---

11   The market price of a product was, until recently, in equilibrium. Now it is falling.

Which of the following is most likely to have caused this?

O   Fall in demand for a complementary product
O   Imposition of an indirect tax on the product
O   Health scares over the effects of consuming a substitute product
O   Rise in the costs of production for the product

---

12   Which of the following changes will cause the demand curve for chocolate to shift to the left?

1   A rise in the price of chocolate
2   Increasing concern about the negative effects chocolate has on health
3   A rise in the price of other confectionery which is a substitute for chocolate
4   A fall in consumers' income

○   Change 1 only
○   Changes 2 and 4 only
○   Changes 3 and 4 only
○   Changes 2 and 3 only

The following information relates to Questions 13–15.

House prices in Erewhon increased rapidly between 20X1 and 20X6, but then fell in 20X7–9.

13   From the three options in the list below, identify the relationship between supply and demand for houses in each of the two periods: 20X1–6, and 20X7–9.

Year	Relationship between supply and demand
20X1–20X6	▼
20X7–20X9	▼

Pull down list:

Supply > Demand
Supply < Demand
Supply = Demand

---

14   The number of new houses being built in 20X7–9 was one of the major factors which affected price.

Which of the following determinants of supply best explain the fall in house prices between 20X7 and 20X9?

1   A reduction in the number of firms building houses
2   Lower raw material costs and labour costs
3   Government subsidies to encourage house building

○   2 only
○   1 and 2
○   1 and 3
○   2 and 3

---

15   Indicate whether the following factors caused a shift in the demand curve or a shift in the supply curve for houses in Erewhon between 20X1 and 20X6:

Increasing household incomes	▼
Reduction in the cost of mortgages	▼
Shortages of available land	▼

Pull down list:

Shift in **demand**
Shift in **supply**

---

4 Price elasticity

1   A firm's product has a price elasticity of demand of –2.

A 10% fall in the price of the product will cause which of the following?

○   Sales volume will increase by 20%
○   Total revenue will decrease by 20%.
○   Sales volume will increase by 5%.
○   Total revenue will increase by 20%.

2   The total yield from an indirect tax levied on a good is likely to be greatest when:

○   Demand is inelastic, supply is elastic.
○   Demand is inelastic, supply is inelastic.
○   Demand is elastic, supply is elastic.
○   Demand is elastic, supply is inelastic.

3   The absolute value of the price elasticity of demand for white wine is greater than one.

A firm currently sells 500 bottles of white wine per day, at a price of $6 per bottle.

The firm has decided to reduce the price of its bottles of wine to $5.70.

Applying the simple (non-average arc) method for calculating price elasticity of demand, which of the following will be true following the change in price?

	Bottles sold per day	Revenue per day
○	More than 525	More than $3,000
○	Between 500 and 525	More than $3,000
○	Between 475 and 500	Less than $3,000
○	Less than 475	Less than $3,000

4   The demand for a good rises from 20,000 to 25,000 following a reduction in price from $20 to $18.

What is the price elasticity of demand, using the average arc (midpoint) method?

(Give your answer to 1 decimal place. Only include the numeric value for the price elasticity of demand. Ignore any minus signs.)

5   Identify whether the following statements are true or false.

If consumers only spend a small proportion of their income on a good, demand for that good will be highly price elastic.

A good for which there are a large number of close substitutes will be highly price elastic.

Pull down list:

True
False

6   The table below shows how the price and quantity supplied of a product changed between two consecutive months:

Date	Price	Quantity
1 January 20X1	$5,000	4,000
1 February 20X1	$5,200	4,400

Using the simple (non-average arc) method, what is the price elasticity of supply of the product?

- ○ 0.5
- ○ 2.0
- ○ 2.36
- ○ 2.5

---

7   Identify whether the following statements are true or false.

Supply is likely to be inelastic if firms have lots of spare capacity.

Supply is likely to be more elastic in the short run than the long run.

Pull down list:

True
False

---

8   If the demand for a good is price inelastic, which of the following is true?

- ○ When the price of the good rises, the quantity demanded falls but total expenditure on the good increases.
- ○ When the price of the good rises, the quantity demanded falls and total expenditure on the good decreases.
- ○ When the price of the good rises, the quantity demanded rises and total expenditure on the good increases.
- ○ When the price of the good rises, the quantity demanded falls but total expenditure on the good is unchanged.

---

9   Which of the following is most likely to reduce the price elasticity of demand for a product?

- ○ Increased passage of time since prices changed
- ○ Greater availability of substitutes
- ○ High costs to consumer of switching to a substitute product
- ○ Lower product differentiation

---

10   Which of the following are likely to mean that the supply of a product is price elastic?

Select all that apply.

- ☐ There is a shortage of a raw material needed to make the product.
- ☐ There are high levels of unemployment among workers with the skills required to make the product.
- ☐ The firm making the product has spare capacity in its manufacturing process.
- ☐ It is difficult for the firm to switch resources away from producing alternative products.
- ☐ The firm has high inventory levels of the finished product.

---

11 A business currently sells 10,000 units of its product each month at a price of $10 per unit.

The product's price elasticity of demand is –0.4.

Calculate the impact on the firm's total revenue per month if the price of the product is increased to $11 per unit.

(Give your answer to the nearest whole number.)

| ▼ | of $ | |

Pull down list:

Increase

Decrease

---

12 A firm currently sells its product at a price of $8 per unit, and generates sales revenue of $7,200 per day.

The firm's management team decided to increase the price of the product to $8.40 but following this increase sales revenues fell to $7,106.40 per day.

What is the price elasticity of demand of the product?

(Give your answer to 1 decimal place. Only include the numeric value for the price elasticity of demand. Ignore any minus signs.)

| |

The following information relates to Questions 13–15.

A firm produces two different products: the Presto and the Lento.

Sales information for the last month is as follows:

Product	Selling price	Quantity sold per day
Presto	$8.25	190
Lento	$5.00	360

13 The firm has noticed that sales of Prestos have been decreasing in recent months and, in order to try to reverse this trend, it has decided to reduce the unit selling price of Prestos to $7.75.

Following this, the firm has noticed that the average quantity of Prestos sold per day has increased to 210.

Calculate the price elasticity of demand for Prestos, using the average arc (midpoint) method.

○ –0.625
○ –1.60
○ –1.63
○ –1.74

14   The firm had previously calculated the price elasticity of demand (PED) for Lentos, using the simple (non-average arc) method for calculating PED. This calculation showed that PED for Lentos (ignoring the minus sign) is 1.875.

With this in mind, the firm has decided to reduce the price of Lentos to $4.80 each.

Calculate the effect of this change on the daily revenues generated by selling Lentos.

- ○   Reduced by $7.20
- ○   Increased by $57.60
- ○   Increased by $62.40
- ○   Increased by $135.00

15   The firm's managers are trying to understand why the price elasticity of demand for Lentos is higher than that for Prestos.

Which of the following will increase the price elasticity of demand for a good?

1   A large and increasing number of substitutes
2   A rise in the proportion of household income spent on the good
3   An increase in consumer incomes
4   A decrease in the price of complementary goods

- ○   1 and 2
- ○   1, 3 and 4
- ○   2 and 4
- ○   2 and 3

16   Last year, a soft drink producer sold two million litres of its drink per month, at a price of $1 per litre.

The government has now introduced a 'sugar tax' on soft drinks, and the drink is now sold for $1.10 per litre. Following the introduction of the tax, sales of the drink have fallen to 1.9 million litres per month.

Using the non-average arc (simple) method, what is the price elasticity of demand for the drink?

- ○   − 1
- ○   − 0.5
- ○   + 0.5
- ○   + 1

17   The demand schedule below shows the quantity of a product sold per day at different prices.

Quantity	Price
	$
40	22
45	21
50	20
55	19

Using the average arc (midpoint) method, what is the price elasticity of demand following a fall in the price of the product from $21 to $20?

- ○ − 2.28
- ○ − 2.21
- ○ − 2.16
- ○ − 2.11

---

18 Following an increase in the price of wheat (from $120 per tonne to $129.60 per tonne), farmers have increased the amount of wheat they grow per year from 2,100 tonnes to 2,184 tonnes.

Using the simple (non-average arc) method, what is the price elasticity of supply of wheat?

(Give your answer to 1 decimal place. Only include the numeric value for the price elasticity of supply. Ignore any minus signs.)

---

19 Following a fall in Essland's exchange rate, the cost of products imported into the country has risen.

A retailer in Essland currently sells one of these products at a price of $80, and demand is 2,500 units per week. The retailer wants to keep the price increase as low as possible, but has decided it has no option but to reduce the price to $84.

The product's price elasticity of demand (calculated using the non-average arc method) is −1.4.

What should the retailer expect weekly demand for the product to be after the price increase?

(Give your answer to the nearest whole number.)

| | units per week
|---|

---

20 Seth Co supplies components. In the coming year, it is forecast that the market price will be $24 and 48,000 components will be demanded by Seth Co's customers.

Currently Seth Co makes 40,000 components per year and the current market price is $20. Seth Co's maximum production capacity is 46,000 components.

What is Seth Co's price elasticity of supply? (to two decimal places)

---

21 If a firm increases its price, which TWO of the following is true, if price elasticity of demand is unitary?

- ○ Total costs will fall.
- ○ Total profit will fall.
- ○ The number of units sold will remain the same.
- ○ Total revenue will stay the same.

5 Cost behaviour

1   The scale of production can lead to economies of scale and diseconomies of scale. These can be internal or external.

From the list below, identify which category of economies or diseconomies of scale the following four statements relate to.

As a firm has grown, workers have been able to specialise in a particular job and become increasingly efficient at that job.

As an industry has expanded, there has become an increasing shortage of skilled labour.

As an industry has developed, banks have developed a better understanding of the industry's requirements.

Management have experienced problems of co-ordination as the number of divisions in a firm has increased.

Pull down list:

Internal economy of scale
External economy of scale
Internal diseconomy of scale
External diseconomy of scale

2   Large firms can benefit from economies of scale, and gain a cost advantage over smaller competitor firms. In spite of this, small firms in industries manage to survive, and there are several reasons for this.

Which of the following help to explain the survival of small firms?

1   The minimum efficient scale of production is at a relatively low level of output.
2   Large firms achieve increasing returns at higher volumes of output.
3   Small firms are able to fragment the market by focusing on specific segments within a market.
4   Large firms are often bureaucratic and inefficient.

    O   1 and 3
    O   1, 2 and 4
    O   2 and 4
    O   1, 3 and 4

3   Which of the following is a source of economies of scale?

Select all that apply.

    ☐   The introduction of specialist capital equipment
    ☐   Purchasing raw materials and other inputs in bulk
    ☐   The employment of specialist managers
    ☐   Cost savings resulting from new production techniques

4   The graph below shows how the cost per unit of producing a good (average cost) varies according to the level of output.

Identify, on the firm's average cost curve, the level of output at which it stops benefiting from economies of scale.

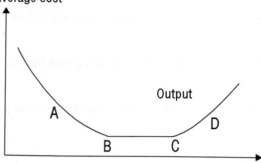

Average cost

- ○   Point A
- ○   Point B
- ○   Point C
- ○   Point D

5   Which of the following is a variable cost to a firm?

- ○   Variable rate mortgage payments
- ○   The cost of raw materials
- ○   Depreciation on a new machine
- ○   Monthly rent payments to lease the firm's warehouse building

6   The table below shows the total volume of sales in four industries, and the number of units which have to be sold per month to enable a firm in each industry to achieve its minimum efficient scale.

Industry	Total industry sales (units sold)	Minimum efficient scale (units sold)
A	14,000	2,000
B	6,000	1,500
C	9,000	1,500
D	2,000	400

Based on the information in the table, which industry would be expected to have the highest level of market concentration?

- ○   Industry A
- ○   Industry B
- ○   Industry C
- ○   Industry D

7   Which THREE of the following are internal economies of scale for a firm?

☐   The firm is able to reduce administration costs per unit of output when it opens a second production plant.

☐   The firm can buy raw materials at lower prices than smaller firms are able to because it buys in bulk.

☐   The firm benefits from working with marketing firms which specialise in advertising and selling similar products.

☐   The firm can obtain finance at lower interest rates than smaller firms which the bank thinks are more likely to default on their loans.

☐   The firm's training costs are reduced because it can draw on a pool of highly skilled labour available in its region.

---

8   A firm is suffering from diseconomies of scale.

Identify whether the following statements about the firm are true or false.

The firm's average costs will decrease as its level of production increases.   [▼]

The firm should increase its level of production in order to increase efficiency.   [▼]

Pull down list:

True
False

---

9   An organisation has been trying to decide whether or not to outsource the payroll function from its finance department. However, the organisation is finding it difficult to devise a contract which controls the uncertainties related to the potential outsourcing arrangement.

Identify whether the following statements are true or false.

The organisation should only outsource the payroll function if the external transaction costs are higher than the internal bureaucratic costs.   [▼]

The difficulties of agreeing the contract and monitoring the outsourcing relationship increase the transaction costs.   [▼]

Pull down list:

True
False

---

10 XYZ Co sells clothes. Currently, it manufactures all of its clothes in-house, but is considering outsourcing the manufacture of some clothes. If XYZ Co decides to proceed with the outsourcing arrangement, the supplier will be paid a monthly fee according to the number of garments it produces.

Which of the following would be consequences, for XYZ Co, of the outsourcing arrangement?

1   Increased transaction costs
2   Reduced control over the quality of its clothes
3   XYZ Co's monthly manufacturing costs will be fixed

- O   1 and 2 only
- O   1 and 3 only
- O   2 and 3 only
- O   1, 2 and 3

11 Which of the terms below describes a situation in which corporate partners work together to supply goods or services through a central hub firm?

- O   Off-shoring
- O   Outsourcing
- O   Network organisation
- O   Shared service centre

12 Which of the following terms best describes the decision by a firm to reduce costs by transferring responsibility for part of the firm's activities to outside providers?

- O   Privatisation
- O   Off-shoring
- O   Outsourcing
- O   Shared service centre

The following information relates to Questions 13–15.

The Government in Essland is concerned about the high levels of market concentration in certain industries, where a small number of firms dominate sales in the industry.

Annual sales figures for four of these industries are shown below, as well as the estimated level of sales required to achieve the minimum efficient scale in that industry.

In Essland, each of the industries shown is currently dominated by five large firms.

Industry	Total industry sales ($m)	Aggregate sales of the five largest firms in the industry ($m)	Level of sales required to achieve minimum efficient scale ($m)
Confectionery manufacturing	612,000	501,840	80,000
Power utilities (electricity and gas)	824,000	659,200	200,000
Supermarkets	968,500	736,060	150,000
Advertising	505,000	393,900	50,000

13 Which of the following statements is/are true?

1 The fixed costs of these large firms will be lower than the fixed costs for smaller firms wanting to join the industry.

2 The high levels of market power these firms hold will make it more difficult and more expensive for them to raise finance.

3 The economies of scale achieved by these large firms can act as a barrier to entry to new firms.

○ 1 and 2
○ 1 and 3
○ 2 and 3
○ 3 only

14 One of the main reasons for the high levels of market concentration in these industries is the significant economies of scale which firms in them benefit from.

Which of the following is an example of an external economy of scale?

○ Minimum efficient scale can only be achieved by producing at a high level of output.

○ Development of a specialist transport and logistics network to support firms in an industry.

○ Combining the administrative functions of two firms after a merger and reducing the overall number of administrative staff employed.

○ A large firm invests in specialist capital machinery which smaller rivals cannot afford.

15 According to the figures for the minimum efficient scale, in which industry are we most likely to see the market being dominated by fewer than five firms in the future?

○ Confectionery manufacturing
○ Power utilities
○ Supermarkets
○ Advertising

16 5,000 units of a product can be produced at a variable cost per unit of $2 per unit and a total cost of $50,000.

If output is doubled how much will the total cost per unit change by?

○ It will fall by 40%.
○ It will rise by 20%.
○ It will not change.
○ It will rise by 100%.

17 Which of the following is an example of a 'trading' economy of scale?

○ Centralising central functions such as R&D.
○ Breaking down complex jobs into simpler individual tasks.
○ Developing a wider product range, to reduce risk and therefore the cost of bank loans.
○ Obtaining bulk purchase discounts from suppliers.

6 Market failure

1   A government introduces a minimum price below free market price.

Which of the following describes the expected consequences of this?

○   There will be no effect on market price or producer incomes.
○   Suppliers will withdraw from the market due to falling incomes.
○   Unsold surpluses of the product will build up.
○   Demand for the product will contract.

2   Which of the following would be expected to occur following the introduction of a maximum price policy?

1   Lower total expenditure by consumers
2   Shortage of the product
3   Higher incomes for producers

○   1 and 2 only
○   1 and 3 only
○   2 and 3 only
○   1, 2 and 3

3   The diagram below illustrates the effect of an indirect tax on the supplier and the consumer of a good. The total amount of the tax is the distance AB.

What proportion of the tax is paid by the consumer of the good?

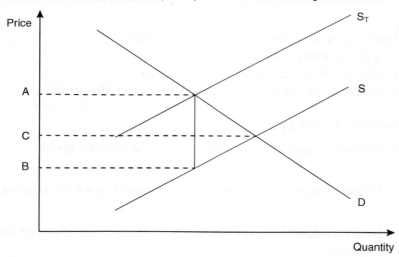

○   AB
○   AC
○   CB
○   None

4   Which of the following is the best example of an external social cost?

    ○   Restrictions on the supply of oil leading to an increase in fuel prices

    ○   Increasing popularity of a holiday destination leading to an increase in the price of holidays at that destination

    ○   People travelling by rail rather than by car, leading to less congestion and fewer accidents on the roads

    ○   Pollution emitted from a factory which has caused local residents to become ill

5   Which of the following types of good is affected by the free rider problem?

    ○   Merit goods
    ○   Public goods
    ○   Demerit goods
    ○   Luxury goods

6   Which of the following is an argument in favour of privatisation?

    ○   It reduces the need for regulation of markets.
    ○   It enables organisations to benefit from greater economies of scale.
    ○   It leads to greater efficiency.
    ○   It leads to an increased provision of merit goods.

7   Which of the following is the most appropriate way for a government to encourage the consumption of a merit good?

    ○   Imposing an indirect tax to increase the price of the good to consumers
    ○   Introducing a tax levy on the producers of the good
    ○   Introducing maximum price policies to regulate the price of the good
    ○   Ensuring that good is provided entirely by the private sector with no state intervention

8   Which of the following best describes a public good?

    ○   A good or service which should be subsidised or provided free in order to encourage its consumption.

    ○   A good or service which is non-diminishable and non-exclusive and therefore will not be provided by the free market.

    ○   A benefit arising from the consumption of a good which is experienced by people other than the immediate consumer of that good.

    ○   A cost arising from the production of a good which is borne by people other than the immediate producer of that good.

9   If the production of a good involves an external social cost, which of the following is the most appropriate policy response for the Government?

○   Take the firm producing the good into state ownership
○   Impose an indirect tax on the good
○   Impose a higher rate of tax on the profits of the producers
○   Provide a subsidy for the consumers of the product

10   Identify the type of good (merit good; demerit good; public good) which each of the comments below relates to.

A 'polluter pays policy' has been introduced to reflect the negative externalities produced.

[▼]

Supply of these goods does not diminish regardless of how many people make use of them.

[▼]

These goods are subsidised because of the benefits they provide to society.

[▼]

Pull down list:

Merit good
Demerit good
Public good

11   Under which of the following circumstances will the primary burden of a tax on a good fall most heavily on consumers?

○   Demand and supply are both elastic.
○   Demand is elastic and supply is inelastic.
○   Demand is inelastic and supply is elastic.
○   Demand and supply are both inelastic.

12   The Government of AAA has recently introduced a minimum wage rate at a level above the existing equilibrium wage rate.

If everything else remains unchanged, which of the following will be true?

○   The equilibrium position between the supply and demand for labour will remain the same.
○   Demand for labour will exceed the supply of labour in AAA.
○   There will be excess supply in the labour market in AAA.
○   The overall number of people employed in AAA will increase.

BPP
LEARNING
MEDIA

The following information relates to Questions 13–15.

The Government in Ostland is becoming increasingly concerned about public health and environmental issues in its country. Two particular issues are: rising levels of obesity in the country, and the potential impact of carbon emissions from large factories.

13   Large fast food producers have been accused of filling their products with excessive amounts of salt and fat to reduce the costs of producing them. This fat and salt later causes health problems that reduce the ability of people to work and require the state to provide health care.

Which of the following are the health problems an example of?

○   Diseconomies of scale
○   External social costs
○   Public goods
○   Positive externalities

14   The Government has introduced a minimum price for all fast food products. The minimum price is above the current market equilibrium price.

Consumer demand for fast food in Ostland is price elastic.

What will be the impact of the minimum price on demand for fast food and total revenue from the sale of fast food products?

Demand   [▼]

Total revenue   [▼]

Pull down list:

Increase
Stay the same
Decrease

15   In response to their concern about the level of emissions from some of the factories in the country, the Government has imposed a tax on carbon emissions.

Which of the following best describes the principle that the Government has applied in looking to tackle the carbon emissions?

○   Social efficiency
○   Public good
○   Polluter pays
○   Negative externalities

16   If the government imposes a minimum price for a good that is above the market price, in which of the following circumstances will the resulting market surplus will be highest?

○   Demand is price inelastic and supply is price elastic.
○   Demand is price elastic and supply is price elastic.
○   Demand is price inelastic and supply is price inelastic.
○   Demand is price elastic and supply is price inelastic.

17   Which TWO of the following statements about private sector, for-profit, producers operating in an unregulated, free-market, economy are TRUE?

    ○   Firms will increase prices to pass on the cost of negative externalities.

    ○   They will consider all costs that they incur when determining the selling price.

    ○   Only when producing a public good will they consider social costs when determining the selling price.

    ○   Externalities will be ignored when determining price and output levels.

7 National income

1   Which of the following is most likely to lead to an increase in aggregate demand in an economy?

    ○   Increased saving
    ○   Increased spending on imports
    ○   Increased taxation
    ○   Increased investment

2   Estland has recently experienced increased levels of spending on imports in place of domestically produced goods and services.

Which of the following will result from this?

    ○   Aggregate supply in Estland will shift to the right; National income will fall
    ○   Aggregate supply in Estland will shift to the left; National income will rise
    ○   Aggregate demand in Estland will shift to the right; National income will rise
    ○   Aggregate demand in Estland will shift to the left; National income will fall

3   Which of the following will result from an increase in the marginal propensity to consume?

    ○   The level of interest rates will increase.
    ○   There will be a fall in the level of national income.
    ○   The size of the multiplier will increase.
    ○   The level of injections into the economy will be reduced.

4   The economy in a country is a closed economy with no government sector.

Consumer expenditure = $50 + 0.6Y$ (where 'Y' = National income)

Investment = 20

What is the equilibrium level of national income in the country?

    ○   50
    ○   70
    ○   125
    ○   175

5   The current equilibrium national income in a country is currently significantly below full capacity.

Which of the following will be most likely to help to increase the equilibrium level of national income?

Select all that apply.

☐   Increasing the trade deficit
☐   Reducing the level of government expenditure
☐   A reduction in labour costs
☐   Increasing investment expenditure by firms
☐   A reduction in consumer spending

---

6   The equilibrium level of national income in a country is $250 billion.

The elements of the aggregate demand in the country are shown below, with the exception of exports:

Consumer expenditure on domestically produced goods and services	$65 billion
Investment expenditure by firms	$20 billion
Government expenditure	$45 billion

Following the principles of Keynesian economics, what is the value of exports in the country?
$ ⬚ billion

---

7   Which of the following will lead to a fall in the value of the multiplier?

○   A decrease in the marginal propensity to consume
○   A fall in the level of public expenditure
○   Consumers saving a lower proportion of their income
○   A decrease in the marginal propensity to import

---

8   Which of the following creates an injection into the circular flow of income?

○   An increase by a firm in its inventories of finished goods, prior to a marketing campaign
○   The purchase by a pension fund of shares in a newly privatised company
○   Individuals depositing cash into an interest-bearing bank account
○   The acquisition of one company by another company

---

9   Which of the following would be expected to cause an increase in national income?

○   An increase in unemployment
○   An increase in exports
○   An increase in saving
○   A fall in consumer spending

10   Which of the following are withdrawals from the circular flow of income?

1   Government spending
2   Exports
3   Taxation
4   Savings

○   1 and 2 only
○   1, 2 and 3
○   2, 3 and 4
○   3 and 4 only

11   How will a steep increase in wage costs be reflected in the model of aggregate demand and aggregate supply used to illustrate the equilibrium level of national income in an economy?

○   Leftward shift in the aggregate supply curve
○   Leftward shift in the aggregate demand curve
○   Rightward shift in the aggregate supply curve
○   Rightward shift in the aggregate demand curve

12   Which of the following will be most likely to lead to a rightward (outward) shift in the aggregate demand curve in an economy?

○   A fall in interest rates
○   A fall in the price of a key raw material, such as oil
○   A fall in the price of imported goods
○   A fall in the level of government spending

The following information relates to Questions 13–15.

The current equilibrium level of national income in Westland is $450 billion, but because this is below the full employment level of national income, of $500 billion, there is currently quite a high rate of unemployment in the country.

13   Following the principles of Keynesian economics, if consumption in Westland is $285 billion, what is the current level of injections into the circular flow of income?

(Give your answer as a whole number, with no decimal places.)

$ [   ] billion

14   In an attempt to reduce unemployment in Westland, the Government is trying to increase aggregate demand in the country. It has increased the level of Government expenditure by $2 billion.

Economists in Westland have identified that 20% of any increase in income will be paid in taxes, 4% will be saved and 16% will be spent on imported goods.

What will be the equilibrium level of national income after the Government's expenditure?

(Give your answer to the nearest $ billion.)

$ [   ] billion

15 Even after the increase in government spending, the equilibrium level of national income in Westland is still below the full employment level.

Which of the following will also help to increase the equilibrium level of national income?

○   An increase in tax rates
○   An increase in exports
○   An increase in interest rates
○   An increase in savings

16 The data below relates to elements of national income in Teeland for the last financial year:

	$m
Exports	384
Imports	407
Investment	208
Government expenditure	359
Savings	194
Taxation	371

Which of the following is true?

○   National income in Teeland is falling
○   National income in Teeland is in equilibrium
○   There is a budget deficit in Teeland
○   National income in Teeland is rising

8 The trade cycle

1   In the last year, Country Q has witnessed a significant increase in its government spending compared to its income from tax receipts ie there has been an increase in its government budget deficit.

Which of the following will be a consequence of this?

○   The level of withdrawals from the economy will increase.
○   The equilibrium level of national income will be reduced.
○   The level of aggregate demand in the economy will increase.
○   The number of people employed in Country Q will be reduced.

2   Which of the following can indicate trade cycle movements?

1   The level of demand-pull inflation
2   Changes in Gross Domestic Product (GDP)
3   The level of seasonal unemployment

○   1 and 2 only
○   2 and 3 only
○   1 and 3 only
○   1, 2 and 3

3   The table below shows some key data about a country's economic performance:

Year	Unemployment rate %	Change in real GDP %	Government income $bn	Government expenditure $bn
1	5.7	1.3	320	410
2	4.8	2.1	365	480

Which of the following statements about the changes in the country's economy from Year 1 to 2 is correct?

○   The economy is contracting and the budget deficit is increasing.
○   The economy is expanding and the budget surplus is increasing.
○   The economy is expanding and the budget deficit is increasing.
○   The economy is contracting and the budget surplus is increasing.

4   Country X is currently suffering from cost-push inflation. Country X has relatively few natural resources, so manufacturing firms in the country have to import a large proportion of the materials they need for their production processes.

Which of the following measures could help to tackle the problem of cost-push inflation in Country X?

1   Introducing a sales tax on manufactured products
2   Weakening the power of trade unions
3   A decision by global oil producers to restrict oil production
4   A revaluation of Country X's currency

○   1, 2 and 3
○   1, 2 and 4
○   2, 3 and 4
○   2 and 4 only

5   Which of the following statements about the recession phase of the trade cycle is correct?

○   It is often caused by excessive consumer expenditure.
○   It is normally characterised by accelerating inflation.
○   It is often characterised by high levels of unemployment.
○   It is usually caused by increasing aggregate monetary demand.

6   In recent years, Country W has enjoyed a sustained period of economic growth. However, this rate of growth has now started to slow.

Which of the following is Country W most likely to have observed when the rate of growth began to slow?

○   The level of imports increased.
○   Inventory levels increased.
○   Inflation rates increased.
○   Investment in new equipment increased.

BPP
LEARNING
MEDIA

7   The economy of a country has been suffering from recession, so the Government's macroeconomic policy objective is to expand the overall level of economic activity in the country.

Which of the following measures are consistent with that objective?

1   Increasing public sector expenditure
2   Lowering interest rates
3   Increasing taxation

O   1 only
O   1 and 2
O   1 and 3
O   2 and 3

8   The trade cycle is typically categorised into four stages: recession, depression, recovery and boom.

Identify which of the four stages the following characteristics relate to.

Low levels of aggregate demand mean the equilibrium level of national income is below the level needed to achieve full employment.

Modest rates of economic growth. Improving consumer and business confidence, leading to greater expenditure.

Falling levels of business and consumer confidence. Falling levels of production. Rising levels of unemployment.

Low levels of unemployment. High inflation due to excess demand for labour and other resources. Increasing deficit in balance of trade.

Pull down list:

Boom
Depression
Recession
Recovery

9   Northland, Southland, Eastland and Westland are four countries. The following economic statistics have been produced for each country for the last financial year.

Country	Northland	Southland	Eastland	Westland
Change in GDP (%)	−0.30	+2.51	−0.55	+2.12
Balance of payments current account ($m)	+550.83	−350.47	−150.90	+220.39
Change in consumer prices (%)	+17.50	+15.37	+1.25	+2.15
Change in working population employed (%)	−2.76	+3.78	+1.76	−3.76

Which country experienced stagflation in the last financial year?

O   Northland
O   Southland
O   Eastland
O   Westland

10 Until recently, the two countries of Effland and Geeland had a similar level of national income per capita. Both are open economies, and the value of goods they import has historically been very similar.

However, they are in different parts of the world, and Effland's economy has recently been enjoying a boom period while Geeland has been suffering from a recession.

Based on the implications of the trade cycle for a country's economy, indicate whether the following are true or false.

The rate of unemployment is likely to be higher in Effland than Geeland.

▼

The rate of inflation is likely to be higher in Effland than Geeland.

▼

The level of imports into Effland is likely to be higher than into Geeland.

▼

Pull down list:

True
False

---

11 The Government in a country is concerned that the national economy is about to enter a recession, and so the Government intends to adjust its macroeconomic policy to try to prevent recession.

Which of the following will result?

○   Government spending will increase; Taxes will be increased; Budget deficit will increase
○   Government spending will increase; Taxes will be cut; Budget deficit will increase
○   Government spending will decrease; Taxes will be increased; Budget deficit will decrease
○   Government spending will decrease; Taxes will be cut; Budget deficit will decrease

---

12 An economy currently has a deflationary gap.

Which of the following would be appropriate measures to close the gap?

1   Increase the economy's trade deficit
2   Increase government spending
3   Increase the interest rate

○   1 and 2
○   2 only
○   1 and 3
○   2 and 3

The following information relates to Questions 13–15.

The economy of Veeland has recently been experiencing a recession, while the economy in Jayland has been experiencing a sustained period of economic growth.

The overall level of global economic growth has remained relatively stable, as have commodity prices and other external factors which might otherwise lead to cost-push inflation.

13 Which of the following would we expect to accompany the recession in Veeland?

   O   An increase in the rate of demand-pull inflation
   O   An increase in the level of national output
   O   An increase in the level of imports
   O   An increase in the level of unemployment

---

14 Prices in Jayland have now started rising significantly due to demand-pull inflation.

Controlling inflation levels is one of the Government's key economic goals, and so it wants to take action to manage the level of aggregate demand in the economy.

Indicate whether the following should be increased or reduced in order to manage aggregate demand in the way the Government requires.

Taxes   [▼]

Government expenditure   [▼]

Pull down list:

Increased
Reduced

---

15 The following economic data has been obtained for four countries for the last financial year.

Country	Country 1	Country 2	Country 3	Country 4
Change in GDP (%)	−1.30	+2.51	−0.05	+1.62
Balance of payments current account ($m)	+150.83	−350.47	−50.90	+120.39
Change in consumer prices (%)	+0.50	+5.37	+2.05	+8.15
Change in unemployment rate (%)	+2.76	−3.78	−0.53	+1.06

Which of the country's statistics is most likely to represent Veeland?

   O   Country 1
   O   Country 2
   O   Country 3
   O   Country 4

16   From the list below, indicate the type of unemployment which is most likely to occur in each of the circumstances described:

Demand for agricultural labour falls during the winter months, so the number of agricultural workers who are unemployed increases during the winter

| ▼ |

Increased supplies of cheap, imported steel have led to a long-term reduction in demand for domestically produced steel in a country

| ▼ |

The onset of a recession has led to a reduction in the level of economic activity in a country

| ▼ |

Pull down list:
Cyclical
Frictional
Structural

17   Which of the following concepts links a fall in unemployment to a rise in inflation?

Select all that apply.

☐   The trade cycle.
☐   Cost-push inflation.
☐   Frictional unemployment.
☐   Automatic stabilisers.
☐   The Phillips curve.

18   Which of the following shows the correct sequence of the phases of the trade cycle?

○   boom, recession, recovery, depression, boom etc.
○   recession, recovery, boom, depression, recession etc.
○   depression, recovery, boom, recession, depression etc.
○   recovery, recession, boom, depression, recovery etc.

9 Index numbers

1   The unit price of a product has increased over the last 4 years as follows:

Year	Price ($)
20X0	8.10
20X1	9.33
20X2	10.26
20X3	11.49

Using the chain base method, what is the price index for the product in 20X3 (to the nearest whole number)?

○   112
○   114
○   115
○   142

2   The current consumer price index is 198.0, with 2007 = 100.

Convert a weekly wage of $421 back to 2007 prices. (Give your answer to 2 decimal places.)

$ [   ]

3   A country measures the rate of inflation using a base weighted index, with 20X1 being the base year.

Three different products are used in the index. The unit prices of these and the quantities purchased (units of each product) are shown below.

Product	Quantity purchased in 20X1 (millions)	Price in 20X1 ($)	Quantity purchased in 20X2 (millions)	Price in 20X2 ($)
Milk	300	1	320	1.10
Beer	150	2	120	2.50
Phones	50	80	75	100.00

What is the weighted average price rise between 20X1 and 20X2, using the country's base weighted index?

○   15.0%
○   24.0%
○   24.3%
○   77.2%

4   Eight years ago, material X cost $5 per kg, and the price index most appropriate to the cost of material X stood at 150.

The same index now stands at 430.

What is the best estimate of the current cost per kg of material X?

○ $1.74
○ $7.50
○ $14.33
○ $21.50

5   The price index in a country is based on the purchases of three products: bread, meat and televisions.

The table below shows the quantities (units) of the products purchased and their unit prices, for the last two years.

Product	Quantity purchased in 20X1 (millions)	Price in 20X1 ($)	Quantity purchased in 20X2 (millions)	Price in 20X2 ($)
Bread	200	1	220	0.9
Meat	150	5	190	5.2
Televisions	10	300	14	350.00

What is the price rise between 20X1 and 20X2 using a current weightings approach?

○   3.6%
○   12.9%
○   13.3%
○   54.1%

6   The average weekly wages paid by a company in recent years are shown below, along with data from the consumer price index (CPI) which is used as a measure of inflation in the country where the company operates.

Year	20X1	20X2	20X3	20X4	20X5	20X6
Wages	215	223	235	247	256	291
CPI	115	118	122	134	133	135

Calculate the average weekly wages in 20X6 at constant 20X1 prices. (Give your answer to 1 decimal place.)

$ [   ]

7   The managers in a company are reviewing its costs. One particular area of concern is the rental cost for the company's head office.

Year	Annual rental ($)	Price index (Base = 100)
Current year	490,000	153.2
Five years ago	320,000	141.6

What is the current year's annual rental in terms of prices 5 years ago? (Give your answer to the nearest $.)

$ [   ]

8   The price index used for measuring the rate of inflation in a country is based on three groups of items: food and drink; travel and leisure; housing.

The relative weight given to each group, and their current index numbers, are shown below.

Group	Base	Weight	Index
Food and drink	100	50	140
Travel and leisure	100	30	130
Housing	100	20	120

Which of the following is the current, overall price index in the country?

O   130.0
O   131.3
O   133.0
O   135.0

9   The average weekly wage costs paid by a firm have increased as follows:

	20X1	20X2	20X3	20X4
Weekly money wages index (20X1 = 100)	200	210	220	230
Index of inflation (Base = 100)	180	190	200	210

Identify whether the following statements are true or false:

Money (ie nominal) wages have increased by at least 5% each year.

Real wages have declined over the period 20X1–20X4.

Pull down list:

True
False

10   In 2014, the consumer price index in Ostland (based on 1995 = 100) stood at 126. In 2014, the index was rebased at 2014 = 100.

By 2017, the new index stood at 109.

If the price index had still been based on the original 1995 figures, what would the 2017 figure have been?

O   109.0
O   115.6
O   135.0
O   137.3

11   The management team at Hiley Co are concerned about rising costs within the company, and the impact these are having on profits.

Over the past five years, Hiley's total wage costs have increased from $64.20 million to $70.33 million.

Over the same period, the base rate index (used to measure inflation) has increased from 120.0 to 126.5.

What has been the real increase in wages over the five year period?

O   1.2%
O   3.9%
O   6.1%
O   9.5%

12   GDP per capita can be used as an indicator of the level of economic growth in a country.

The following figures show nominal GDP per capita figures for three countries, as well as the inflation index numbers for each country.

All three countries use the same currency ($).

Year	Ayland	Ayland	Beeland	Beeland	Ceeland	Ceeland
	GDP per capita	Price index	GDP per capita	Price index	GDP per capita	Price index
20X4	$15,000	115.9	$20,120	118.6	$28,241	117.5
20X7	$16,174	119.4	$20,621	122.4	$29,604	120.3

Which country had the highest real growth (% growth) between 20X4 and 20X7? ▼

Which country experienced negative real growth between 20X4 and 20X7? ▼

Pull down list:

Ayland
Beeland
Ceeland

The following information relates to Questions 13–15.

The rate of inflation in Ostland is measured using a consumer price index (CPI). The index is measured against prices in 20X1, where 20X1 = 100.

The CPI at the end of each of the last five years was:

20X3	106.4
20X4	109.0
20X5	111.5
20X6	113.6
20X7	116.3

13   What was the annual rate of inflation in Ostland for 20X7?

○   2.10%
○   2.38%
○   2.70%
○   2.72%

---

14   In which year was the rate of inflation highest?

○   20X4
○   20X5
○   20X6
○   20X7

---

15   National income figures (GDP) are used as a measure of economic growth in Ostland.

GDP figures for 20X6 and 20X7 are shown below. These are nominal figures.

20X6 $5,750 billion
20X7 $6,230 billion

By how much did the economy of Ostland grow, in real terms, between 20X6 and 20X7?

- ○   5.51%
- ○   5.83%
- ○   7.18%
- ○   8.35%

16   An index of average gross earnings with base year 20X1, and at constant 20X1 prices, has been calculated to be 108 by 20X5.

Which of the following statements is true?

- ○   Average earnings have risen by 1.08% between 20X1 and 20X5
- ○   The average price of goods and services has increased by 8% between 20X1 and 20X5
- ○   Average earnings can buy 8% more goods and services in 20X5 than they could in 20X1
- ○   Average gross earnings have fallen 8% between 20X1 and 20X5

17   The nominal GDP of Nortland for the financial year 20X7 was $8,040 billion.

The GDP deflator for 20X7 was 103.63. The GDP deflator is measured against a base of 100 in 20X5.

Under the same index, the GDP deflator for 20X3 was 95.38

What is Nortland's GDP for 20X7 in terms of 20X3 prices? (Give your answer to the nearest $ billion.)

$ [   ] billion

18   An index number in a country is made up of three items: food, housing and transport.

Group	Weight	Index
Food	50	116
Housing	30	124
Transport	20	?
All items	100	118

To the nearest whole number, which of the following is the index number for transport?

- ○   23
- ○   114
- ○   119
- ○   122

10 Government economic policy

1   Which of the following will be the most likely consequences of an increase in the money supply?

    ○   Interest rates rise, investment spending rises, and aggregate demand rises
    ○   Interest rates rise, investment spending falls, and aggregate demand falls
    ○   Interest rates fall, investment spending falls, and aggregate demand falls
    ○   Interest rates fall, investment spending rises, and aggregate demand rises

2   Mixiland is currently suffering from high levels of inflation, and the Government of Mixiland wants to use deflationary fiscal policy to bring inflation levels under control.

Which of the following measures would be expected in Mixiland?

1   Tax increases
2   Increasing the budget deficit
3   An interest rate rise

    ○   1 only
    ○   1 and 3 only
    ○   2 and 3 only
    ○   1, 2 and 3

3   Bali Co is based in a country whose government wants to pursue an expansionary fiscal policy in response to current economic conditions in the country.

Which of the following should Bali Co expect to see specifically as a result of the Government's policy?

Select all that apply.

    ☐   Increases in the rates of taxation on company profits
    ☐   Increases in tax allowances for investment in capital equipment
    ☐   Increasing levels of government expenditure
    ☐   Reductions in interest rates
    ☐   Reductions in the level of borrowing

4   Which TWO of the following are ways a government may seek to reduce the rate of demand-pull inflation in an economy?

    ☐   Reducing interest rates
    ☐   Increasing direct taxes
    ☐   Applying more stringent controls over bank lending
    ☐   Increasing the budget deficit
    ☐   Increasing the money supply ('quantitative easing')

5   Ipland has been suffering from increasing levels of cyclical (demand-deficient) unemployment in recent years, and the Government is considering ways to reduce the unemployment level.

Which of the following is likely to be the best way to tackle cyclical unemployment?

- ○   Reduce the level of government spending in the economy
- ○   Make more training available for the unemployed
- ○   Reduce the level of interest rates
- ○   Manage the foreign currency reserves to increase the exchange rate

6   The central bank of Bosland implements monetary policy in the country on behalf of the Government. The bank has adopted a policy of inflation targeting to help control inflation levels in the country.

Currently, the rate of inflation in Bosland is above the target level, as a result of the high levels of aggregate demand in the country.

Which of the following is most likely to happen as a result of this?

- ○   The bank will raise interest rates.
- ○   The bank will increase the money supply.
- ○   The budget deficit will increase.
- ○   Unemployment will fall.

7   Bizzi Co manufactures and sells consumer electronic goods, such as refrigerators, microwave ovens and washing machines.

The Government in the country in which Bizzi Co operates has recently increased interest rates.

Indicate whether the following statements about the consequences of the change in interest rates are true or false.

The level of investment Bizzi Co makes in new capital equipment will be expected to fall.

The level of consumer demand for Bizzi Co's products will be expected to fall.

Pull down list:

True
False

8   Which of the following correctly describes the purpose of supply side policy?

- ○   To raise the level of aggregate demand in an economy
- ○   To manage the money supply in an economy
- ○   To improve the ability of an economy to produce goods and services
- ○   To reduce unemployment by reducing the supply of labour

9   Identify whether the following taxes are regressive, proportional or progressive.

Income tax in Kayland is charged at 20% on a person's salary, regardless of what their salary is.

Income tax in Essland is charged at 25% on earnings of up to $50,000 and then at 40% on any excess over $50,000.

The price of petrol in Veeland includes a petrol duty of 30% of the net cost of the petrol.

Pull down list:
Progressive
Proportional
Regressive

10   The figures below show the amount of income that workers receive after tax at different levels of salary in three countries.

	Income before tax ($)	Income after tax ($)
Country X	20,000	16,000
	40,000	30,000
Country Y	20,000	14,000
	40,000	29,000
Country Z	20,000	18,000
	40,000	34,000

Which of the countries have a progressive tax system?

○   Country X and Country Y
○   Country X and Country Z
○   Country Y and Country Z
○   Country X, Country Y and Country Z

11   Which of the following statements are valid criticisms which could reduce the effectiveness of fiscal policy in managing aggregate demand in an economy?

1   Government expenditure may replace private expenditure rather than providing additional expenditure.

2   Increased government borrowing, required to fund additional expenditure, could lead to higher interest rates.

3   Fiscal policy is slower to implement than monetary policy.

○   1 and 2 only
○   1 and 3 only
○   2 and 3 only
○   1, 2 and 3

12 The country of Norland has enjoyed significant economic growth in recent years. However, recently, the rate of inflation has started to increase and the Government has responded to this by raising interest rates.

In response to the high levels of consumer demand for its product in recent years, B Co moved to larger premises. The company used loan funding from its bank to acquire the premises and to install new equipment in it.

What impact will the Government's interest rate policy be most likely to have on B Co's sales and pre-tax profit margin?

- ○ Sales will decrease; Net profit margin will decrease
- ○ Sales will decrease; Net profit margin will increase
- ○ Sales will increase; Net profit margin will decrease
- ○ Sales will increase; Net profit margin will increase

The following information relates to Questions 13–15.

The economy of Beeland has been suffering from recession in recent years. A new government has just been elected, and one of its priorities is to restore economic growth in the country.

13 The new Government of Beeland is operating an expansionary fiscal policy.

Which of the following is this most likely to include?

- ○ Reducing interest rates
- ○ Increasing corporation tax
- ○ Increasing government expenditure
- ○ Increasing the money supply

14 In addition to its expansionary fiscal policy, the Government has also decided to pursue an expansionary monetary policy.

XXX Co is a company based in Beeland.

Which of the following will XXX Co expect to result from the Government's recent policy initiatives?

1 Increased revenue
2 Increased interest charges
3 Increased profitability

- ○ 1 only
- ○ 1 and 2
- ○ 1 and 3
- ○ 2 and 3

15 The Government's critics have argued that, rather than trying to control the economy through fiscal or monetary policy, it would be more effective to use supply side policy.

Which TWO of the following proposals are consistent with the principles of supply side policy?

- ☐ Increase government involvement in the provision of services (for example through nationalising key services)
- ☐ Reduce income taxes in order to increase the incentives for people to work
- ☐ Increase money supply in order to stimulate an increase in consumer spending
- ☐ Increase flexibility in the labour market by reducing the power of trade unions

BPP LEARNING MEDIA

16 Which TWO of the following are examples of an indirect tax?

☐ Capital gains tax.
☐ Motorway tolls levied by the government.
☐ Corporation tax.
☐ Inheritance tax.
☐ Tax on carbon emissions from firms.

17 Which TWO of the following government actions are part of its fiscal policy?

☐ Decreasing interest rates in order to stimulate private sector investment.
☐ Using official foreign currency reserves to buy the domestic currency.
☐ Borrowing money from the capital markets and spending it on capital goods.
☐ Reducing indirect taxation while maintaining public spending.

11 International economics

1 Which of the following is most likely to cause a country's balance of payments current account to move towards a deficit?

○ A devaluation of that country's currency
○ An expansionary fiscal policy
○ Government subsidies to domestic producers
○ A rise in the rate of domestic saving

2 BBB Co is based in the UK, but it can only obtain one of the key inputs into its production process from a supplier in the US.

Last month, when the exchange rate between UK£ and US$ was £1 : $1.5, BBB paid the supplier £32 million for the products it supplied.

BBB needs to buy the same quantity of the product this month, and the price of the product (in $) remains the same. However, the exchange rate has now fallen to £1 : $1.45.

How much, in £, will BBB have to pay the supplier this month? (Give your answer to 1 decimal place.)

£ [   ] billion

3 Identify whether the following statements are true or false.

A marked deterioration in the UK's balance of trade will lead to an increase in the value of £ sterling.   [▼]

A deterioration in the balance of trade will lead to a reduction in demand for foreign currency to pay for imports.   [▼]

Pull down list:

True
False

4 Which of the following will typically raise (appreciate) the exchange rate for a country's currency?

1 A fall in the value of imports into the country
2 A rise in foreign investment in the country
3 A fall in interest rates in the country

- O 1 and 2 only
- O 1 and 3 only
- O 2 and 3 only
- O 1, 2 and 3

5 The exchange rate for Japanese yen against the US dollar has moved from 110 yen per $ to 120 yen per $. Demand from US customers for goods imported from Japan is price elastic.

What will be the impact of the movement in the exchange rate?

- O US customers will find Japanese goods more expensive and expenditure on goods imported from Japan will increase.

- O US customers will find Japanese goods cheaper and expenditure on goods imported from Japan will increase.

- O US customers will find Japanese goods more expensive and expenditure on goods imported from Japan will decrease.

- O US customers will find Japanese goods cheaper and expenditure on goods imported from Japan will decrease.

6 Under a system of freely floating exchange rates, what will be the most likely outcome of a fall in the inflation rate in Exland relative to the rates of inflation in Exland's major trading partners?

- O A fall in demand for exports from Exland
- O An increase in the foreign exchange rate of Exland's currency
- O A decrease in the supply of the currencies of Exland's trading partners
- O An increase in Exland's interest rate

7 Which of the following will be expected to result from a decision to reduce interest rates in a country?

1 Increased sales as result of higher disposable income for customers

2 Higher business profits as a result of increased sales and lower interest expenses for businesses

3 Lower import costs for companies in the country as the value of the country's currency strengthens against other currencies

- O 1 and 2 only
- O 1 and 3 only
- O 2 and 3 only
- O 1, 2 and 3

8   Which of the following could cause a country's balance of payments current account to move towards a surplus?

     ○   A rise in the volume of commodity imports
     ○   An inflow of foreign capital into the economy
     ○   An increase in foreign tourism into the country
     ○   An increase in the Government's tax receipts

9   The high rate of inflation in Country D's economy has led to a deterioration in its balance of payments current account.

Which of the following are valid reasons which could explain this?

1   Export sales have fallen as the rate of inflation has made Country D's exports less competitive.
2   Higher domestic prices have made imported goods more attractive in Country D.
3   Excess demand from consumers in Country D has reduced the volume of goods available for export.

     ○   1 and 2 only
     ○   1 and 3 only
     ○   2 and 3 only
     ○   1, 2 and 3

10   Companies in Country B rely on exports to surrounding countries for a significant proportion of their revenue, because their productive capacity is greater than that required to satisfy domestic demand. However, in recent years, Country B has had a small deficit on its balance of payments current account due to the volume of products and services it imports.

Following a change in the Government's macroeconomic policy, the economy in Country B is now growing more rapidly than that of its trading partners.

Identify whether this change in growth rates will be expected to increase or decrease the following:

Quantity of exports from Country B to its trading partners   [▼]

Quantity of imports into Country B from its trading partners   [▼]

Balance of payments current account deficit   [▼]

Pull down list:
Increase
Decrease

11   Country DDD has an open economy (ie it trades with other countries). Consumers in Country DDD purchase products from firms in foreign countries, while firms in Country DDD export products to consumers in other countries.

The value of Country DDD's currency relative to other currencies is determined through a floating exchange rate.

Identify whether the following would be expected to lead to an appreciation (increase) or depreciation (decrease) in the value of Country DDD's currency.

A contractionary fiscal policy in Country DDD causing a reduction in the level of consumer spending in Country DDD

[▼]

A reduction in the rate of inflation in Country DDD making exports from Country DDD more competitive in foreign countries

[▼]

Pull down list:

Appreciation
Depreciation

---

12   Assume that demand for imports in the UK is elastic.

Indicate what would be expected to happen to the following if £ sterling depreciates in value against the currencies of other countries.

The price, in £ sterling, of imported goods

[▼]

Total spending by the UK on imported goods

[▼]

Pull down list:

Decrease
Increase

The following information relates to Questions 13–15.

Under a system of floating exchange rates, the value of Country B's currency (the 'B') has fallen from 1B : $1.125 to 1B : $1.10.

Companies XXX and YYY are both based in Country B.

Company XXX exports a large proportion of its products. The raw materials it uses to manufacture its products are all local.

Company YYY does not export any of its products, but it imports a significant number of the raw materials used to manufacture its products and it cannot obtain substitutes for these raw materials in its own country.

13   Which of the following statements will be correct, following the fall in the exchange rate?

○   Demand for Company XXX's products will increase and Company YYY's profitability will increase.
○   Demand for Company XXX's products will increase and Company YYY's profitability will decrease.
○   Demand for Company XXX's products will decrease and Company YYY's profitability will increase.
○   Demand for Company XXX's products will decrease and Company YYY's profitability will decrease.

---

14   The price per unit of a key raw material Company YYY uses in its production process is $337.50.

What impact has the change in the exchange rate had on the cost per unit (in Bs) of the raw material?

○   Decrease by 8.44
○   Decrease by 6.82
○   Increase by 8.44
○   Increase by 6.82

---

15 Following the change in the exchange rate, Company XXX and other companies in Country B have experienced an increase in demand from customers in foreign countries for their products.

Identify the impacts this will have on demand for currency B and on its exchange rate.

Demand for currency B | ▼ |

Value of currency B (exchange rate) | ▼ |

Pull down list:

Decrease

Increase

No change

---

16 Consider the following figures which have been extracted from a country's balance of payments accounts:

Exports of tangible goods	$36,248 million
Imports of tangible goods	$38,197 million
Exports of services	$27,853 million
Imports of services	$24,619 million

What is the country's balance of trade? (Include a minus sign in the drop down box if the balance is negative).

$ | ▼ | [   ] billion

Pull down list:

+

−

---

17 Which one of the following will appear in the financial account of Teeland's balance of payments accounts?

○   Insurance cover provided by a Teeland insurance company for a customer based in Exland

○   A loan provided by the Teeland government to the government of Wyeland

○   Direct investment in a new factory in Zedland by a company based in Teeland

○   Foreign holidays purchased by residents of Teeland

---

18 Cave Co is based in Country A where the currency is the A$.

Cave Co has just agreed two foreign currency transactions. In both cases the transactions involve companies in Country B where the currency is the peso.

Transaction 1. The sale of goods by Cave Co: 100,000 peso payment due to be made..

Transaction 2. The purchase of supplies by Cave Co: A$6,000 payment to be paid.

The exchange rate is currently 1A$ = 20 peso.

What would be the impact on Cave Co's profit (in A$s) if the value of the A$ was 10% higher when the transactions take place?

○   Decrease by $455.

○   Increase by $91.

○   Increase by $455.

○   Decrease by $91.

19 Mike Co is based in Country C where the currency is the C$.

Mike Co has just agreed a purchase of 100,000 units of component A from a company based in Z-land where the currency is the Euro.

The price of each unit will be 1.20 euros and the invoice will be paid in euros in 6 months' time.

The current exchange rate is 1C$ = 0.50 euros.

What would be the impact on Mike Co's costs (in C$s) if the value of the C$ was 20% higher when the transaction takes place? (to the nearest C$)

C$ [   ]

[▼]

Pull down list:
Higher
Lower

12 International trade

1   Which of the following is a benefit for a country which adopts a flexible exchange rate system?

   O   It provides certainty for organisations engaged in international trade.
   O   There will be little or no currency speculation.
   O   Monetary policy can be used to manage the exchange rate.
   O   It reduces the need for central banks to keep reserves of foreign exchange.

2   Which of the following policies for correcting a country's balance of payments current account deficit is an expenditure-reducing policy?

   O   Increasing the rate of direct tax in the country
   O   Devaluation of the country's currency
   O   The imposition of an import tax
   O   The use of import quotas on goods and services coming into the country

3   Which of the following are 'protectionist measures' in international trade?

   Select all that apply:

   ☐   Import quotas
   ☐   Trade deficits
   ☐   Subsidies for local producers
   ☐   Outsourcing
   ☐   Fixed exchange rates
   ☐   Tariffs

4   Which THREE of the following are benefits to a country from joining a single currency area?

☐   Reduced transaction costs
☐   Lower interest rates
☐   Elimination of exchange rate uncertainty
☐   Reduced price transparency
☐   Single monetary policy across the currency area
☐   Increased competition and efficiency

---

5   Country X is a major producer and exporter of steel.

Country M imports steel from Country X, but the Government of Country M is trying to protect its domestic steel industry, and has imposed a tariff on steel imported from Country X.

Demand in Country M for steel imported from Country X is relatively price inelastic.

Identify whether the following will increase or decrease as a result of the Government imposing the tariff.

Demand in Country M for steel from Country X   [▼]

Expenditure in Country M on steel imported from Country X   [▼]

Total revenue in Country X from steel exported to Country M   [▼]

Pull down list:
Decrease
Increase

---

6   Which of the following are characteristics of a customs union?

1   Common external tariffs
2   Consumption is diverted away from goods produced outside the union
3   A common system of taxation between members
4   Free trade among members

○   1, 2 and 3
○   1, 2 and 4
○   1, 3 and 4
○   2, 3 and 4

---

7   Which of the following statements best expresses the difference in the role played by the World Bank compared to the IMF?

○   The IMF provides loans whereas the World Bank is where governments keep deposits to help them conduct international currency transactions.

○   The World Bank focuses on regulation and stabilisation of the financial system whereas the IMF focuses on economic development and trade.

○   The IMF lends at subsidised rates whereas the World Bank lends at market rates.

○   The World Bank provides longer-term funding for developing and building economies whilst the IMF seeks to stabilise countries that are in crisis.

8 Which of the following has been a significant driver of globalisation?

○ Divergent consumer tastes in different national consumer markets
○ Growth opportunities and weak competition for firms within domestic markets
○ Tariffs and import quotas being imposed by national governments
○ Developments in information and communication technologies

9 Organisations in a country will benefit from which of the following if the country joins a free trade area?

1 Organisations can import raw materials from countries inside the free trade area tariff-free.
2 There will be exchange rate stability between the member countries.
3 Prices of rival, imported products from countries outside the free trade area would rise.

○ 1 only
○ 1 and 2 only
○ 3 only
○ 2 and 3

10 XXX Co, a company based in Erewhon, manufactures cars. It sells some of its cars to consumers in Erewhon, but many of its customers are in foreign countries.

Until recently, XXX Co has manufactured all of its cars in Erewhon, but it has recently relocated its global manufacturing plant to Keyland to take advantage of lower production costs.

Indicate whether this change will cause the following to increase or decrease:

GDP in Erewhon

Foreign direct investment in Keyland

Exports from Keyland

Pull down list:

Decrease
Increase

11 Which of the following best describes the function of the World Trade Organization (WTO)?

○ To encourage economic growth through providing loans and technical assistance to countries

○ To smooth out trade imbalances between countries and to promote a structured growth in world trade

○ To create an area of freedom without internal frontiers and an internal market where competition is free and undistorted

○ To liberalise trade by persuading countries to abolish tariffs and other barriers

12   An accountant has been asked to use the PESTEL framework to analyse the opportunities and threats facing a company.

Which FOUR of the following should the accountant include in their analysis?

☐   A newly elected government intends to increase tariffs on imports.

☐   Rising production costs have led to a fall in the company's profit margin.

☐   Interest rates are expected to increase soon.

☐   Changes in tastes and trends are increasing demand for a product.

☐   The company's highly skilled workforce means the quality of its products is superior to competitors' products.

☐   New technologies have led to the development of substitute products.

The following information relates to Questions 13–15.

LLL Co is a large manufacturing company based in Homeland. Currently, all of LLL Co's operations are based in LLL Co, and nearly all of its sales are to domestic customers.

However, the senior managers at LLL Co are currently considering opportunities for the company to expand internationally. They are also concerned at the relatively high wage costs in Homeland compared with those in other countries.

13   Which of the following are drivers encouraging LLL Co to expand internationally?

1   Economic growth and increasing disposable income among consumers in Homeland
2   Higher wage costs and lower staff productivity in Homeland compared to other countries
3   Improved transport and communication links between Homeland and other countries

○   1 and 2 only
○   1 and 3 only
○   2 and 3 only
○   1, 2 and 3

---

14   In recent years, the market for LLL Co's products has become increasingly competitive, and LLL has seen its market share fall in recent years.

Which of the following factors could have contributed to this?

1   Competitors in Homeland moving production offshore
2   Multinational companies from outside Homeland entering the market
3   Reduction in the level of tariff barriers on imports entering Homeland

○   1 and 2 only
○   1 and 3 only
○   2 and 3 only
○   1, 2 and 3

---

15 LLL Co's management accountant has been using PESTEL analysis to help identify external influences which could affect the company's performance.

Identify which category in the analysis is most appropriate for each of the following influences.

Consumer demand in Homeland is expected to fall following an increase in unemployment.

There is a trend among consumers in Homeland to buy domestically produced goods in preference to imported ones.

The Government is expected to impose a quota on the volume of manufactured goods being imported into Homeland.

Pull down list:

Political
Economic
Social
Technological

---

16 A group of countries have entered a trade agreement under which there are no restrictions on the movement of goods and services between the countries, nor on the movement of any of the other factors of production between the countries. However, the counties have imposed common external tariffs on imports from non-member countries.

Despite entering the agreement though, the countries have no plans to share a common currency.

What type of trade agreement have the countries entered?

○   Common market
○   Customs union
○   Economic union
○   Free Trade Area

---

17 Which of the following is NOT a consequence of international trade?

○   Countries can specialise in products in which they have a natural advantage.
○   It may lead to the purchase of dangerous or unethical imported products.
○   The creation of external economies of scale.
○   An increase in the impact of the recession phase of the trade cycle.

---

18 A group of countries have imposed a common external tariff on imports from non-member countries. There are no restrictions on the movement of goods and services between the countries, although there are some restrictions on the movement of labour.

What type of trade agreement have the countries entered into?

○   A single market.
○   A customs union.
○   A free trade area.
○   A common market.

19   Which of the following correctly describes the main aim of the IMF?

  ○   To be an organization for liberalizing trade.

  ○   To support the stability of the international monetary system by providing support to countries with balance of payments problems.

  ○   To be a place for governments to settle trade disputes.

  ○   To provide financial and technical assistance to support developing countries.

20   Which of the following is NOT a key feature of globalisation?

  ○   Companies with production facilities in more than one country.
  ○   Reduced economic divisions between countries.
  ○   Increased commonality of tastes across countries.
  ○   Improved communications.

13 Functions of the financial system

1   When a financial intermediary (such as a bank) provides short-term facilities for savers and long-term ones for borrowers, which of the following services is it performing?

  ○   Maturity transformation
  ○   Risk transformation
  ○   Aggregation
  ○   Interest transformation

2   Which of the following is the most suitable source of finance for a company undertaking a major long-term investment project?

  ○   Bank overdraft
  ○   Three year bank loan
  ○   Bill of exchange
  ○   Share issue

3   Which of the following are appropriate sources of long-term debt finance for an organisation?

  Select all that apply.

  ☐   Mortgages
  ☐   Overdrafts
  ☐   Bonds
  ☐   Issuing shares
  ☐   Bills of exchange

4   Which TWO of the following correctly describe the functions of financial intermediaries?

  ☐   Decreasing the level of liquidity in the economy
  ☐   Reducing the amount of debt which firms have
  ☐   Channelling funds from depositors to borrowers
  ☐   Providing advice on alternative ways of obtaining finance

5   In the global banking crisis of 2007–2010, some commercial banks needed injections of government funds to avoid them becoming insolvent. This was because the bank had loaned too much money to the property market and, when the property market collapsed, the banks could not recover the funds they needed to repay customers who had placed deposits with them.

Which of the following functions of a financial intermediary had the banks failed to perform in this situation?

- ○   Maturity transformation
- ○   Risk transformation
- ○   Aggregation
- ○   Provision of a transmission mechanism

6   What is the main function of the money market?

- ○   To enable businesses and government to obtain liquidity
- ○   To encourage saving by individuals and businesses
- ○   To permit the efficient buying and selling of shares
- ○   To deal in credit instruments of more than 1 year maturity

7   Identify whether each of the six sources of finance listed below is short-term or long-term.

Place each source of finance under the correct heading in the table.

Convertible bonds   **Shares**   **Commercial Paper**

Debentures   **Bills of exchange**   **Overdraft**

Short-term finance	Long-term finance

8   A bond with a nominal value of $100 has a coupon rate of interest of 4% per year.

If the current market price of the bond is $95, what is the annual interest yield on the bond?

- ○   3.8%
- ○   4.0%
- ○   4.2%
- ○   5.0%

9   Which of the following correctly describe the functions of financial intermediaries?

1   Linking people who wish to borrow and people who wish to lend
2   Regulating capital and money market activities
3   Matching the supply of funds to the demand for funds

- ○   1 only
- ○   1 and 2
- ○   1 and 3
- ○   2 and 3

10   Which TWO of the following are the most appropriate sources of short-term finance for an organisation?

☐   Finance leases
☐   Bank overdrafts
☐   Bills of exchange
☐   Mortgages
☐   Share issue

---

11   ZZZ Co's liquidity position has been getting worse in recent months, despite its sales increasing. The company's auditors have highlighted weaknesses in ZZZ Co's credit control function as a major cause of its cash flow problems.

Which of the following is the most appropriate course of action for ZZZ Co?

○   Obtain a new bank loan
○   Increase its overdraft
○   Sell bills of exchange
○   Re-mortgage its factory

---

12   Zelda plc has decided to use long-term debt to finance its expansion, in order to benefit from the tax relief on the interest payments.

Given this, which of the following sources of finance is most appropriate for Zelda plc?

○   Preference shares
○   Debentures
○   Commercial bills of exchange
○   A new issue of ordinary shares

The following information relates to Questions 13–15.

Highfly Co is looking to raise finance to fund the construction of a new airport terminal. This is a major, long-term investment, and Highfly expects the new terminal will take approximately 10 years to complete.

However, Highfly's financial gearing ratio is already high as a result of it substantially enlarging its existing terminal a few years ago.

13   Which TWO of the functions of financial intermediaries will be most useful to Highfly, given its need for a large amount of finance to fund a long-term project?

☐   Maturity transformation and Risk transformation
☐   Maturity transformation and Aggregation
☐   Aggregation and Risk transformation
☐   Liquidity and Risk transformation

---

14   Which of the following is the most appropriate source of finance for Highfly to fund the construction of the new terminal?

○   Issuing new shares
○   Debenture loans
○   A mortgage secured on the new terminal
○   Certificates of deposit

BPP
LEARNING
MEDIA

15 In the context of its high gearing ratio, Highfly is looking more generally at possible sources of finance for the future which are not debt finance.

Which of the following is NOT an example of debt finance?

O   Finance lease
O   Retained earnings
O   Five year loan
O   Trade credit

16 Which of the following are issued on the capital market to raise finance for a company?

O   Treasury Bonds.
O   Gilts.
O   Treasury Bills.
O   Debentures

17 Which of the following will NOT be traded on the money market?

O   Ordinary shares.
O   Bills of Exchange.
O   Treasury Bills.
O   Certificates of deposit.

14 Commercial and central banks

1   BST Bank operates a 12.5% liquidity ratio.

BST has just received an initial deposit of $2.1 million from a new customer.

Including this initial deposit, how much will the bank's total deposits rise by?

(Give your answer to 1 decimal place.)

$ [   ] million

2   Which of the following describes the bank credit multiplier?
O   The relationship between an injection of government spending into the economy and the increase in national income
O   The relationship between the value of an initial increase in a bank's deposits and the total rise in deposits
O   The process by which cash leaks out of the banking system into less formal accumulations
O   The process by which government controls the creation of credit in the banking system

3   There has recently been an increase in the money supply in Country S.

Identify whether this increase in the money supply will be expected to cause the following to rise or fall.

The rate of interest in Country S

▾

Levels of borrowing and investment

▾

Pull down list:

Fall

Rise

---

4   Which of the following are functions of a central bank?

1   Maintaining monetary stability in an economy

2   Providing long-term finance for capital investment

3   Acting as banker to the Government

4   Acting as lender of last resort

O   1, 2 and 3

O   1, 2 and 4

O   1, 3 and 4

O   2, 3 and 4

---

5   If all the commercial banks in a national economy operated on a cash reserve ratio of 20%, how much cash has to be deposited with the banks for the money supply to increase by a further $300 million, in addition to the initial deposit?

O $60 million

O $75 million

O $225 million

O $240 million

---

6   Which of the following are functions of a central bank?

Select all that apply:

☐   Setting interest rates at an appropriate level to meet the Government's inflation target

☐   Using open-market operations to influence interest rates and the size of the money supply

☐   Transforming customer deposits into loans with a longer maturity

☐   Buying and selling currencies on the foreign exchange market in order to manage the exchange rate

☐   Packaging individual amounts deposited by savers and lending them on to borrowers in bigger amounts

---

7   Which of the following correctly identifies the three main aims of a commercial bank?

O   Aggregation, Liquidity, Security

O   Liquidity, Profitability, Responsibility

O   Liquidity, Profitability, Security

O   Profitability, Responsibility, Security

BPP
LEARNING
MEDIA

8   Which THREE of the following are functions of a central bank?

☐   Managing fiscal policy
☐   Maintaining price stability
☐   Controlling the balance of payments current account
☐   Holder of the foreign exchange reserves
☐   Acting as lender of the last resort

9   The reserve requirement for banks in Country A is 10%. The Central Bank of Country A has sold $20 million of government bonds but has not subsequently spent the money it raised from the sale.

What will the impact of this be on money supply in Country A?

○   Increase by $2 million
○   Decrease by $200 million
○   Decrease by $20 million
○   Decrease by $2 million

10   Identify whether a decision by a central bank to use its open-market operations to sell government bonds will be expected to cause an increase or a decrease in the following.

Commercial banks' balances with the central bank

▼

Money supply

▼

Interest rates

▼

Pull down list:

Decrease
Increase

11   Which of the following statements about quantitative easing are true?

1   Quantitative easing involves the central bank injecting large amounts of money into the economy to try to stimulate aggregate demand.

2   In the process of quantitative easing, a central bank creates new money electronically and uses it to buy financial assets, such as government bonds.

○   Neither of them
○   Statement 1 only
○   Statement 2 only
○   Both of them

12   Last year, the current market rate of interest in Country X was 5%, and the Government issued some new bonds at $100 each, offering a nominal yield of 5%.

Since then, the rate of economic growth in Country X has slowed significantly, and the market interest rate has now fallen to 2%.

What is the maximum price a rational investor will now be prepared to pay for the government bonds?

○ $40
○ $97
○ $100
○ $250

The following information relates to Questions 13–15.

The commercial banks operating in Country D are required to maintain a liquidity ratio of 8%, and they all comply with this requirement exactly.

There have been some suggestions recently that this ratio should be increased to 10%, but there have not yet been any changes to the banking regulations in Country D.

13   One of the commercial banks in Country D has received a cash deposit of $1 million from a new investor.

What is the maximum **additional** increase in total bank deposits which will result from this initial investment?

(Give your answer to 1 decimal place.)

$ [   ] million

---

14   The banking regulator in Country D has now ruled that commercial banks must keep a liquidity ratio of 10%.

Identify the impact that this change will be expected to have on the following:

The level of the bank (or credit) multiplier   [▼]

The extent of the increase in total deposits resulting from an initial deposit   [▼]

Pull down list:
Decrease
Increase
No change

---

15   The central bank in Country D is concerned about the current rapid rate of growth in the economy, and it intends to use open-market operations to control the money supply.

Which of the following statements most appropriately describes the course of action the central bank should take?

○   The bank should buy government securities in order to reduce the money supply and increase interest rates.

○   The bank should buy government securities in order to increase the money supply and increase interest rates.

○   The bank should sell government securities in order to reduce the money supply and increase interest rates.

○   The bank should sell government securities in order to increase the money supply and reduce interest rates.

15 Financial mathematical techniques

1   How much will an investor have after 5 years if they invest $5,000 at 12% simple interest per annum?

(Give your answer as a whole number, with no decimal places.)

$ [   ]

2   $2,000 is invested in a bank account which earns compound interest at 5% per year.

What will the cash value of the account be, to the nearest $, at the end of 5 years?

○ $2,431
○ $2,500
○ $2,553
○ $2,680

3   Jane invests $10,000 now. For two years it will earn 8% per year (compound interest) and then for an additional five years it will earn 10% per year (compound interest).

What is her investment worth at the end of year seven? (Give your answer to the nearest $.)

$ [   ]

4   $10,000 is invested now at a nominal interest rate of 12% with interest compounded monthly.

To the nearest $, what is the value of the investment at the end of the second year?

○ $12,000
○ $12,400
○ $12,544
○ $12,697

5   An investor requires an annual (year-end) income of $15,000 in perpetuity.

Assuming a fixed rate of interest of 4% each year, and ignoring administrative charges, what is the sum required now to purchase the annuity?

Give your answer to the nearest $.

$ [   ]

6   A saver invests $1,500 now and at the end of each of the next four years.

If the annual interest rate is 6%, what is the present value (to 2 decimal places) of this investment? (Use tables)

$ [   ]

7   A firm has arranged a 10 year lease, at an annual rent of $8,000.

The first rental payment has to be paid immediately, and the others are to be paid at the end of each year.

What is the present value of the lease (to the nearest $) based on a discount factor of 12%? (Use tables)

$ [   ]

8   A company has taken out a $400,000 mortgage to help it acquire a new warehouse.

Interest on the mortgage is compounded at 6% each year, and the mortgage is to be repaid by 15 equal year-end repayments.

To the nearest whole $, the annual repayment will be which of the following?

○ $26,667
○ $41,186
○ $50,667
○ $63,908

9   Deeside Co is considering whether or not to invest in a project which would cost $200,000 now, but would then yield $20,000 per annum every year in perpetuity, starting 1 year from now.

Deeside's cost of capital is 8%.

Calculate the present value of the future cash inflows the project will generate.

(Give your answer as a whole number, with no decimal places.)

$ [   ]

10   XYZ Co is evaluating four mutually exclusive projects. The projects all require the same initial investment, but will generate different cash inflows as shown in the table below.

Project	Year 1 $'000	Year 2 $'000	Year 3 $'000	Year 4 $'000
A	10,000	8,000	6,000	6,000
B	8,000	8,000	8,000	8,000
C			16,000	14,000
D				35,000

The cash inflows from each project will be received on the last day of the year.

XYZ Co's cost of capital is 8%.

Which of the projects will generate the highest net present value?

○   Project A
○   Project B
○   Project C
○   Project D

11   An investment has a net present value of $8,000 at 10% and one of -$2,000 at 17%.

What is the approximate IRR on the investment? (Give your answer to 1 decimal place.)

[   ] %

12   A company invested $40,000 into a bank deposit account which pays interest at 4% per year.

      At the end of Year 3, the company withdrew $20,000.

      The remaining balance was reinvested for another two years, at 4%.

      What is the value of the company's investment at the end of Year 5?

      O $26,784.00
      O $27,034.12
      O $27,866.18
      O $28,000.00

The following information relates to Questions 13–15.

Poch Co has been growing rapidly in recent years, and is considering a range of additional new projects which could help to sustain this growth in future.

Poch is already committed to Project A, but the company's management team are still uncertain about which of Projects B–E to invest in.

13   Project A will cost $500,000 to set up initially, but will generate cash inflows of $38,400 per year. These are expected to continue in perpetuity.

      The company's cost of capital for Project A is 6%.

      What is the net present value of Project A?

      (Give your answer to the nearest $, and indicate in the drop down box whether the net present value is positive or negative.)

      $ [▼] [   ]

      Pull down list:

      +

      –

---

14   Projects B, C and D will each require initial capital expenditure of $250,000.

      The table below shows the expected cash inflows generated by the three projects, and this cash will be received by Poch Co on the last day of each year.

	Year 1 ($'000)	Year 2 ($'000)	Year 3 ($'000)	Year 4 ($'000)
Project B	80	90	75	65
Project C	90	100	80	-
Project D	60	80	100	50

None of the projects are expected to generate any further income after the end of Year 4.

A cost of capital of 8% is to be used to evaluate Projects B, C and D.

On the basis of their net present values, which of the projects should Poch Co invest in?

      O   Project B only
      O   Projects B and D
      O   Projects B and C
      O   Projects C and D

---

15 Using a cost of capital of 10%, the net present value of Project E is $12,000, but at a cost of capital of 18% its net present value is –$4,000.

What is the internal rate of return (IRR) of Project E?

○   12%
○   14%
○   16%
○   22%

---

16 A company is buying a new piece of machinery which will increase the amount of its product the company can produce.

The business case for the machinery identified the following:

Initial cost	$500,000
Useful life	4 years
Scrap value of the machinery at the end of Year 4	$20,000

Additional income generated from additional production:

Year 1	$140,000
Year 2	$170,000
Year 3	$160,000
Year 4	$150,000

The company uses a cost of capital of 6% to evaluate new projects, and assumes the income from additional production will be received at the end of each year.

What is the net present value of the machinery?

○ $36,520
○ $51,460
○ $52,360
○ $56,520

---

17 Company A invests $600,000 now with compound interest at 5% but at the end of year 3 withdraws $100,000. The remainder of the investment is invested for another two years at 2%.

What is the value of the remaining investment at the end of year 5? (to the nearest $100)

$ [ ]

---

18 A bank loan has been taken out which costs an effective annual rate of 6% per year, however the actual interest payments are made each quarter (ie four times a year).

Calculate the interest rate that is payable each quarter (as a percentage, to 2 decimal places).

[ ] %

BPP
LEARNING
MEDIA

16 Impact of interest and exchange rate changes on business performance

1   The exchange rate (spot rate) for the Euro against the US dollar is currently €1 : $1.1152.

However, dealers in the foreign exchange markets expect the spot rate in 3 months' time to be €1 : $1.0977.

Based on this information, the Euro is expected to:

○   Depreciate by 1.57% against the US dollar over the next 3 months
○   Depreciate by 1.59% against the US dollar over the next 3 months
○   Appreciate by 1.57% against the US dollar over the next 3 months
○   Appreciate by 1.59% against the US dollar over the next 3 months

2   Sten Co is based in a Eurozone country, but sells large quantities of its product in the UK, where the sales price is quoted in £.

Last month, the exchange rate between the Euro and the £ was €1 : £0.8, and the selling price of Sten's product in the UK was £400.

The exchange rate between Euro and £ has now changed to €1 : £0.85.

Assuming the sales price in the UK changes in line with movements in the exchange rate, what will the price of Sten's product be in the UK now (to the nearest £)?

○   £340
○   £376
○   £425
○   £588

3   Henna Co is a US company but some of its customers are based in the UK.

The price of the products for customers in the UK is listed in £. Henna Co allows customers 30 days' credit before they have to pay for their products.

In its financial statements, Henna Co records the amount receivable from a sale in US$, based on the exchange rate at the time of the sale.

When customers settle their accounts, the amount they pay is based on the exchange rate at the current time (not the rate when the original purchase took place).

Last month, Edwards Ltd, a UK customer, bought a product priced £5,000. The exchange rate at the time of the transaction was £1 : $1.50.

Edwards Ltd settled its account with Henna Co yesterday, by which time the exchange rate was £1 : $1.40.

How did the actual cash amount (in $) received from the sale to Edwards Ltd compare to the receivables amount Henna Co originally recorded?

○ $500 less
○ $238 less
○ $238 more
○ $500 more

4   A UK retail company buys products from a supplier in China.

The unit price of product X is 4,700 Chinese yuan.

The retailer pays for the goods after 30 days.

The exchange rate at the time of the purchase was £1 : 9.4 Chinese yuan.

By the time the UK company settled its account with the supplier the exchange rate was £1 : 9.0 Chinese yuan.

Calculate the foreign currency gain or loss the UK company makes on each unit of product X as a result of the movement in the exchange rate.

(Give your answer to 2 decimal places.)

£ [   ]   [▼]

Pull down list:

gain
loss

---

5   If a country's currency strengthens (appreciates), identify whether this will make its exporters and importers better or worse off in the following situations.

Exporters who have made sales on credit but have not yet received payment for those sales   [▼]

Importers who have made purchases on credit but have not yet paid for these purchases   [▼]

Pull down list:

Better off
Worse off

---

6   Which of the following are true of forward contracts?

1   They fix the rate for a future transaction.
2   They are a binding contract.
3   They are flexible once agreed.
4   They are traded openly.

O   1, 2 and 4 only
O   1, 2, 3 and 4
O   1 and 2 only
O   2 only

---

7   Which TWO of the following are true in relation to futures contracts, in comparison to forward contracts?

☐   They are more expensive.
☐   They are only available in a small amount of currencies.
☐   They are less flexible.
☐   They may be an imprecise match for the underlying transaction.

8   A company based in Farland (with the Splot as its currency) is expecting a US customer to pay $1,000,000 in 3 months' time and wants to hedge this transaction using currency options.

What of the following are appropriate options for the company based in Farland to use?

1   A Splot put option
2   A US dollar put option
3   A Splot call option
4   A US dollar call option

○   2 or 3
○   2 only
○   1 or 4
○   4 only

9   Company Z (based in a Eurozone country) recently purchased goods for $770,000 from Stayt Co (a US company), with payment due in 30 days.

The exchange rate at the date of the purchase was €1 : $1.10.

If the exchange rate at the date of payment is €1 : $1.13, which of the following is correct?

○   Company Z will make an exchange loss of €18,584.07.
○   Company Z will make an exchange loss of €16,894.61.
○   Company Z will make an exchange gain of €16,894.61.
○   Company Z will make an exchange gain of €18,584.07.

10   Interest rates in Isopia have recently been reduced.

Identify whether the following will be expected to increase or decrease as a result of the lower interest rates.

Consumer spending   [▼]

Borrowing   [▼]

Saving   [▼]

Business investment   [▼]

Pull down list:

Decrease
Increase

11   Sunrise Co manufactures consumer electronics products, which are considered by most consumers to be
      luxury items.

      It is currently evaluating a potential new product and has prepared an investment appraisal as part of the
      evaluation process.

      However, interest rates in Sunrise's country have now been increased, and the company is concerned about
      the potential impact this could have on its investment appraisal.

      Identify the expected impact of the interest rate change on the following.

      Expected revenues from the new product   [▼]

      Cost of capital used to discount future revenues   [▼]

      Net present value of the investment in the new product   [▼]

      Pull down list:

      Decrease
      Increase
      No change

12   Which of the following are most likely to occur following an increase in interest rates in Country Y?

      Select all that apply:

      ☐   The amount of capital expenditure by businesses in Country Y will decrease.
      ☐   The amount of net government borrowing will increase.
      ☐   The demand for exports from Country Y will decrease.
      ☐   The level of saving relative to the level of consumption in Country Y will decrease.
      ☐   The level of aggregate demand in Country Y will increase.

The following information relates to Questions 13–15.

Multon Co is based in Country M, whose currency is the M$.

Country M is not part of the Eurozone (whose currency is the Euro), but Multon makes a number of sales to
customers in the Eurozone. Competition in the European market is tough, however, and demand for Multon's
product is sensitive to variations in price.

In addition, Multon has to import one of the key raw materials for its production process from China. However, it
does not make any sales to Chinese customers.

13   Which combination of exchange rate movements will be most beneficial for Multon Co?

      O   The value of the M$ strengthens (appreciates) against the Euro and also strengthens against the
            Chinese yuan.

      O   The value of the M$ strengthens (appreciates) against the Euro but weakens (depreciates) against the
            Chinese yuan.

      O   The value of the M$ weakens (depreciates) against the Euro and also weakens against the Chinese
            yuan.

      O   The value of the M$ weakens (depreciates) against the Euro but strengthens (appreciates) against the
            Chinese yuan.

14 The current exchange rate between the M$ and the Euro is M$1 : €1.5.

Multon has just made a €1,000 sale to a European customer, on credit.

By the time the customer pays, the M$ has strengthened by 10% against the Euro.

What will the amount Multon receives, in M$, be?

- ○ $606.06
- ○ $740.74
- ○ $1,350.00
- ○ $1,650.00

15 Multon Co has to pay 10 million Chinese yuan to a major supplier in three months' time.

The current exchange rate between the M$ and the Chinese yuan is M$1 : 10 Chinese yuan.

What should Multon Co do to reduce the risk of an unfavourable movement in the exchange rates between the M$ and the Chinese yuan before the payment is made?

- ○ Enter into a call option in $, at an option rate of M$1 : 10 Chinese yuan
- ○ Enter into a forward contract to buy M$1 million in 3 months
- ○ Enter into a forward contract to buy 10 million Chinese yuan in 3 months
- ○ Arrange a put option in Chinese yuan, conferring the right to sell 10 million yuan in 3 months' time

16 Country X operates a system of floating exchange rates. The government's fiscal deficit and the country's trade deficit are both high.

Which of the following is LEAST likely to result from an increase in interest rates by the central bank?

- ○ A fall in private sector investment.
- ○ A fall in government spending on capital goods.
- ○ An increase in the price of imported goods.
- ○ A rise in consumer saving.

17 Data and information

1 Which of the following correctly describes the difference between data and information?

- ○ Data is quantitative and information is qualitative.
- ○ Data is information that has been processed.
- ○ Information is data that has been processed.
- ○ Data is qualitative and information is quantitative.

2 The management accountant for a supermarket group has produced a report analysing revenue for all the stores in the group for the last year. The figures in the report have been summarised from the daily transaction records from each store.

The group's senior management team use annual revenues as a key factor when deciding whether to close any stores.

The group acquired some new stores halfway through the last year, but the accountant's report doesn't distinguish between these stores and ones which were open for the full year.

Which of the characteristics of good information does the report fail to provide?

- ○ Relevance
- ○ Completeness
- ○ Accuracy
- ○ Timeliness

3   Which of the following is the best form of presentation to illustrate the relative sizes of different categories of cost incurred in running a factory?

A   Component bar chart
B   Frequency distribution
C   Simple bar chart
D   Ogive

4   The table below shows the average salaries for the different regions in a country.

Region	Average salary
	$
South-East	21,500
Midlands	20,800
North-East	18,200
North-West	17,500
South-West	16,700

Which of the following will be the most appropriate type of diagram to draw to illustrate the regional differences in average salary?

- ○ A component bar chart
- ○ A multiple bar chart
- ○ A percentage component bar chart
- ○ A simple bar chart

5   Which of the scatter diagrams A–D (below) shows no relationship between the level of unemployment (U) and the national income (NI)?

- ○ Diagram A
- ○ Diagram B
- ○ Diagram C
- ○ Diagram D

6   One of the key macroeconomic policy targets in a country is that the annual rate of inflation should not exceed 2%.

The chart below shows the actual inflation figures for each month (comparing the price index in that month to the equivalent figure a year earlier).

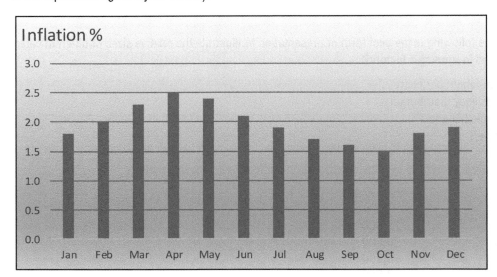

For how many months in the year was the inflation target achieved?

○   4
○   5
○   7
○   8

BPP
LEARNING
MEDIA

7   The scatter diagram below illustrates the level of weekly sales of Delph Co's product at different price points.

When explaining the figures to their colleagues, the Sales Director pointed out that, at one stage, sales had been affected when a competitor launched a new product.

Identify the point on the graph which corresponds to this point where the competitor launched the rival product.

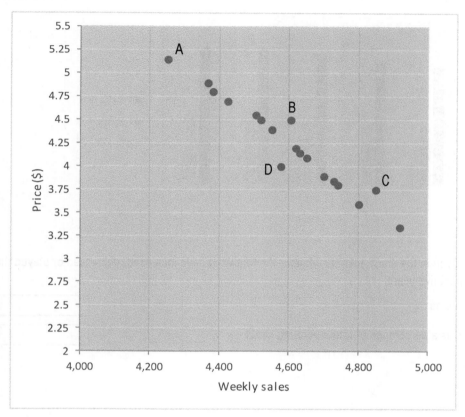

○   Point A
○   Point B
○   Point C
○   Point D

8   Smit Co allocates its operating costs into three categories: production costs, logistics costs and marketing costs.

Costs for the past five years are shown in the following diagram. (Year 5 is the most recent year.)

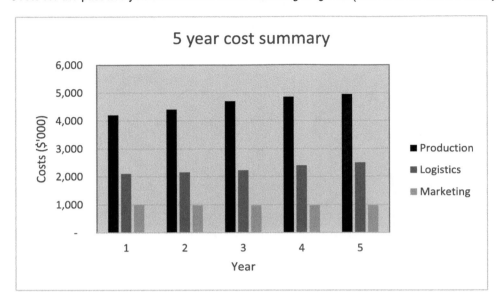

Using the data given in the chart, identify whether the following have increased, decreased or stayed the same over the past five years.

Total operating costs

Marketing costs as a percentage of total operating costs

Pull down list:

Decreased
Increased
Stayed the same

9   One of the performance indicators a building society uses to monitor performance is the number of new mortgage offers it makes per week.

The graph below provides a cumulative summary of these weekly figures for the 52 weeks in the last year.

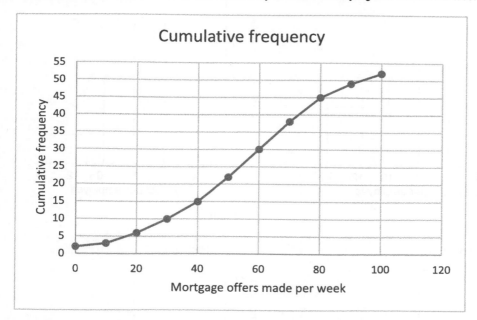

How many weeks in the last year did the building society make more than 60 mortgage offers per week?

| | weeks

10   A company is concerned about falling productivity levels among its staff, and has recorded the following data on days lost through employee sickness in a year.

Days lost per employee		Number of employees
At least	Less than	
0	6	18
6	8	30
8	10	18
10	14	12

Which of the following histograms represents the data most accurately?

O   Graph A
O   Graph B
O   Graph C
O   Graph D

Graph A

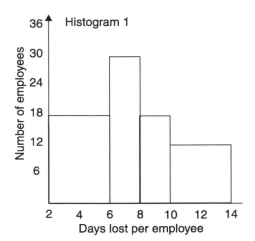

Graph B

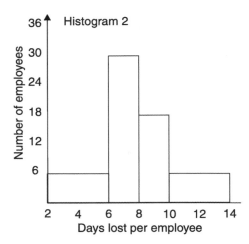

Graph C

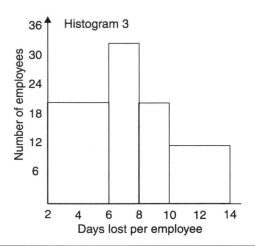

Graph D

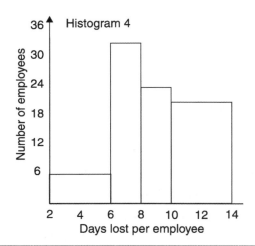

11   Which of the following statements are true?

1   Big data analytics allows businesses to analyse and reveal insights in data which they have previously been unable to analyse.

2   In order for organisations to analyse big data and to gain insights from it, the source data needs to be structured within a software package.

3   One of the key features of big data is the speed with which data flows into an organisation, and with which it is processed.

O   1 and 2 only
O   1 and 3 only
O   2 and 3 only
O   1, 2 and 3

12   Seon Co runs a chain of fashion retail stores. A key element of its commercial success comes from being able to identify customer trends, and responding to them, more quickly than its competitors.

Which of the following are potential sources of big data for Seon Co?

Select all that apply:

☐   Online video clips of clothes being shared by customers
☐   Daily transactions records from stores
☐   Inventory records from the chain's central warehouse
☐   Keywords from conversations about fashion on social media
☐   The number, and level, of discounts Seon Co has to offer on its products

---

The following information relates to Questions 13–15.

One of the key performance indicators a supermarket uses for evaluating the performance of its stores is the weekly revenue each store generates.

The graph below provides a cumulative summary of the weekly figures for the store in Dorville for the 52 weeks in the last year.

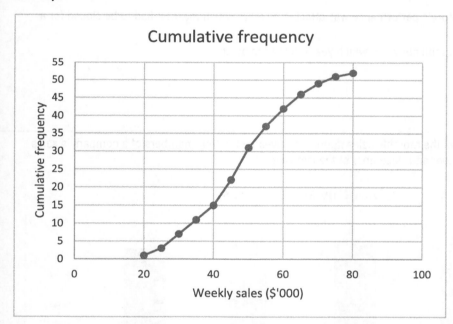

13   For how many weeks in the last year was the Dorville store's revenue less than or equal to $40,000?

[   ] weeks

---

14   What was the most common level of weekly sales in the Dorville store in the last year?

○ $40,000–$45,000
○ $45,000–$50,000
○ $50,000–$55,000
○ $75,000–$80,000

---

15   The graph below shows the Dorville store's annual sales and operating profits for the last five years. (Year 5 is the most recent.)

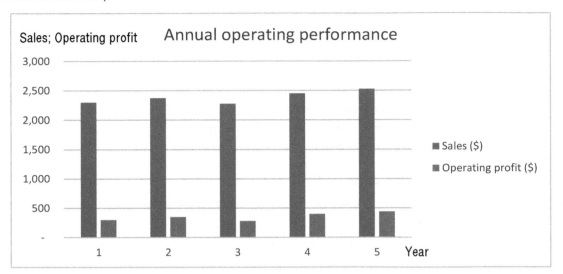

In one of the years, the store's performance was affected by a fire which meant it had to be closed for a week.

Based on the data in the graph above, in which year did the fire occur?

O   Year 2
O   Year 3
O   Year 4
O   Year 5

16   The following chart shows the monthly sales figures achieved by the four members of a company's sales team for October, November and December of the last year.

Which member of the team achieved the highest sales for December?

- ○ Dylan
- ○ Rory
- ○ Sergio
- ○ Alana

---

17   A company employs 40 staff, but there are significant variations in their wages. The following table shows a frequency distribution of the employees' weekly wages:

Weekly wage	Frequency
Above $150 but less than $200	4
Above $200 but less than $300	8
Above $300 but less than $400	10
Above $400 but less than $500	9
Above $500 but less than $700	6
Above $700 but less than $1,000	3

This information is plotted in a histogram, in which the rectangle representing weekly wages between $200 and $300 is 8 cm high.

What is the height of the rectangle representing weekly wages between $500 and $700?

- ○ 3 cm
- ○ 4 cm
- ○ 6 cm
- ○ 12 cm

---

18 Forecasting

1   A company launched a new product last year, and the management team are monitoring sales of the product closely.

Over the first 10 months of this year, they have noticed that demand for the product has been increasing in a way which can be described using the equation $y = a + bx$, where $b = 10.05$.

If $\Sigma x = 60$, $\Sigma y = 1,048$, $\Sigma xy = 7092$, $\Sigma x^2 = 440$ and $n = 10$, what is the value of 'a' in the equation $y = a + bx$?

(Give your answer to 1 decimal place, and indicate in the drop down box whether the value of 'a' is positive or negative.)

▼	

Pull down list:

+

−

2   Economists working for the Government in Ecobia have been trying to identify if there is any relationship between the level of unemployment in the country and the rate of inflation.

They have calculated the following values from the data they have collected, where 'x' is the rate of unemployment and 'y' is the rate of inflation:

Σx = 210
Σy = 187
Σx^2 = 4,634
Σy^2 = 3,865
Σxy = 4,208
n   = 10

What is the value of the correlation coefficient?

(Give your answer to 2 decimal places and indicate in the drop down box whether the value of the coefficient is positive or negative.)

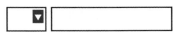

Pull down list:

+
–

---

3   DEF Co has monitored how demand for its product has varied at a range of different prices, as shown in the following diagram.

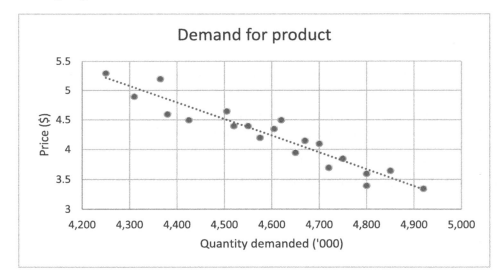

From the diagram, which of the following is the correlation coefficient between price and quantity demanded?

O   +0.95
O   +0.47
O   –0.47
O   –0.95

4   The sales department in XXX Co has noticed that some of the company's products appear to sell better than others in different countries. To investigate this further, they have undertaken some market research looking at customer awareness of five of their main products.

The results of the research are shown below. (The product ranked '1' is the product which had the highest customer awareness score in each survey.)

Product	Country A – rank	Country B – rank
Alpha	1	4
Beta	3	1
Camma	4	3
Delta	5	2
Epsilon	2	5

What is the value of the rank correlation coefficient between the findings from the two countries?

(Give your answer to 1 decimal place and indicate in the drop down box whether the value of the coefficient is positive or negative.)

[▼] [   ]

Pull down list:

+

−

---

5   Using data from 12 European countries, it has been calculated that the correlation between the level of car ownership and the number of road deaths is 0.83.

Which of the statements shown follow from this?

1   High levels of car ownership cause high levels of road deaths.

2   There is a strong relationship between the level of car ownership and the number of road deaths.

3   69% of the variation in the level of road deaths from one country to the next can be explained by the corresponding variation in the level of car ownership.

4   83% of the variation in the level of road deaths from one country to the next can be explained by the corresponding variation in the level of car ownership.

○   1 and 2 only
○   1 and 3 only
○   2 and 3 only
○   2 and 4 only

6   A company uses regression analysis to establish a total cost equation for budgeting purposes.

Data for the past 4 months is as follows:

Month	Total cost	Quantity produced
	$'000	$'000
1	57.5	1.25
2	37.5	1.00
3	45.0	1.50
4	60.0	2.00
	200.0	5.75

The company has identified that the gradient of the regression line (Y = a + bX) is 17.14.

What is the value of 'a' in the equation?

○   25.36
○   48.56
○   74.64
○   101.45

7   Over an 18-month period, XYZ Co's sales have been found to have an underlying linear trend of y = 7.112 + 3.949x, where y is the number of items sold and x represents the month.

Monthly deviations from trend have been calculated, and volume of sales in month 19 is expected to be 1.12 times the trend value.

What is the forecast number of items to be sold in month 19?

○   73
○   82
○   92
○   94

8   Using an additive time series model, the quarterly trend in a company's operating profit is given by Y = 65 + 7t, where Y is the forecast profit (in $'000) and t is the quarter (starting with t = 1 in the first quarter of 20X5).

If the seasonal component in the fourth quarter is –30, what is the forecast for the company's operating profit for the fourth quarter of 20X6, to the nearest $'000?

○   63
○   151
○   123
○   91

9   A company analyses the time series of its quarterly sales using a multiplicative model.

Based on its data analysis from previous years, the company has identified that Quarter 3 has a seasonal factor of 0.97.

Seasonally adjusted figures for Quarter 3 in the current year were $47.92 million.

What were the actual sales for Quarter 3 in the current year?

- ○ $46.48 million
- ○ $46.95 million
- ○ $48.89 million
- ○ $49.40 million

10   Which of the following scenarios best illustrates the concept of the residual component in a time series model?

- ○   A long-term increase in a company's production costs of 2% per year
- ○   An increase in unemployment figures caused by a global recession over the past two years
- ○   The impact on sales of a fire which destroyed part of a company's warehouse and the inventory in it
- ○   An increase in visitor numbers of a tourist destination during the main holiday season

11   Which of the following are necessary if forecasts obtained from a time series analysis are to be reliable?

1   The trend must not be increasing or decreasing.
2   The trend must continue as in the past.
3   Extrapolation must not be used.
4   The same pattern of seasonal variation will continue as in the past.

- ○   1 only
- ○   1 and 2 only
- ○   2 and 4 only
- ○   1 and 3 only

12   The accountant at Hopwood Autos has carried out a time series analysis of the number of cars sold ('Sales'), calculating the moving average trend and average seasonal variations using the additive method. She has only partially completed this analysis. The calculations carried out so far are shown in the following table.

Year	Quarter	Sales	Moving total of 4 quarters' sales	Moving average of 4 quarters' sales	Trend	Seasonal variation
20X2	1	200				
	2	110				
			870	217.5		
	3	320			219	+101
			884	221.0		
	4	240			222	+18
			892	223.0		
20X3	1	214			225	−11
			906	226.5		
	2	118			229	−111
			926	231.5		
	3	334			232	+102
			932	233.0		
	4	260			234	+26
			938	234.5		
20X4	1	220			235	−15
			944	236		
	2	124			238	?
			962	240.5		

The seasonal variation figure for Quarter 2 in 20X4 is currently missing from the analysis.

What should the correct figure be?

○   −116.5
○   −114
○   +114
○   +116.5

The following information relates to Questions 13–15.

For each month in the last year, a utility company has monitored the monthly volume of gas consumed in an area against the average temperature in that area. The following results have been obtained.

X Average temperature (°C)	Y Gas consumption (Million kWh)	X^2	Y^2	XY
2.5	26.70	6.25	712.89	66.75
0.8	33.10	0.64	1,095.61	26.48
4.6	28.60	21.16	817.96	131.56
8.9	22.40	79.21	501.76	199.36
14.6	17.30	213.16	299.29	252.58
15.1	10.10	228.01	102.01	152.51
18.3	5.10	334.89	26.01	93.33
21.2	4.20	449.44	17.64	89.04
20.3	4.40	412.09	19.36	89.32
14.2	11.60	201.64	134.56	164.72
10.6	23.50	112.36	552.25	249.10
6.5	24.50	42.24	600.25	159.25
137.60	**211.50**	**2,101.10**	**4,879.59**	**1,674.00**

13   Using the data obtained, what is the correlation coefficient between average monthly temperature and gas consumption for the last year?

(Give your answer to 3 decimal places and indicate in the drop down box whether the value of the coefficient is positive or negative.)

[▼] [   ]

Pull down list:

+

−

14   Based on the data collected so far, the gas company's management accountant has plotted the following graph of the relationship between temperature and gas consumption.

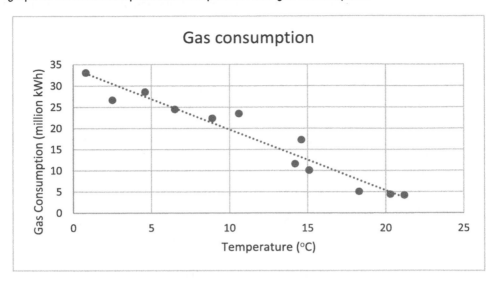

The average figure for the month just ended was 17°C.

To the nearest million kWh, how much gas will the gas company expect to have been consumed in that month?

[   ] million kWh

---

15   The management accountant at the utility company has identified that the company's revenues are subject to the following quarterly seasonal variations:

Quarter	Quarter 1	Quarter 2	Quarter 3	Quarter 4
Seasonality	+45%	+65%	−50%	−35%

Revenue for Quarter 2 this year followed the expected pattern, and the actual revenue figure was $350 million.

Assuming a multiplicative model for the time series, what are the quarterly revenues expected to be for Quarter 3 this year?

O $318.18 million
O $288.75 million
O $175.00 million
O $106.06 million

16 Zena Co has identified that monthly sales for a product are closely related to the number of times it advertises in the national press. Zena Co uses regression analysis to help forecast monthly sales.

The data used for the analysis is as follows:

Month	Number of adverts	Product sales
1	5	46,200
2	3	35,400
3	6	51,000
4	4	41,750
5	3	34,340

The gradient of the regression line is 5,400. Using regression analysis, what would be the forecast monthly sales for month 6, if Zena only places two adverts in that month?

○　19,058
○　22,680
○　26,930
○　29,858

17 Endelby Co's revenue for the last month was $74,000.

The underlying trend was $85,000 and the seasonal factor is 0.87.

What is the seasonally-adjusted figure for Endelby's revenue for the last month, assuming a multiplicative model for seasonal adjustment?

○　$73,950
○　$64,380
○　$85,057
○　$97,701

18 A retail company uses time series analysis, and the multiplicative model, to help forecast sales. The retailer has identified that the following seasonal (annual) factors apply, due to external factors such as inflation.

20X0	20X1	20X2	20X3	20X4	20X5	20X6	20X7
100	104	109	116	124	132	143	153

The company has decided to rebase the index so that 20X5 = 100.

What will the index for 20X7 now be, to the nearest whole number?

[   ]

19   A hotel company operates 12 different hotels, which charge different prices based on their location and quality. The company is evaluating the extent to which the price charged by the hotels corresponds to occupancy levels (ie the % of rooms which are booked each night).

The company's management accountant has ranked price against occupancy rates for the 12 hotels, and identified the difference ('d') between the rankings for each hotel. The resulting value of d^2 was 196.

What is the Spearman's rank correlation coefficient ('R') between price and occupancy rates for the company's hotels?

(Give your answer to 2 decimal places, and indicate in the drop down box whether the value of the coefficient is positive or negative.)

▼	

Pull down list:

+

−

---

20   A hospital is trying to forecast demand for its accident and emergency services using a combination of time series and regression analysis models.

Based on an analysis of the demand in previous quarters, the hospital has produced the following equation for the predicted number of admissions:

$y = 15x + 7{,}230$

where 'x' represents the number of the quarter, and 'y' represents the predicted number of admissions.

The value of 'x' for the first quarter of the next year will be 21.

The hospital has identified that the following seasonal (quarterly) variations, using the multiplicative model:

Quarter 1:   1.1
Quarter 2:   0.95
Quarter 3:   0.9
Quarter 4:   1.05

What is the difference between the predicted numbers of admissions for Quarter 1 and Quarter 4 for the next year?

○   45
○   330
○   359
○   369

---

21   The correlation coefficient between two variables (x and y) has been calculated as 0.9.

Which TWO of the following statements about x and y are correct?

☐   There is a weak relationship between x and y
☐   Values of y increase as values of x increase
☐   If the values of x and y were plotted on a graph, the line relating them would have a gradient of 0.9
☐   81% of the variation in y can be explained by the corresponding variation in x
☐   Increases in x cause corresponding increases in y

22 A restaurant company is looking to analyse the extent to which customer satisfaction levels affect sales in its restaurants. The company owns five restaurants, and the following table shows their customer satisfaction levels and sales growth over the last year.

Customer satisfaction scores are given on a scale of 1-5, where '5' is 'Excellent' and '1' is 'Very poor'.

Restaurant	Average customer satisfaction score	Sales growth (%)	Rank	Rank
Holly	4.1	2.4	3	1
Ivy	3.8	2.0	4	3
Juniper	4.4	2.2	2	2
Kirsch	3,2	1.9	5	4
Lemon	4.5	1.6	1	5

What is the coefficient of rank correlation between customer satisfaction and sales growth for the restaurants?

- ○ −0.1
- ○ −0.05
- ○ 0
- ○ 0.1

---

23 Unemployment numbers actually recorded in a town for the first quarter of 20X7 were 18,200.

The underlying trend at this point was 22,400 people and the seasonal factor (based on the multiplicative model) is 0.80.

Using the multiplicative model for seasonal adjustment, what is the seasonally-adjusted unemployment figure for the quarter?

- ○ 22,750
- ○ 28,000
- ○ 14,560
- ○ 22,400

---

24 A firm has identified the following equation for the predicted costs in the next quarter:

$y = 225x + 250$

where 'x' represents the output (in 000s) and 'y' represents the total cost in $000s.

Assuming that output is forecast to be 2,000 units, which of the following statements is true?

- ○ The variable cost per unit is $225,000.
- ○ The fixed cost per unit is $250.
- ○ Fixed costs will be higher than variable costs.
- ○ Total cost is expected to be $700,000.

25   A company is looking to analyse the extent to which customer satisfaction scores affect profits. The company has four divisions, and the following table shows their customer satisfaction scores and profits over the last year.

Customer satisfaction scores are given on a scale of 1-4, where '4' is 'Excellent' and '0' is 'Very poor'.

Division	Profits ($m)	Average customer satisfaction score
A	3.6	3.6
B	2.5	2.5
C	1.8	0.8
D	4.0	2.0

What is the Spearman's rank correlation coefficient between satisfaction and profits? (to one decimal place)

Answers

1 Organisations and stakeholders

1   The correct answer is: The owners of a firm cannot be sure that managers will pursue the strategy which is most appropriate to achieving the owners' goals.

The principal-agent problem highlights the issue that the owners (shareholders) of a company (ie the principals) cannot be sure that the strategies being pursued by the managers of the company (ie the agents) are the ones which are most appropriate to achieving the owners' goals.

Monitoring managers' performance should improve shareholders' control over managers, which should reduce the principal-agent problem. Similarly, linking rewards to performance should help to reduce the problem (because managers' interests will be better aligned to shareholders' interests).

The large number of shareholders in a company describes a joint stock company, but this is not, in itself, a factor in the principal-agent problem.

2   The correct answers are: Employees and volunteers, Donors and Beneficiaries.

Charities, unlike companies, do not have shareholders. Charities could not operate without the work of employees and volunteers, or without donations from their donors, so these are both important stakeholder groups. The objective of a charity is to provide help or support for its beneficiaries, so beneficiaries are also an important stakeholder group.

3   The correct answer is: Shares in a private limited company have to be sold privately.

The essential difference between the two types of company is that shares in private limited companies have to be sold privately and cannot be offered for sale publicly (for example, on a stock exchange). By contrast, public limited companies can offer new shares publicly, and many public limited companies are quoted on a stock exchange meaning that existing shareholders can sell their shares on the stock exchange.

A state-owned enterprise is in the public sector, but it is not a public limited company.

4   The correct answer is: 4 only

A QUANGO is a state-owned organisation. However, public limited companies are private enterprises. The 'public' element relates to the fact that their shares can be publicly traded on a stock exchange.

Although charities are not-for-profit organisations, they are not state-owned and so are not public sector organisations. Likewise, producer co-operatives are owned by their workers rather than the state.

5   The correct answer is: High power: Low interest

Shareholders with high power and low interest need to be kept satisfied. While they are satisfied, they are likely to remain passive, but if they become dissatisfied, they will become more active and their level of interest in the company will increase.

Stakeholders with high power and high interest are key players. An organisation needs regular communication with its key players to ensure that any decisions are acceptable to them.

Stakeholders with low power but high interest need to be kept informed of any decisions, while an organisation only needs to give minimal effort to the needs of stakeholders with low power and low interest.

6   The correct answer is: 1 and 2 only

In contrast to commercial organisations, not-for-profit and public sector organisations do not have a simple primary objective, such as profit maximisation. Primary objectives are likely to be based around value or quality of service – but this may mean many things eg quick response times, high-quality service, high levels of usage. In addition, there will be financial constraints which need to be managed and may conflict with quality objectives. So, objectives are difficult to set because of the range of different interests which have to be considered (point 1).

In addition, it can often be difficult to identify the output of not-for-profit and public sector organisations, and consequently to measure performance in a way that is meaningful (point 2). For example, are good exam results an adequate measure for the quality of teaching – given that they depend on the aptitude of the students as well as the input of the teachers?

In contrast to commercial organisations whose strategic objectives will reflect changes in the competitive environment, the broad strategic objectives of not-for-profit organisations tend not to change over time, so point (3) is incorrect.

7   The correct answer is: 1 and 3 only.

A frequent performance objective in not-for-profit organisations is achieving value for money, where value for money is assessed in relation to economy, efficiency and effectiveness.

Point (1) relates to economy – keeping input costs as low as possible while still being able to achieve the level of quality required.

Point (3) relates to efficiency – generating the maximum output possible from the resources being used.

Not-for-profit organisations do not have shareholders, and their aims are not primarily financial. Therefore, point (2) is not correct.

8   The correct answers are: The Chief Executive of DEF Co, DEF Co's non-executive directors, The Chairman of DEF Co

Any member of the Board should be working in the shareholder's best interests. This is the point highlighted in the principal-agent problem, where the shareholders are the principals and a company's directors and managers are the agents.

A bank has a duty to operate in the best interests of their own shareholders, as do supplier companies.

9   The correct answers are: Private sector, Co-operative.

A co-operative is a private sector business which is owned by its workers or customers, who share the profits.

Sometimes co-operatives are not primarily profit seeking, but this may not be the case here. Other features of co-operatives include open membership, democratic control, distribution of surplus in proportion to purchases and promotion of education.

10   The correct answers are: A local authority hospital, a school run by the local education authority.

Measures such as value for money or efficiency are often used in not-for-profit organisations or public sector organisations, such as hospitals or state-funded schools, due to the lack of an underlying profit motive.

Private sector organisations (private college, retailer, public limited company) all have an underlying objective to generate profit and maximise the wealth of their owners.

11   The correct answer is: Customers.

Customers will be the group who are most adversely affected by the change, and are therefore most likely to object to it, because they will have to pay higher prices to buy the products.

The directors' motivation in increasing prices would appear to be to improve profitability following the increase in the cost of the raw materials. Shareholders would be likely to support actions designed to improve profitability rather than to oppose them.

Suppliers are responsible for the rising cost of the raw materials, but would have no direct reason to oppose an increase in the price of the final product.

Employees as a group are unlikely to be affected by the change.

12   The correct answers are: Shareholders, Bankers.

Return on investment will be of greatest importance to shareholders and bankers – both of whom have a direct financial interest in how well the company is performing.

13   The correct answers are:

Client 1 – 'Shareholders vote against directors' remuneration at AGM' | Profit-seeking |

Client 2 – 'Dividends increased despite slight fall in sales' | Profit-seeking |

Client 3 – 'Hospital forced to cut staff in face of government funding cuts' | Not-for-profit |

One of the characteristics which distinguish profit-seeking organisations from not-for-profit ones is their ownership structure. By definition, companies (profit-seeking organisations) are owned by shareholders – therefore, Client 1 must be a profit-seeking organisation.

Similarly, dividends are paid to shareholders, meaning that Client 2 is also a company (a profit-seeking organisation).

By contrast, the hospital (Client 3) appears to be government funded (public sector), meaning that it is a not-for-profit organisation.

14   The correct answers are:

A company whose shares are bought and sold on a stock market | Private sector |

A police force | Public sector |

A football club controlled by its supporters | Mutually owned |

Although a company whose shares are bought and sold on a stock market is referred to as a public limited company, it operates in the private sector where it seeks to generate a profit for its shareholders.

Police forces are public sector organisations, which are funded by local authorities and whose primary objectives will be to ensure that law and order are maintained in local communities rather than to make a profit.

The key feature of mutual organisations is that they are owned by their customers. A football club's supporters are its customers, so a club run by its supporters will be mutually owned.

15   The correct answers are:

Organisation 1 – To prevent crime and protect local communities, and bring to justice those people who commit offences   `Not-for-profit`

Organisation 2 – Maintain recent growth rates in order to increase market share   `Profit-seeking`

Organisation 3 – Achieve favourable pay, benefits and safe working conditions for members   `Not-for-profit`

Organisation 1 is describing some of the typical aims of a police force. Police forces are not-for-profit, public sector organisations.

For organisation 2, although there isn't any specific reference to 'profit', the reference to increasing market share indicates that this organisation is directly competing against other organisations. This is one of the key characteristics of commercial, profit-seeking organisations.

Organisation 3 is describing some of the typical aims of a union. Although unions are not public sector organisations, they are still not-for-profit. The reference to 'members' is the key word here – highlighting that the union is working to support the interests of its members, rather than to generate a profit for owners.

16   The correct answers are:

Stakeholder group	Type of stakeholder
Perway's customers	Connected
Perway's staff	Internal
Trade unions representing Perway's staff	External
Perway's bank	Connected
Environmental pressure groups complaining about pollution from Perway's factories	External
Perway's suppliers	Connected

Employees and management are internal stakeholders.

Connected stakeholders typically include customers, suppliers, shareholders and other providers of finance (eg a company's bank)

External stakeholders include pressure groups, governments and regulators, and local communities.

17   The correct answers are: Organisational goals that are aligned with the individual goals of the managers, Formal control systems such as budgets.

Organisational goals should reflect common goals that individuals work towards.

Control systems may be informal, especially for small organisations; not all organisations have budgets.

18   The correct answer is: 1 and 2 only.

Directors' pay should be controlled by non-executive directors (working as part of a remuneration committee).

Share option schemes encourage directors to care about the share price.

Investment will increase costs in the short-term and may reduce profit. This in turn may damage shareholder wealth in the long-term.

2 Measuring returns to shareholders

1   The correct answer is: $3,230,000

Free cash flow to the firm indicates the cash flows generated by a business in a particular year after tax and investment spending (but before interest).

	$
PBIT	4,000,000
Taxes	170,000
Capital expenditure	600,000
Free cash flow to the firm	**3,230,000**

2   The correct answer is: 25.0%

$$ROCE = \frac{PBIT}{Capital\,employed} = \frac{\$200m}{\$800m} = 0.25 \quad (ie\ 25.0\%)$$

3   The correct answer is: 38.3%

If you are asked to calculate ROCE and you are given 2 years' worth of capital employed figures, you should use an average capital employed figure for the later year.

So capital employed is: (560,000 + 535,500)/2 = 547,750

ROCE = Profit before interest and tax / Capital employed.

So, for 20X9, this is: 210,000 / 547,750 = 38.3%

4   The correct answer is: 20%

$2 / 0.08 = $25

$2 / 0.1 = $20

The value of the shares has fallen from $25 to $20, which represents a 20% fall (5/25).

5   The correct answer is: $0.29

EPS measures profit after tax and preference dividends, divided by the number of equity shares in issue

	$
PBIT	4,000,000
– Interest expenses	(400,000)
PBT	3,600,000
– Taxes	(170,000)
Net income	3,430,000
– Preferred dividends	(500,000)
Earnings	2,930,000
No of shares	10,000,000
EPS	0.293

6   The correct answer is: Poorer outlook for business in general.

The poorer outlook will reduce forecasts of returns and so increase the required rate.

The rate of return investors require will increase as risk increases. So, investors will require a higher average dividend as a company's gearing increases, and they will require a higher return if a business adopts riskier business strategies.

7   The correct answer is: a fall in the level of interest rates in the country.

The fall in interest rates would increase share prices for two reasons: firstly, it would reduce the required rate and so increase the present value of free cash flows; secondly, it would lead investors to take funds from interest-bearing investments and put the funds into equities to get a better return and so bid up the price of shares.

The bankruptcy of a competitor would reduce competition in the industry, which might prompt a rise in the firm's share in the expectation that the reduction in competition will help it to will earn increased profits. However, the reasons for the firm leaving the industry (ie bankruptcy due to problems in the industry), may raise doubts over the future profitability of the industry as a whole. If shareholders are uncertain over the future of the industry, this could cause them to sell their shares, leading to a fall in share prices across the industry as a whole.

If a firm has high borrowing, the interest payments it incurs could make it difficult to maintain the level of dividend payments shareholders require (and hence they will sell their shares, reducing the price of the firm's shares).

Similarly, if the firm's earnings are falling, this could reduce investors' confidence in it (which would reduce share price rather than increasing it).

8   The correct answer is: The investment should not be undertaken as it will lead to a fall in the share price of the company.

The value of the company will reflect the present value of its future cash flows; this will fall if the investment is undertaken.

A negative NPV indicates that discounted future cash flows are not expected to cover the cost of the investment so it should not be undertaken. Even if the firm has no other projects planned, it would be better to keep its capital invested in a bank, rather than investing in a project with a negative NPV.

The time period used should reflect the expected life of the project. There is no justification for increasing the project's life in order to change a negative NPV into a positive one.

Increasing the cost of capital increases the discount rate used in the NPV calculation. If the NPV is already negative, then increasing the cost of capital will make the NPV figure more negative.

9   The correct answer is: 1 and 3 only

Tax rates would affect the cash flows that shareholders will expect to receive, not the discount factor they apply to those cash flows.

10   The correct answer is: Share price.

An important aspect of profit and EPS is that they ignore the capital required to generate the earnings (net income).

ROCE does take capital into account, but is based on historic performance, not future performance. This is also true of profit and EPS.

The share price is determined by discounting future cash flows. The higher the share price, the greater the wealth of shareholders.

11 The correct answers are: A fall in interest rates, Increasing demand for some of XYZ's key products, News of better economic stability in XYZ's home country.

Increasing demand for XYZ's products would be expected to increase revenues and profits, and the expectation of increasing profits will lead to an increase in the price of the company's shares.

Lower interest rates increase the relative yield on shares and investors buy them and bid their price up. This price increase is likely to affect the market as a whole, so XYZ's share price will increase as part of this general market increase. Prices are also likely to rise in response to greater investor confidence in the economy as a whole.

Falling ROCE indicates lower profitability which will likely lead to a fall in the share price.

Increasing levels of borrowing (financial gearing) could be seen as increasing the level of financial risk in the company, which will typically be expected to reduce, rather than increase, the share price.

12 The correct answer is: 0.26

EPS measures profit after tax, divided by the number of equity shares in issue. Although the company's issued share capital is $4 million, the face value of its shares is 50 cents each, meaning that it has 8 million shares in issue.

	$
PBIT	22,800,000
– Interest expenses	(240,000)
PBT	2,560,000
– Taxes	(480,000)
Profit after tax	2,080,000
No of shares	8,000,000
EPS	0.26

13 The correct answer is: 0.33

Capital employed = debt + equity = $30.0m + ($7.5m + $49.5m) = $87.0m

$$ROCE = \frac{Profit\ before\ interest\ and\ tax}{Capital\ employed}$$

$$= \frac{\$29m}{\$87m} = 0.33$$

14 The correct answer is: $1.07

Number of shares = $7.5m / 0.5 = 15m

$$Earnings\ per\ share = \frac{Profit\ after\ tax\ and\ preference\ dividends}{Number\ of\ equity\ shares\ in\ issue}$$

$$= \frac{\$16m\ (being\ \$29m - \$3m - \$8m - \$2m)}{15m}$$

$$= \$1.07$$

15   The correct answer is: $7.45 million.

The shareholders expect a return of 15% on their investment in the company, represented by the share capital of $7.5m plus the retained profits (of $49.5m). Therefore the minimum level of return needed to satisfy the shareholders will be $8.55m ($57m × 15%).

The level of profit which this needs to be compared against is the company's profit after tax and after preference dividends, which in this case is $16.0m ($29.0 – $3.0 – $8.0 – $2.0).

So, the company is currently generating $7.45m ($18.0m – $2.0m – $8.55m) more than the minimum amount it needs in order to satisfy its equity shareholders.

16   The correct answer is: 21.8%

The investors benefitted from the increase in share price as well as the dividend received.
Therefore, their total return over the year is $0.60 per share ($0.35 capital growth, plus $0.25 dividend).

The rate of return in based on the share price at the start of the year (ie $2.75), so the rate of return is $0.60/$2.75 = 21.8%.

17   The correct answer is: 3.6%

Dividend yield = Dividend per share / market price per share.

Therefore dividend yield = $0.1 / $2.80 = 3.6%

Note. The dividend yield is based on the market price of the shares ($2.80 each) not their nominal price ($1 each).

3 Demand, supply and price

1   The correct answer is: Point B

The effect of the increase in household income will be to increase the demand for all normal goods at any given price, meaning that the demand curve will shift to the right (to D_1).

Similarly, the effect of the fall in average unit costs of production will mean that the supply curve shifts to the right (to S_2).

Point B represents the new equilibrium, ie the intersection between D_1 and S_2.

2   The correct answer is: The supply curve for DVD discs will shift to the right. The price of the discs will fall and more discs will be supplied.

A reduction in the cost of producing the discs will cause the supply curve for DVD discs to shift to the right. If their costs are lower, then suppliers are prepared to supply more at the prevailing market price. More generally, an outward (rightward) shift in the supply curve means that output will increase at all prices. Consequently, the price of the discs will fall and more discs will be supplied.

3   The correct answer is: 1, 2 and 3.

An advertising campaign for foreign holidays will be expected to lead to a rise in the demand for foreign holidays (ie the demand curve shifts to the right). Similarly, a rise in the price of domestic holidays will make foreign holidays relatively more attractive – meaning the demand curve for foreign holidays shifts to the right.

A fall in the disposable incomes of consumers will be expected to lead to a fall in the demand for foreign holidays, because although consumers might still want a holiday they will be less able to pay for one. In this case, the demand curve shifts to the left.

However, a rise in the price of foreign holidays will lead to a movement along the demand curve, rather than a shift in the demand curve.

4   The correct answer is: A fall in the price of a substitute.

As the price of a substitute falls, demand will transfer to the substitute, leading to a fall in demand for the original product.

The other options would be expected to lead to an outward (rightward) rise in the demand curve.

If the price of a complement falls, this will lead to an increase in demand for it. In turn, this will also be expected to lead to an increase in demand for products associated with it.

5   The correct answer is: 2 and 4.

The introduction of a government subsidy, and the development of new technology which makes production quicker and cheaper, will both be expected to shift a supply curve to the right. A shift to the right indicates that the supply of the good will be increased at every price.

A rise in the cost of factors of production, or the introduction of an indirect tax on the good will have the opposite effect – they will cause the supply curve to shift to the left. So, even though the market price of the good remains the same, firms will be prepared to supply less of the good at that price.

6   The correct answer is: Demand for Q will increase, leading to a shortage of Q and causing the price of Q to rise.

As the supply of Finto increases, there is an increase in demand for factors of production (like Q). As Q's market was previously in equilibrium, the increase in demand for Q will cause a shortage of Q (demand > supply) which in turn will cause the price of Q to rise.

7   The correct answers are:

| Supply of Zebops | Increase |
| Price of Zebops | Decrease |

Because the market for FFF is initially in equilibrium, an increase in the supply of FFF will lead to a surplus (supply > demand). Consequently, the price of FFF will fall.

This fall in the price of FFF will lower the costs of production of firms using FFF to make Zebops. In turn, this will lead to an increase in the supply of Zebops, such that supply of Zebops now exceeds demand.

The resulting surplus of Zebops will lead to a fall in their price.

8   The correct answers are: A government subsidy for A1, A reduction in the cost of raw materials used to make A1.

A rightward shift in the supply curve of A1 corresponds to an increase in the supply of A1, where that increase is due to any factor other than price of A1.

In this case, a government subsidy for A1 and a reduction in the cost of the raw materials used to make A1 would both increase supply of A1 at any price level, because they will make A1 more profitable.

Increasing the price of A1 will lead to a movement along its supply curve, not a shift in the supply curve.

Increasing the price of B2 and reducing the cost of producing B2 are both likely to increase production of B2. However, because A1 and B2 are goods in joint supply, an increase in the production of B2 is likely to be accompanied by a leftward shift (reduction) in the production of A1, not a rightward shift.

9   The correct answer is: 1 and 3 only.

You must distinguish between factors that cause a shift in the supply curve (a change in the number of people who will offer themselves for the work at any given wage level) and a movement along the supply curve (changes in the number of people who will offer themselves for work in response to changes in the wage level).

A fall in the real wage levels of professional scientists will cause a movement along the supply curve; fewer people will offer to do the work as the wages they receive for doing it falls.

By contrast, a reduction in government spending on science education will mean there are less people who are qualified and able to do the work (regardless of how much they would be paid).

An increase in salaries being paid for non-science jobs means that these become relatively more attractive, meaning the number of people who want to become professional scientists falls.

10   The correct answer is: The supply curve for the good will shift to the right, prices will fall and demand will increase.

A fall in the cost of producing the good will lead to an increase in supply at every price, which means the supply curve will shift to the right.

The conditions of demand have not changed so the demand curve for the good has not shifted. However, the increased supply will lead to a lower equilibrium price. A surplus of supply over demand and a lower price will lead to an increase in demand (to restore the market clearing equilibrium for the product).

11   The correct answer is: Fall in demand for a complementary product.

A fall in demand for the complement will lead to an inward shift in the demand for this product. For example, if the demand for beach holidays falls, this will reduce demand for associated goods (complements) such as swimwear. In turn, this will cause a surplus of swimwear and its price will begin to fall.

The imposition of an indirect tax on the product, and rising costs of production will both lead to an inward shift in the supply curve. This will lead to a shortage of the product, which in turn will lead to an increase in the price in order to restore the market equilibrium.

The health scare is likely to lead to a reduction in demand for the substitute product, meaning that demand for our product could increase. This will lead to an outward shift in the demand curve, resulting in an increase in price, not a fall.

12   The correct answer is: Changes 2 and 4 only.

A change in attitudes towards a product will lead to a shift in the demand curve. If the change is a negative one (as in increased health concerns), the demand curve will shift to the left, indicating that demand for the good at any given price level is less than before. A fall in consumers' income will have the same effect (assuming a normal good, not an inferior good). The fall in income means that consumers' ability to purchase goods is reduced at each price.

A rise in the price of substitute products will cause the demand curve to shift to the right, as chocolate becomes relatively cheaper and more is demanded at each price.

A change in the price of a good itself causes a movement along the demand curve, not a shift in it.

13   The correct answers are:

Year	Relationship between supply and demand
20X1–20X6	Supply < Demand
20X7–20X9	Supply > Demand

The fact that house prices are rising between 20X1 and 20X6 indicates there must be a shortage of houses during that period. Therefore, supply is less than demand (or, alternatively, demand is greater than supply).

By contrast, between 20X7 and 20X9, the falling price indicates there is a surplus of houses, so supply is greater than demand.

Supply only equals demand when the market is in equilibrium, at which point prices remain stable.

14   The correct answer is: 2 and 3.

In order for prices to fall, the supply of houses must increase – in other words, there is an outward shift in the supply curve.

Lower input costs and government subsidies will both reduce the costs of production and thereby encourage builders to build more houses at every price – prompting an outward shift in the supply curve.

However, reducing the number of firms building houses would be expected to restrict supply, rather than increase it.

15   The correct answers are:

Increasing household incomes   Shift in **demand**

Reduction in the cost of mortgages   Shift in **demand**

Shortages of available land   Shift in **supply**

As household incomes increase, many people are likely to spend their extra income either buying a house for the first time, or moving to a more expensive one. Therefore the increase in income leads to an outward shift in the demand curve for houses.

The low cost of mortgages (low interest rates) will also increase demand, because people who may not have been able to afford mortgage repayments when the cost was higher are now able to do so. This again will lead to an outward shift in the demand curve.

A shortage of available land is likely to mean that construction companies are not able to build the number of houses they might otherwise want to at any given price. In effect, this will lead to an inward shift in the supply curve.

4 Price elasticity

1   The correct answer is: Sales volume will increase by 20%.

A 10% fall in the price of a product will lead to a 20% increase in sales volume where the price elasticity is –2.

Note that elasticity of demand measures percentage change in quantity demanded in relation to percentage change in price.

Elasticity of –2 indicates that the product is elastic and therefore total revenue will increase following a fall in price. However, it will not rise by 20%.

2   The correct answer is: Demand is inelastic, supply is inelastic.

Imposing an indirect tax will increase the price paid by a consumer, but could reduce the amount received by a supplier (because they receive the price net of tax).

The total yield from an indirect tax is likely to be greatest when demand for the good is relatively unaffected by the addition of a tax onto the price (ie demand is inelastic) and also when supply is relatively unaffected, even though suppliers will be receiving the price net of the tax (ie supply is also inelastic).

3   The correct answer is: more than 525, More than $3,000

Price elasticity of demand is greater than one, meaning that a fall in price results in a greater than proportional increase in the quantity being demanded.

The price of a bottle of wine has fallen by 5% ($0.3/$6), therefore the quantity demanded will increase by more than 5% – that is, by more than 25.

Price elasticity greater than one indicates that demand is elastic, and therefore total revenue will increase following a reduction in price.

4   The correct answer is: 2.1

The average arc method involves assessing changes in quantity demanded (or price) in relation to the average level of quantity demanded (or price).

Average quantity = (20,000 + 25,000) / 2 = 22,500

Average price = (18 + 20) / 2 = 19

Price elasticity of demand:

$$\frac{(5,000/22,500)\times100}{(-2/19)\times100} = \frac{22.22}{-10.53} = -2.1; \text{ but ignoring the minus sign} = 2.1$$

Note. For standard 'fill the gap' (numeric entry) questions in the computer based assessment, it is not possible to include a minus sign in your answer, as it is a special character. You can only input numbers into the answer for such questions, hence the instruction in this question to ignore the minus sign in your answer.

5   The correct answers are:

If consumers only spend a small proportion of their income on a good, demand for that good will be highly price elastic.

False

A good for which there are a large number of close substitutes will be highly price elastic.

True

If we only spend a very small proportion of our income on a good, then a rise in the price of that good will have very little impact on the amount of it we consume. For example, salt has a very low price elasticity of demand. We spend a very small proportion of our income on salt, so even if there was a large percentage increase in the price of salt we would have relatively little difficulty in paying this, and so demand for salt would not fall substantially. By contrast, if mortgage interest rates rise, then demand for mortgages would be expected to fall substantially, because – given their income constraints – people will no longer be able to afford a mortgage.

Goods which have a large number of close substitutes will be highly price elastic, because if the price of the good rises consumers will simply switch to one of the substitutes rather than paying the higher price.

6   The correct answer is: 2.5.

Price elasticity of supply is calculated as: % change in quantity supplied / % change in price.

Price has increased by 4% ($200/$5,000).

In response to that, quantity supplied has increased by 10% ($400/$4,000).

Price elasticity of supply = 10% / 4% = 2.5

7   The correct answers are:

Supply is likely to be inelastic if firms have lots of spare capacity.

False

Supply is likely to be more elastic in the short run than the long run.

False

Supply is likely to be elastic if a firm has lots of spare capacity, because the spare capacity means it can quickly and easily increase the amount it supplies following the price rise.

Supply is likely to become increasingly elastic the longer the time period being considered. In the immediate aftermath of a price rise, supply is likely to be almost fixed, or could only increase according to any inventory of finished goods already available to sell.

In the longer term, existing firms will have time to increase their production capacity, while new firms may also enter the industry in response to a price rise making production more profitable.

8   The correct answer is: When the price of the good rises, the quantity demanded falls but total expenditure on the good increases.

If demand is price inelastic, then demand responds by a less than proportional amount to a change in price. So, for example, if price rises by 5%, demand will fall by less than 5%. Consequently, total expenditure on a good which is inelastic rises if price rises and decreases if price decreases.

However, although the response is less than proportional, the quantity demanded will still fall following an increase in price.

The only circumstance in which total expenditure on a good remains unchanged following a change in the price of the good is if price elasticity of demand is exactly equal to 1. This is known as unity or unit elasticity.

9   The correct answer is: High costs to consumer of switching to a substitute product.

If the price of a product rises, say mobile phone call rates, some consumers will conclude that they might spend more changing their contract and so on that they would save by switching to a cheaper provider. This reduces price elasticity of demand.

Consumers are more likely to respond to price rises if there are <u>more substitutes</u> which are <u>similar</u> to the product whose price has risen.

Over time, consumers are more likely to become aware of price rises and to respond to them.

10   The correct answers are:

- There are high levels of unemployment among workers with the skills required to make the product,
- The firm making the product has spare capacity in its manufacturing process,
- The firm has high inventory levels of the finished product.

Supply is likely to be elastic if firms have spare capacity or if they can easily obtain additional supplies of the raw materials or labour required to make a product. If the price of the product increases, and therefore becomes more profitable for a firm to make and sell, the firm will respond by obtaining the necessary additional resources to increase the amount it supplies.

Similarly, if a firm has large quantities of a finished product in stock, it can easily increase the amount of the product it supplies to the market.

A shortage in raw materials will make it harder for the firm to increase the amount of the product it makes following an increase in the price of the product. This will mean that the price elasticity of supply for the product is likely to be low. Similarly, if it is difficult for the firm to switch resources away from alternative products, this will make it harder to increase the supply of any given product following an increase in its price.

11   The correct answer is: Increase of $5,600

CIMA have said that when the method for calculating price elasticity of demand is not given in the question, candidates should use the non-average arc (simple) method.

No method is specified in this question, and therefore you should have used the non-average arc (simple) method in your calculations.

The non-average arc method involves assessing changes in quantity demanded (or price) in relation to the initial level of quantity demanded (or price), not in relation to average levels.

$$PED = \frac{\% \text{ change in quantity demanded}}{\% \text{ change in price}}$$

$$-0.4 = \frac{\% \text{ change in quantity demanded}}{+10\%}$$

Therefore, % change in quantity demanded is $(-0.4 \times 10\%) = -4\%$

New quantity demanded at $11 is 96% of 10,000, which is 9,600 units.

Total revenue at the price of $11   = $105,600 (9,600 units @ $11)

Total revenue at the price of $10   = $100,000 (10,000 units @ $10)

Change in total revenue   = Increase of $5,600 (from $100,000 to $105,600)

12   The correct answer is: 1.2

CIMA has said that when the method for calculating price elasticity of demand is not given in the question, candidates should use the non-average arc (simple) method.

No method is specified in this question, and therefore you should have used the non-average arc (simple) method in your calculations.

At the original price of $8, the firm sold 900 units per day ($7,200 / 8)
Following the increase in price, the amount sold has fallen to 846 units per day ($7,106.40 / 8.40)
The percentage change in quantity demanded = –6% (–54/900)
Percentage change in price = 5% (0.4/8)
Price elasticity of demand = –6% / 5% = –1.2; but ignoring the minus sign = 1.2.

13   The correct answer is: –1.60

Price elasticity of demand (PED) = % change in quantity demanded / % change in price

Under the average arc (midpoint) method, the percentage changes are based on the average prices and average quantities demand (from before and after the price change).

Average quantity demand = (190 + 210) / 2 = 200
So, % change in quantity demanded = –10% (–20/200)

Average price = ($8.25 + $7.75)/2 = $8
So, % change in price 6.25% (0.5/8)

PED = –10% / 6.25% = –1.60

If you selected –1.74, this suggests you used the simple point (non-average arc) method for calculating price elasticity of demand, rather than the average arc (midpoint) method.

14   The correct answer is: increased by $57.60

The price of Lentos has been reduced by 4% compared to the initial price ($0.2/$5).

Given a price elasticity of demand of 1.875, this means that the resulting percentage increase in quantity demanded, following the price reduction, is 7.5% (4% × 1.875).

This means the number of Lentos sold per day is now 387 (360 × 107.5%).

387 Lentos sold at a price of $4.80 each generates a daily revenue of $1,857.60.

The original revenue, from selling 360 units per day at $5 each, was $1,800.

Therefore the price reduction has resulted in a revenue increase of $57.60 per day.

15   The correct answer is: 1 and 2.

The number of substitutes for a good, and the proportion of household income spent on it, are major determinants of a good's price elasticity of demand.

Goods which have a large number of substitutes are likely to be price elastic, because if the price of the good rises consumers will be likely to switch to buying one of the substitutes, rather than paying the higher price.

The price elasticity of demand for a good increases as the proportion of household income spent on it increases.

Increasing income and a decrease in the price of complementary goods will both lead to a shift in the demand curve but, in themselves, they will not affect the price elasticity of demand of a good.

16   The correct answer is: – 0.5

Price elasticity of demand (PED) = % change in quantity demanded / % change in price

Under the non-average arc (simple) method, the percentage changes are based on the original price and quantity (ie before the price change occurred).

% in change in quantity demand = -0.1m litres / 2m litres = -5%

% change in price = $0.1 / $1 = 10%

Therefore, price elasticity of demand = -5%/10% = -0.5

17   The correct answer is: – 2.16

Price elasticity of demand (PED) = % change in quantity demanded / % change in price

Under the average arc (midpoint) method, the percentage changes are based on the average prices and average quantities demand (from before and after the price change).

Average quantity demand = (45 + 50) / 2 = 47.5
So, % change in quantity demanded = –5/47.5 = –10.53%

Average price = ($21 + $20)/2 = $20.50
So, % change in price = 1/20.50 = 4.88%

PED = –10.53% / 4.88% = –2.16

18   The correct answer is: 0.5

Price elasticity of supply = % change in quantity supplied / % change in price

Under the simple (non-average arc) method, the percentage changes are based on the initial quantity and price, before the price changed occurred.

So, % change in quantity supplied = 84 / 2,100 = 4%

Percentage change in price = $9.60/$120 = 8%

Price elasticity of supply = 4% / 8% = 0.5

Note. Price elasticity of supply is automatically positive, so there is no need to adjust for the minus sign here.

19   The correct answer is: 2,325

The price of the product has been increased by 5% from the original price ($4/$80).

Given a price elasticity of demand of –1.4, this means that the expected % change in quantity demanded will be 5% × –1.4 = –7%.

The initial quantity demand was 2,500, a 7% reduction will amount to 175.

Therefore, the revised weekly demand will be 2,500 – 175 = 2,325.

20   The correct answer is: 0.75.

Price elasticity of supply (PES)= % change in quantity supplied / % change in price

As no method is specified for this calculation, the simple method should be used.

% change in price = 4 / 20 × 100 = 20%

Supply will only be able to rise to 46,000, so the % change in supply = 6,000 / 40,000 × 100 = 15%

PES = 15 / 20 = 0.75

21   The correct answers are:

- Total costs will fall.
- Total revenue will stay the same.

If price elasticity of demand is unitary (ie = 1) then number of units demanded will fall by the same percentage as price has risen. This means that total revenue will be unchanged.

Because the number of units demanded falls, the number of units produced will fall too meaning that costs fall. Since revenue will be unchanged and costs will fall then profits will rise.

5 Cost behaviour

1   The correct answers are:

As a firm has grown, workers have been able to specialise in a particular job and become increasingly efficient at that job.

| Internal economy of scale |

As an industry has expanded, there has become an increasing shortage of skilled labour.

| External diseconomy of scale |

As an industry has developed, banks have developed a better understanding of the industry's requirements.

| External economy of scale |

Management have experienced problems of co-ordination as the number of divisions in a firm has increased.

| Internal diseconomy of scale |

Internal economies of scale arise when a firm's costs per unit of output decrease as the firm's scale of production increases. Specialisation, and division of labour, only become possible once a firm reaches a certain size.

Internal diseconomies of scale arise when a firm's cost per unit of output increases as the firm's scale of production increases. The increasing scale of production could make it more difficult for management to co-ordinate production across the firm.

External economies of scale arise where a firm's costs per unit of output decrease as a result of the increasing size of its industry as a whole. The facilities and support services that can be shared by all firms in an industry contribute to external economies of scale.

External diseconomies of scale arise when a firm's costs per unit of output increase as the size of the industry as a whole increases. The shortage of skilled labour, resulting from the growth of the industry, means that the cost of hiring staff will increase, so this is an external diseconomy of scale.

2   The correct answer is: 1, 3 and 4.

Large firms achieving higher returns is, in effect, describing economies of scale, which could give large firms a competitive advantage against smaller firms.

Targeting a specific segment within a market can often be a key part of a small firm's competitive strategy.

The minimum efficient scale (MES) is the size beyond which no significant economies of scale can be achieved (because unit costs have already reached their lowest level). If the MES occurs at a relatively low level of output, then large firms may not achieve any additional economies of scale compared to larger firms. Moreover, if the large firms start to suffer diseconomies of scale (by becoming bureaucratic and inefficient) this actually leads to their unit costs being higher than those of smaller firms.

3   The correct answers are:

- The introduction of specialist capital equipment
- Purchasing raw materials and other inputs in bulk
- The employment of specialist managers

Technical improvements from new production techniques could apply at any scale of operations, and so are not a source of economies of scale.

Specialisation is one of the main sources of economies of scale, either in relation to efficiency gains from using specialist equipment, or through a more structured division of labour (eg specialist managers).

Purchasing in bulk can help firms obtain inputs more cheaply, if they are able to obtain bulk discounts.

4   The correct answer is: Point B.

A firm benefits from economies of scale if increasing the level of output leads to a lower cost per unit of output. This means that economies of scale will lead to falling average costs.

The firm stops benefiting from economies of scale at the point at which its average cost curve becomes horizontal. After this point, average costs remain constant as output increases, instead of decreasing as they would do if the firm continued to benefit from economies of scale.

The rising average cost curve in turn signifies the point at which the firm would start to suffer from diseconomies of scale.

5   The correct answer is: The cost of raw materials.

A variable cost is one which varies with the amount of output being produced.

The amount of raw materials required will increase as the amount of output being produced increases. Therefore the cost of raw materials is a variable cost.

The interest paid on a variable rate mortgage will vary if interest rates change, but this is not related to the level of output, therefore this should not be classified as a variable cost.

Similarly, the rental paid to lease the warehouse does not vary with the level of output. Therefore, even if the landlord increases the rent, this would still be classified as a fixed cost.

Similarly, the amount of depreciation charged on the machine is a fixed cost.

6   The correct answer is: Industry B.

The minimum efficient scale (MES) is the lowest level of output at which a firm can achieve minimum average cost. We would expect the firm with the highest market concentration to be the one in which the MES constitutes the highest proportion of total industry sales. The higher the MES as a proportion of total industry sales, the lower the number of firms in that industry which can operate at their minimum average cost.

Industry A: MES is 1/7 of total sales, suggesting that up to 7 firms could operate in the industry and all achieve their minimum average costs.

Industry B: MES is 1/4 of total sales, suggesting that a maximum of 4 firms could operate in the industry and still minimise their average costs.

In Industry C, MES is 1/6 of total sales; while in Industry D MES is 1/5 of total sales.

As such, we would expect the highest level of market concentration in Industry B.

7   The correct answers are:

- The firm is able to reduce administration costs per unit of output when it opens a second production plant.

- The firm can buy raw materials at lower prices than smaller firms are able to because it buys in bulk.

- The firm can obtain finance at lower interest rates than smaller firms which the bank thinks are more likely to default on their loans.

Internal economies of scale occur when a firm expands its output and as a result its average costs per unit fall.

The distinction between internal and external economies of scale is that internal economies result from the size of the individual firm, whereas external economies arise when an industry as a whole grows. External economies of scale can benefit all the firms in an industry, rather than being restricted to a single firm.

The availability of labour with specific skills and marketing firms which specialise in the industry are both factors which relate to the industry as a whole, and so they are external economies of scale.

Although financial economies of scale (such as lower interest rates) don't relate directly to the firm's operation and production, they are still internal economies of scale because the lower interest rate is a function of the firm's own size, rather than being a function of the industry's size.

8   The correct answers are:

The firm's average costs will decrease as its level of production increases.	False
The firm should increase its level of production in order to increase efficiency.increase the transaction costs.	False

Diseconomies of scale mean that costs per unit of output (ie average costs) increase as the scale of production increases. Consequently, the firm should reduce (rather than increase) its level of production in order to reduce costs and increase profitability.

9   The correct answers are:

The organisation should only outsource the payroll function if the external transaction costs are higher than the internal bureaucratic costs.	False
The difficulties of agreeing the contract and monitoring the outsourcing relationship increase the transaction costs.	True

In this case, the transaction costs will be the costs of outsourcing the payroll function, while the costs of maintaining the function in-house will be the bureaucratic costs.

It will only be economically beneficial for the organisation to outsource the payroll function if the cost of doing (ie the transaction cost) is lower than the cost of keeping it in-house.

10   The correct answer is: 1 and 2 only.

The decision to outsource any functions increases transaction costs. Transaction costs are incurred when a firm buys goods or services from other firms, rather than producing them in-house.

The decision to outsource the manufacturing process means XYZ Co will have reduced control over manufacturing operations, and consequently the quality of the clothes being manufactured. This is one of the disadvantages of outsourcing.

BPP
LEARNING
MEDIA

XYZ Co will still produce some of its clothes in-house, and its manufacturing costs would be expected to vary according to the quantity of clothes produced. In addition, the costs it pays to the outsourcing company will be variable costs, because the amount of the monthly fee depends on the number of garments produced.

11   The correct answer is: Network organisation.

In a network organisation, corporate partners work together to supply goods or services through a central hub firm. In this way, a network of relatively small firms can present the appearance of a large firm.

In effect, the central hub firm outsources activities to the partner firms, but the description relates to the organisational structure (of a network organisation) rather than the process (of outsourcing).

A shared service centre relates to the situation in which one part of an organisation provides a service for the whole group, where that service had previously been provided in a number of different places across the group. For example, instead of each division within a company having its own finance department, there could be one single finance department for the whole company.

Off-shoring relates to the process of relocating a business activity to another country to take advantage of lower costs there.

12   The correct answer is: Outsourcing.

Off-shoring looks like a plausible answer but off-shoring can be to a division of the same company rather than to an outside provider. The question did not say this provider was in a different country (which would be the key characteristic of off-shoring).

By definition, outsourcing refers to a firm employing an external provider to carry out an activity that the firm had previously carried out internally.

Shared service centres typically involve a consolidation in the way services are provided within a firm, rather than transferring responsibility to an outside provider.

13   The correct answer is: 3 only.

Economies of scale can give a large firm a potential source of competitive advantage against smaller rivals by enabling it to achieve lower costs per unit. The low costs per unit which large firms achieve can act as a barrier to entry, because if new, smaller firms joining the market can't achieve the same levels of cost, then it will be difficult for them to compete successfully against the existing, large firms. So statement 3 is correct.

Although average fixed costs per unit in a large firm would be expected to be lower than in a small firm, statement 1 refers to fixed costs as a whole, rather than the costs per unit. Therefore it is not correct. In total, the fixed costs in a large, multinational firm will be larger than those in a smaller firm. The benefit which large firms gain – relative to smaller firms – is that they can apportion those costs over a larger volume of output, meaning that their unit costs are lower than those of smaller firms.

Typically it will be cheaper and easier for large firms to raise finance, because they are perceived to be less risky than smaller firms. The notion of financial economies of scale refers to this point. Statement 2 is therefore incorrect.

14   The correct answer is: Development of a specialist transport and logistics network to support firms in an industry.

The improved transport and logistics network could help all the firms in the industry reduce their costs, which is the key characteristic of an external economy of scale.

Combining administrative functions and investing in specialised machinery are both internal economies of scale, because the benefits are restricted to a single firm.

If minimum efficient scale can only be achieved by producing a high level of output, this would be a reason for firms to want to grow, and could be a reason why the industries are dominated by a small number of large firms. However, it is not, in itself, an economy of scale.

15   The correct answer is: Power utilities.

As there are currently five large firms dominating the industry, in order for each of them to have achieved their minimum efficient scale (MES), the MES must be less than 1/5 of the total industry sales.

However, in the power utility industry the MES is nearer ¼ of the total industry sales ($200 billion / $824 billion), which suggests that at least one of the firms is currently operating below their optimum level, meaning that it is vulnerable to the forces of competition driving it from the industry.

16   The correct answer is: It will fall by 40%.

Total cost at 5,000 units = $50,000 and total cost per unit = $50,000 / 5,000 = $10. Of the $50,000 total cost, $10,000 is variable cost ($2 × 5,000) and the remainder ($40,000) is fixed. So, total cost at 10,000 units = $40,000 fixed cost + $20,000 variable (10,000 × $2) = $60,000 and total cost per unit = $60,000 / 10,000 = $6.

This is a fall of $4/ $10 × 100 = 40%.

This shows the impact of technical economies of scale, where a high proportion of costs are fixed.

Notes on incorrect answers:

Total costs will rise from $50,000 to $60,000 ie an increase of 20%, but the question asks for total cost per unit.

Variable cost per unit will not change, but this is not what the question is asking.

17   The correct answer is: Obtaining bulk purchase discounts from suppliers.

All are examples of internal economies of scale, but only obtaining bulk purchase discounts from suppliers relates to the company's trading.

Centralising central functions such as R&D is a managerial economy of scale.

Breaking down complex jobs into simpler individual tasks is a technical economy of scale (arising from the production process).

Developing a wider product range, to reduce risk and therefore the cost of bank loans is a financial economy of scale.

6 Market failure

1   The correct answer is: There will be no effect on market price or producer incomes.

The free market price will not change. A minimum price will only affect supply and demand for a good if it is above the free market price. Unsold surpluses, and a contraction in demand for the product, refer to this scenario (ie where minimum price is set above free market price).

Suppliers withdrawing from the market, confuses a maximum price with a minimum price; suppliers would be likely to withdraw from the market if maximum price is set below the free market price.

2   The correct answer is: 1 and 2 only.

Maximum pricing policies (or 'ceiling prices') mean that the maximum price for which a good can be sold is set below the market price.

As a result, the amount suppliers will be prepared to supply will fall. The lower price means that consumers will be willing and able to purchase more of a good. However, because the amount suppliers are prepared to supply has fallen, there will be a shortage. (This can be the basis for 'black market' economies.)

Under free market conditions, this shortage will lead to a rise in price under market equilibrium is restored. However, because the price cannot go above the prescribed maximum, the equilibrium cannot be restored here.

Because the amount which customers can actually buy (rather than how much they might like to buy) has fallen, due to the restrictions in supply, total expenditure by consumers will fall.

Similarly, the fact that price has been reduced and supply has fallen means that producers' incomes will fall, not rise.

3   The correct answer is AC.

The consumer bears the increase AC. The producer incurs the cost CB.

The initial equilibrium price is at price C, at the intersection of supply (S) and demand (D). The imposition of the tax leads to a restriction in supply, single not double space as illustrated by the supply curve shifting to S_T. This shift in the supply curve results in a new equilibrium price being reached at price A. This means that consumers will pay a higher price than they did before the tax was introduced, shown by the gap between A and C.

The gap between the two supply curves is A–B so the amount not paid by the consumer ie B to C is paid by the producer.

4   The correct answer is: Pollution emitted from a factory which has caused local residents to become ill.

An external social cost arises when an economic activity produces negative externalities, meaning the total cost of the activity to society is greater than the private cost to the people or firms involved in it.

When the factory analyses its costs it will only consider its own private costs of production. However, its production processes have a wider impact on society through the pollution it emits.

Travel by rail could be viewed as an external social benefit, because the choices of individual people (to switch their modes of transport) have benefits to people other than themselves.

Although restrictions on the oil supply and increasing popularity of a holiday destination will lead to consumers incurring higher costs, these are not external social costs. Instead, they are direct functions of the interaction of supply and demand in the marketplace.

5   The correct answer is: Public goods.

The free rider problem relates to a situation where it is not possible to exclude third parties from consuming a good that someone else has bought. Non-excludability is one of the characteristics of public goods (and hence is one of the main reasons why such goods would not be provided by the free market).

6   The correct answer is: It leads to greater efficiency.

One of the main arguments in favour of privatisation is that, as a result of being exposed to market forces, privatised industries become more efficient and responsive to the wishes of consumers.

Regulation will be required once an industry has been privatised, because the regulator monitors the behaviour of the privatised firms to ensure, for example, that they do not set excessively high prices for their products or services.

Nationalised industries are likely to be monopolies, therefore they should already be benefiting from economies of scale.

A merit good is one whose consumption should be encouraged – for example by subsidising the provision of it, or providing it free at the point of consumption. Given such circumstances, it may often be more appropriate for merit goods to be provided through the public sector, rather than by private companies.

7   The correct answer is: Introducing maximum price policies to regulate the price of the good.

Merit goods are ones which will have positive externalities, but where the level of consumption will be too low if their provision is left to the free market. Therefore the action the government takes should be one which encourages an increased level of production and/or consumption of the good.

Introducing a maximum (or 'ceiling') price will prevent the price of the good becoming too high, and should therefore help to encourage consumption of it.

By contrast, imposing an indirect tax, and increasing the price to consumers, will reduce demand for the good. In order to encourage consumption of the good, a government should subsidise production, or provide it free – as with state education, for example.

Introducing a tax levy on producers will be expected to reduce supply of the good, which in turn will be expected to increase price and reduce consumption.

8   The correct answer is: A good or service which is non-diminishable and non-exclusive and therefore will not be provided by the free market.

Non-diminishability and non-exclusivity (non-excludability) are the two main defining characteristics of a public good. The 'free rider' problem (which arises as a result of non-exclusivity) means that private enterprises will not be prepared to provide the good. Consequently, it has to be provided through the public sector (national or local government).

A good or service which should be subsidised or provided free in order to encourage its consumption - this is a merit good.

A benefit arising from the consumption of a good which is experienced by people other than the immediate consumer of that good - this is a positive externality

A cost arising from the production of a good which is borne by people other than the immediate producer of that good - this describes a negative externality.

BPP
LEARNING
MEDIA

9   The correct answer is: Impose an indirect tax on the good.

An example of an external social cost is air pollution caused by manufacturing activities, that impose health and clean-up costs on the whole society. An indirect tax is a tax on spending and should raise prices and thereby directly lead to a **reduction** in demand, which should be the purpose of the government policy.

State ownership does not, in itself, act as a mechanism for controlling output (although it could be used in this way, this is unlikely in reality).

Imposing a tax on profits in itself, does not control demand for the good (although imposing the tax may lead to producers charging a higher price for the good, thereby reducing demand for it. Nonetheless, imposing an indirect tax directly on the good is a more appropriate way of incorporating the external social cost into market decisions (supply and demand).

A subsidy will increase production and demand for the good, rather than reducing it, which is what the Government wants to achieve.

10   The correct answers are:

A 'polluter pays policy' has been introduced to reflect the negative externalities produced.

Demerit good

Supply of these goods does not diminish regardless of how many people make use of them.

Public good

These goods are subsidised because of the benefits they provide to society.

Merit good

The generation of negative externalities as a consequence of their production or consumption is the key characteristic of a demerit good. A polluter pays policy is one way of trying to reduce the production of negative externalities generated by a demerit good.

The fact that supply doesn't diminish regardless of how many people use a good or service defines the characteristic of non-diminishability. Along with non-exclusivity, non-diminishability is one of the key characteristics of a public good.

The generation of a wider benefit for society as a result of the consumption of a good or service is a positive externality. Merit goods (such as education and health care) generate positive externalities. However, unlike public goods, the provision of merit goods is diminishable.

11   The correct answer is: Demand is inelastic and supply is elastic.

When demand is inelastic, the reduction in consumer demand for a product will be less than proportional to the rise in price. Consequently, producers are able to pass much of the price rise on to consumers.

When supply is inelastic, the burden of tax will fall primarily on the producer, therefore the burden shifts to the consumer the more elastic supply is.

Therefore, when demand is inelastic and supply elastic, the primary burden of a tax will fall most heavily on consumers.

12   The correct answer is: There will be excess supply in the labour market in AAA.

The introduction of the minimum wage above the equilibrium rate will mean that more people will want to work than firms will want to employ. This will mean there is an excess of labour supply over demand for labour.

13   The correct answer is: External social costs.

The health issues mean that additional burden will be placed on the health services in Ostland, who were not part of the original transactions between the consumer and the fast food companies. As such, they are external social costs (or negative externalities) because the 'costs' resulting from the consumption of the food are being borne by society as a whole (via the health service), not by the producers or consumers.

14   The correct answers are:

Demand | Decrease |

Total revenue | Decrease |

Imposing a minimum price above the current market price will mean that the price increases. This will lead to a fall in demand.

In this case, since demand is price elastic, the increase in price will lead to a greater than proportional fall in demand, so total revenue from the sale of fast food will decrease.

15   The correct answer is: Polluter pays.

The 'polluter pays' principle argues that the firms which produce emissions and other pollution should bear the costs of managing in order to prevent damage to human health or the environment.

In this case, by imposing a tax on carbon emissions, the Government has created a financial incentive for the firm to reduce the level of emissions it generates (because this will, in turn, reduce the amount of the emissions tax the firm has to pay).

The emissions themselves are negative externalities , but the concept of externalities doesn't specifically describe the principle the Government has applied to tackle the emissions.

16   The correct answer is: Demand is price elastic and supply is price elastic.

If supply is price elastic then the high price will cause a large rise in supply.

If demand is price elastic then the high price will cause a large fall in demand.

A combination of a large fall in demand and a large rise in supply will result in the highest market surplus.

17   The correct answers are:

- They will consider all costs that they incur when determining the selling price.
- Externalities will be ignored when determining price and output levels.

Firms consider all costs that they incur when determining the selling price.

Externalities are costs (or benefits) experienced outside the firm and therefore are not costs that are directly incurred or considered by the firm.

Notes on incorrect answers:

Firms will only increase prices to pass on the cost of negative externalities if the government is imposing an indirect tax to force the firm to recognise the social costs associated with the production of its goods – this will not be happening in an unregulated, free-market, economy.

Public goods are unlikely to be produced in an unregulated economy due to the free-rider problem but if they are then, as with all goods, only costs incurred by the firm will be considered when determining the selling price.

7 National income

1   The correct answer is: Increased investment.

Investment is an injection into the circular flow of income in an economy, and therefore will be expected to increase aggregate demand.

Saving, imports and taxation are all withdrawals, and so will reduce (rather than increase) aggregate demand.

2   The correct answer is: Aggregate demand in Estland will shift to the left; National income will fall.

The increased level of spending on imports leads to a reduction in spending on domestically produced goods (consumption of domestically produced goods). Consumption is one of the elements of aggregate demand, so this change will lead to a reduction in aggregate demand.

Spending on imports is a withdrawal from the circular flow. So increasing the level of imports will lead to a fall in national income.

3   The correct answer is: The size of the multiplier will increase.

The multiplier is calculated as $1 / (1 - MPC)$. Therefore an increase in the marginal propensity to consume will lead to an increase in the size of the multiplier.

An increase in the marginal propensity to consume (and, in turn, in the level of consumption) would be expected to lead to an increase in the level of national income, rather than a fall.

A change in MPC, by itself, will not lead to a change in interest rates or to the level of injections into the economy.

4   The correct answer is: 175.

Equilibrium occurs where income = expenditure.

In this case, expenditure comprises consumption plus investment (because there are no imports or exports, and no government expenditure).

So $Y = 50 + 0.6Y + 20$, therefore $0.4Y = 70$

$70/0.4 = 175$

5   The correct answers are:

- A reduction in labour costs
- Increasing investment expenditure by firms

The equilibrium level of national income is determined by the intersection of aggregate demand and aggregate supply.

As the equilibrium level in this scenario is currently below full capacity, then outward shifts in both aggregate demand and aggregate supply could help to generate the growth required to increase the equilibrium level.

Increasing investment will help to increase aggregate demand, because investment is an injection into the circular flow of income.

Increasing the trade deficit means that imports will increase more than exports. Imports are a withdrawal out of the circular flow, therefore an increase in the trade deficit will reduce aggregate demand rather than increasing it.

Similarly, reducing government spending or consumer spending will both reduce aggregate demand rather than increasing it.

Reducing labour costs should encourage firms to increase production levels, contributing to an outward shift in aggregate supply.

6   The correct answer is: $120 billion

Equilibrium occurs when income = expenditure.

Expenditure is represented by aggregate demand.

Aggregate demand here, excluding exports = 65 + 20 + 45 = $130 billion.

This means that exports must be $250 billion − $130 billion = $120 billion.

7   The correct answer is: A decrease in the marginal propensity to consume.

The multiplier effect describes the fact that the resulting rise in national income is greater than an initial increase in aggregate demand in an economy.

The formula for the multiplier is $1/(1 - MPC)$ which means that the value of the multiplier will fall when the marginal propensity to consume (MPC) falls.

A fall in public expenditure may lead to a fall in the aggregate expenditure $(C + I + G + X - M)$ but will not, in itself, affect the value of the multiplier itself, because it will not affect the marginal propensity to consume.

Lower saving and a decrease in the propensity to import will both lead to an increase in the marginal propensity to consume domestically produced goods, and will therefore lead to a rise in the value of the multiplier (rather than a fall).

8   The correct answer is: An increase by a firm in its inventories of finished goods, prior to a marketing campaign.

Increasing inventory levels is an investment in terms of the aggregate demand function $(C + I + G + X)$, because the firm will have incurred expenditure to produce the extra items of inventory.

Although the purchase of shares or making a corporate acquisition are both investments for the individuals or organisations concerned, they are merely the transfer of ownership of already-existing assets, and there is no creation of new non-current asset capital investment or inventories. From the point of view of the national economy as a whole, these do not count as investment and therefore do not provide an injection into the circular flow.

An individual depositing cash has chosen to save, rather than to spend, their cash. In economic terms, saving represents a withdrawal from the circular flow of income, rather than an injection into it.

9   The correct answer is: An increase in exports.

Exports are an injection into the circular flow, and so an increase in the level of exports increases the level of injections into the economy, thereby leading to an increase in national income.

Savings are a withdrawal from the circular flow and so an increase in savings would be expected to reduce national income.

Consumer spending is one of the components of aggregate demand, so a fall in spending will reduce aggregate demand (and consequently would be expected to reduce national income).

Unemployment suggests that the equilibrium level of national income is below the full employment level. As unemployment levels rise, this suggests the equilibrium level of national income is falling increasingly below the full employment level – which would indicate a decrease in national income, rather than an increase.

BPP
LEARNING
MEDIA

10 The correct answer is: 3 and 4 only.

Taxation and savings (as well as imports) are withdrawals from the circular flow.

Government spending and exports (as well as investment) are injections into the circular flow.

11 The correct answer is: Leftward shift in the aggregate supply curve

An increase in wage costs will lead to a supply side adjustment, not a demand side adjustment. If wage costs rise, firms will try to reduce the number of staff they employ, meaning the aggregate supply curve will shift inwards (to the left).

12 The correct answer is: A fall in interest rates.

Reducing interest rates would be expected to lead to an increase in consumption (rather than saving) and also an increase in investment (due to the reduction in the cost of borrowing required to fund capital expenditure). Consumption and investment are both elements of aggregate demand, so this will lead to a rightward shift in the aggregate demand curve.

A fall in the price of a key raw material, such as oil, is a supply side adjustment and so will lead to a rightward shift in the supply curve, not the demand curve.

A fall in the price of imported goods would be expected to lead to an increase in demand for imports. However, imports are a withdrawal from the circular flow of income, and so reduce aggregate demand rather than increasing it.

Government spending is an injection into the circular flow in the economy. Reducing the level of government spending would therefore reduce aggregate demand rather than increasing it.

13 The correct answer is: $165 billion

The principles of Keynesian economics hold that, at the equilibrium level of national income, expenditure equals income (E = Y).

So, in Westland's case:

$450 billion = $285 billion + injections

Rearranging this equation, injections = $450 billion – $285 billion = $165 billion.

Note. The calculation needs to be based on the current, equilibrium level of national income, not the full employment level.

14 The correct answer is: 455 ($455 billion)

In an open economy (such as Westland's) the value of the multiplier will be 1 / MPW.

The withdrawals from the economy are taxation, savings and imports.

So, in this case, the multiplier is 1 / (0.20 + 0.04 + 0.16) = 1 / 0.4 = 2.5

Therefore, the initial government expenditure of $2 billion will lead to an overall increase of $5 billion in the equilibrium level of national income.

The level was previously $450 billion, so after this increase it is now $455 billion.

15 The correct answer is: An increase in exports.

In order to increase the equilibrium level of national income, additional injections into the circular flow are required.

Exports are an injection (as government expenditure and investment would also be).

Taxation and savings (as well as imports) are withdrawals.

An increase in interest rates is likely to make saving more attractive to consumers, whilst also reducing the amount of investment by firms into new equipment (because of the higher cost of borrowing). Consequently, an increase in interest rates would be expected to reduce injections and increase withdrawals – which is the opposite of what is required here.

16   The correct answer is: National income in Teeland is falling.

The amount of injections into the economy (exports; investment and government expenditure) is less than the withdrawals from it (imports; savings and taxation). This means national income will fall.

	Injections $m	Withdrawals $m
Exports (X)	384	
Imports (M)		407
Investment (I)	208	
Government expenditure (G)	359	
Savings (S)		194
Taxation (T)		371
Total	951	972

National income will rise if injections are greater than withdrawals; while the economy will be in equilibrium if the value of injections and withdrawals is equal.

A budget deficit occurs when a government spends more than it receives in tax (ie when G > T). In this case, tax proceeds are greater than government expenditure, so there is currently a budget surplus.

8 The trade cycle

1   The correct answer is: The level of aggregate demand in the economy will increase.

A budget deficit (when government spending is greater than government income from tax receipts) is designed to boost aggregate demand in the economy, and consequently to increase the equilibrium level of national income and reduce the level of demand-deficient or cyclical unemployment.

Government spending is an injection into the circular flow.

2   The correct answer is: 1 and 2 only.

Changes in GDP can measure the rate of growth in an economy, which is the key variable when looking at the trade cycle (ie how is the rate of growth fluctuating over time?).

A number of economic indicators show movements in the trade cycle. For example, during a period of expansion some will rise (eg raw material prices as a result of demand-pull inflation) while others will fall (eg demand-deficient unemployment, bankruptcies).

However, seasonal unemployment will rise or fall according to the season of the year (eg jobs for ski instructors) but these seasonal variations are not indicative of any business cycle movements.

3   The correct answer is: The economy is expanding and the budget deficit is increasing.

The increase in real GDP indicates that the economy is growing, and the falling unemployment rate is consistent with this.

Government expenditure is greater than government revenue, meaning the country is running a budget deficit. The deficit was $115 billion in Year 2, compared to $90 billion in Year 1, meaning that the budget deficit is increasing.

4   The correct answer is: 2 and 4 only.

Cost-push inflation is inflation caused by higher unit costs of production being passed through into higher prices.

Increases in wages are one of the main causes of cost-push inflation, and aggressive wage demands made by trade unions on behalf of their members could contribute to this wage inflation. Weakening the power of trade unions could therefore be one way of reducing the size of wages increases.

A revaluation of the currency (measure 4) will make imported goods and raw materials cheaper for firms in Country X to buy. This could be particularly important in Country X, since imported goods are likely to make up a significant proportion of firms' production costs.

Introducing a sales tax on manufactured products would lead to an inward shift in the supply curve for those products and so would be expected to increase cost-push inflation rather than decreasing it.

Similarly, a decision by oil producers to restrict supply would be expected to increase the price of oil, which in turn will have a knock-on effect on the price of other goods. Again, this will increase cost-push inflation rather than decreasing it.

5   The correct answer is: It is often characterised by high levels of unemployment.

A recession is a period in which there is negative economic growth (ie national income declines).

During a recession, the level of aggregate demand will be too low relative to aggregate supply. As a result, firms are likely to reduce the amount they produce, with the result that they need a smaller labour force. This leads to increases in the level of unemployment.

Some of the other key characteristics of economic recession are:

- Low business confidence, investment spending and reduced business profits

- Low household income and widespread drop in consumer spending (this means statement A cannot be correct)

- Falling inflation rate (this means statement B cannot be correct)

Reductions in investment spending and consumer spending both contribute to the low levels of aggregate demand.

6   The correct answer is: Inventory levels increased.

Initially, firms will carry on producing the same level of output as they did when the economy was growing quickly. However, the slowdown in the rate of growth means that demand will reduce, and so goods will be held as inventory rather than being sold.

The slowdown in the rate of growth is likely to mean that both the overall demand for goods and the demand for imported goods are likely to fall rather than rise.

7   The correct answer is: 1 and 2.

Increasing public sector expenditure provides an injection into the circular flow and so should increase the level of aggregate demand in the economy, particularly if the impact of the initial injection is then boosted by the multiplier effect. As such, increasing public sector expenditure is a key component of a demand management policy.

Lowering interest rates should stimulate investment (by companies) and consumer expenditure – which again will help to boost aggregate demand.

Increasing taxation lowers demand in the economy because people will have less money available (after tax) for consumption. Similarly, increasing taxation could also mean that firms have less money available for investment.

8   The correct answers are:

Low levels of aggregate demand mean the equilibrium level of national income is below the level needed to achieve full employment.	Depression
Modest rates of economic growth. Improving consumer and business confidence, leading to greater expenditure.	Recovery
Falling levels of business and consumer confidence. Falling levels of production. Rising levels of unemployment.	Recession
Low levels of unemployment. High inflation due to excess demand for labour and other resources. Increasing deficit in balance of trade.	Boom

Recessions are characterised by falling levels of national income (negative economic growth). As national income falls, business and consumer confidence also falls. One of the main factors behind the negative growth is typically falling levels of aggregate demand. In turn, firms respond to the lower demand by producing less, and reducing their workforce.

During the depression phase of the trade cycle, an economy will be stuck at low levels of national income, giving rise to a deflationary gap (where the level of aggregate demand is below that needed to assure full employment in the economy).

During a recovery phase, the level of national income will begin to rise again. This economic growth will help to reduce unemployment levels, and will help to improve consumer and business confidence. In turn, this confidence will lead to greater expenditure, which will help to sustain the recovery.

The boom phase of a trade cycle will be characterised by high levels of demand – both for products and for factors of production (such as labour). If aggregate demand exceeds aggregate supply this will lead to inflation. Also, if aggregate demand for products cannot be met from domestic production, the level of imports will increase to help make up the shortfall.

9   The correct answer is: Northland.

Stagflation occurs when economic growth (defined by the change in national income in a period) is low or negative, and inflation is high.

The relevant figures to look at to identify whether a country is experiencing stagflation are: percentage change in GDP (level of economic growth) and change in consumer prices (rate of inflation).

The percentage changes in GDP indicate that Northland and Eastland both experienced negative growth, while Northland also had a high level of price inflation. This combination of negative growth and high inflation means that Northland is the correct option.

10   The correct answers are:

The rate of unemployment is likely to be higher in Effland than Geeland.	False
The rate of inflation is likely to be higher in Effland than Geeland.	True
The level of imports into Effland is likely to be higher than into Geeland.	True

Effland is experiencing a boom, and therefore we would expect the rate of unemployment to be low, whereas Geeland (which is suffering a recession) would be expected to have a higher rate of unemployment.

In a boom period, we would expect inflation to be relatively high, due to the high levels of aggregate demand compared to aggregate supply. In turn, these high levels of aggregate demand for goods and services would also be expected to lead to high levels of imports into Effland (because the imports will be necessary to satisfy the high levels of demand).

11   The correct answer is: Government spending will increase; Taxes will be cut; Budget deficit will increase

Government expenditure is an injection into the circular flow of income, while taxes are a withdrawal from the circular flow.

In order to avoid recession, the Government will want to boost aggregate demand in the economy. Increasing injections and reducing withdrawals will help to achieve this.

The budget deficit measures the excess of government spending over its tax receipts. Reducing taxes while increasing government spending means the budget deficit will increase.

12   The correct answer is: 2 only.

A deflationary gap indicates that the aggregate demand in the economy is below that needed for the equilibrium level of national income to be the full-employment level of national income. Consequently, the measures needed to address a deflationary gap are ones which will increase aggregate demand – by increasing injections into the economy, or reducing withdrawals from it.

Government spending is an injection into the economy.

A trade deficit represents a net withdrawal from an economy, because it means imports are greater than exports.

Increasing interest rates is typically a measure for reducing aggregate demand (or trying to reduce inflation rates) which is the reverse of the situation here.

13   The correct answer is: An increase in the level of unemployment

In a recession, we would expect there to be a decline in the level of aggregate demand, with the result that slack develops in the economy (ie the equilibrium level of national income is less than the full employment level). One of the consequences of this is likely to be an increase in the level of unemployment. As demand for firms' products or services falls, they will need fewer staff to satisfy that demand.

As aggregate demand falls we would expect the rate of inflation to fall rather than increase. Similarly, we would expect a reduction in demand to affect imported goods as well as domestically produced goods. Therefore we would expect the level of imports to decline rather than to increase.

14   The correct answers are:

Taxes	Increased
Government expenditure	Reduced

The existence of demand-pull inflation means that any actions the Government takes will need to reduce aggregate demand in the economy.

Taxes are a withdrawal from the circular flow, so increasing taxes will help to reduce aggregate demand.

Government spending is an injection into the circular flow, so this should be reduced in order to reduce aggregate demand.

15   The correct answer is: Country 1.

Veeland has been suffering from a recession, which means its economic growth (% change in GDP) will be negative. This means that Veeland has to be either Country 1 or Country 3.

In a recession, we would expect unemployment levels to be rising, not falling (as in Country 3).

In a recession we would also expect the balance of payments current account (trade balance) to improve as the demand for imports falls. (Given the global economic stability, we would expect the level of exports from Veeland to remain relatively stable.) Again, this suggests Veeland is Country 1, not Country 3.

In a recession, there is little pressure on prices from demand-pull inflation. Coupled with the absence of external cost-push inflation, then the rate of inflation should be low. Again, this is consistent with the data for Country 1.

16   The correct answers are:

Demand for agricultural labour falls during the winter months, so the number of agricultural workers who are unemployed increases during the winter.	Frictional
Increased supplies of cheap, imported steel have led to a long-term reduction in demand for domestically produced steel in a country.	Structural
The onset of a recession has led to a reduction in the level of economic activity in a country.	Cyclical

Cyclical unemployment is caused by a decline in the general level of economic activity (for example, due to a downturn in the trade cycle.)

Whereas cyclical unemployment results from the level of demand in the economy as a while, structural unemployment results from a reduction in demand for any individual good, service or industry.

Seasonal unemployment is a type of frictional unemployment. Although seasonal unemployment (like structural unemployment) can affect specific industries, the difference between the two is that seasonal unemployment is short-term, whereas structural unemployment is long-term. Seasonal unemployment is particularly associated with industries (such as agriculture, or leisure and tourism) where demand for labour rises and falls regularly over the year.

17   The correct answers are:

- The trade cycle
- The Phillips curve.

The boom phase of the trade cycle is characterised by falling unemployment and rising inflation.

The Phillips curve suggests that there is a trade-off between unemployment and inflation ie if one is falling then the other is rising.

Notes on incorrect answers:

With cost-push inflation prices are rising due to factors that are not linked directly to demand and therefore are not directly linked to output or employment levels.

A fall in frictional unemployment will not be linked to demand levels and therefore is not directly linked to output or employment levels.

Automatic stabilisers are factors that help to support the economy during a recession eg unemployment benefits.

18   The correct answer is: depression, recovery, boom, recession, depression etc.

The starting point does not matter, but a depression follows a recession, and a boom follows a recovery.

9 Index numbers

1   The correct answer is: 112

As you have been asked to use the chain base method, the price index for 20X3 needs to be calculated with respect to the price in the previous year (20X2) only, not against a base year as would be the case if you had been asked to use the fixed base method.

11.49 / 10.26 × 100 = 111.98 (which is rounded up to 112)

2   The correct answer is: $212.63

Deflated (base) wage = Actual (current) wage × Index number for base year / Index number of given year.

Base wage   = $421 × 100 / 198

            = $212.63

Note. The question specifically asked you to give your answer to 2 decimal places, so you must do this for your answer to be correct.

3   The correct answer is: 24.0%

As you have been asked to use the base weightings approach, the weightings need to be based on quantities purchased in 20X1 (the base year).

	Quantity (m) – 20X1	Price in 20X1			Price in 20X2
	Q_0	P_0	$P_0 \times Q_0$	P_n / P_0	$P_0 \times Q_0 \times$ price relative
Milk	300	1	300	1.1/1 = 1.1	330
Beer	150	2	300	2.5/2 = 1.25	375
Phones	50	80	4,000	100/80 = 1.25	5,000
			4,600		5,705

Index in 20X2 = 5,705 / 4,600 × 100 = 124.0

So the weighted average price rise is 24.0%.

If you selected Option 24.3%, this suggests you used the quantities from the current year (20X2) to determine your weightings, rather than the quantities from the base year (20X1).

4   The correct answer is: $14.33

The current price per kg = $5 × 430/150 = $14.33

5 The correct answer is: 13.3%

As you have been asked to use the current weightings approach, the weightings need to be based on quantities purchased in 20X2 (the most recent year).

	Quantity (m) – 20X2	Price in 20X1		Price in 20X2	
	Q_n	P_0	$P_0 \times Q_n$	P_n / P_0	$P_0 \times Q_n \times$ price relative
Bread	220	1	220	0.9/1 = 0.9	198
Meat	190	5	950	5.2/5 = 1.04	988
Televisions	14	300	4,200	350/300 = 1.1667	4,900
			5,370		6,086

Index in 20X2 = 6,086 / 5,370 × 100 = 113.3

So the weighted average price rise is 13.3%.

If you selected 12.9%, this suggests you used the quantities from 20X1 as the basis of your weightings, rather than the quantities from 20X2.

6 The correct answer is: $247.9

CPI in 20X6 = 135

CPI in 20X1 = 115

Average wages at constant 20X1 prices = 291 × 115/135 = 247.9

(**Note.** The question specifically asked you to give your answer to 1 decimal place, so you must do this for your answer to be correct.)

7 The correct answer is: $452,898

Current rental payments deflated to prices 5 years ago:

$490,000 × 141.6 / 153.2 = $452,898

(Remember you were asked to give your answer to the nearest $, so you should not have included any decimal places.)

8 The correct answer is: 133.0

(50/100 × 140) + (30/100 × 130) + (20/100 × 120)

= 133.0

9 The correct answers are:

Money (ie nominal) wages have increased by at least 5% each year.	False
Real wages have declined over the period 20X1–20X4.	True

Increase in money wages:

20X1–20X2:	210/200 – 1 = 5%
20X2–20X3:	220/210 – 1 = 4.8%
20X3–20X4:	230/220 – 1 = 4.5%

Real wages:

20X1:	200/180 = 1.111
20X2:	210/190 = 1.105
20X3:	220/200 = 1.1
20X4:	230/210 = 1.095

10 The correct answer is: 137.3

The indices show that prices in 2014 were 26% higher than in 1995, and that prices in 2017 were 9% higher than in 2014.

Prices in 2017 were therefore 1.26 × 1.09 = 1.3734.

Using a continuous sequence, the index number in 2017 would therefore have been 137.3.

11 The correct answer is: 3.9%

Nominal wage cost	Price index	Real wage cost
64.20	120.0	64.2 × (100/120) = 53.5
70.33	126.5	70.33 × (100/126.5) = 55.6

Real wage increase = (55.6 − 53.5) / 53.5 = 3.9%

The nominal increase over the 5 year period was 9.5%; so if you chose Option 9.5% you calculated your answer using nominal rather than real rates.

12 The correct answers are:

Which country had the highest real growth (% growth) between 20X4 and 20X7? | Ayland |

Which country experienced negative real growth between 20X4 and 20X7? | Beeland |

Ayland: Real GDP per capita 20X4: 15,000/115.9 × 100: $12,942.19
Real GDP per capital 20X7: 16,174/119.4 × 100: $13,546.06   **Growth: 4.7%**

Beeland: Real GDP per capita 20X4: 20,120/118.6 × 100: $16,964.59
Real GDP per capital 20X7: 20,621/122.4 × 100: $16,847.22   **Growth: −0.7%**

Ceeland: Real GDP per capita 20X4: 28,241/117.5 × 100: $24,034.89
Real GDP per capita 20X7: 29,604/120.3 × 100: $24,608.48   **Growth: 2.4%**

13 The correct answer is: 2.38%

The annual rate of inflation in 20X7 is calculated as the percentage increase between the index figure at the end of 20X6 and at the end of 20X7.

$$\text{Therefore:} \quad = \frac{116.3 - 113.6}{113.6} \times 100$$

$$= 2.38\%$$

14 The correct answer is: 20X4.

Year	Price index	% change
20X3	106.4	
20X4	109.0	**2.44**
20X5	111.5	2.29
20X6	113.6	1.88
20X7	116.3	2.38

15   The correct answer is: 5.83%.

The GDP figures shown are nominal figures. To convert them into real figures, they need to be adjusted for inflation, in line with the CPI figures.

Real GDP for 20X6 = $5,750 / 113.6 × 100 = $5,061.62 billion
Real GDP for 20X7 = $6,230 / 116.3 × 100 = $5,356.84 billion

% growth = (5,356.84 − 5,061.62)/5,061.62 = 5.83%

16   The correct answer is: Average earnings can buy 8% more goods and services in 20X5 than they could in 20X1

The use of constant prices means the index measures the amount of goods and services which earnings can buy in 20X5 compared to what they could have bought in 20X1. The fact that the index is greater than 100 means that average earnings have increased more rapidly than the average price of goods and services.

The base year index = 100, so an increase from 100 to 108 represents an increase of 8% (not an increase of 1.08%).

The index is relative, so we can only tell how earnings have increased relative to the price of goods and services. As such, we cannot tell how much the price of goods and services have increased overall − nor, for that matter, how much earnings have increased overall.

17   The correct answer is: $7,400 billion.

The relevant GDP deflator to use (to convert 20X7 figures into 20X3 figures) is 95.38 / 103.63

$8,040 billion × 95.38/103.63 = $7,399.93 billion; rounded to the nearest billion = $7,400 billion.

18   The correct answer is: 114

All items = food + housing + transport

If we assume the index for transport = 't'

$118 = (116 \times 0.5) + (124 \times 0.3) + (t \times 0.2)$

$118 = 58 + 37.2 + 0.2t$

$0.2t = 118 − 58 − 37.2$

$0.2t = 22.8$ so $t = 114$

10 Government economic policy

1   The correct answer is: Interest rates fall, investment spending rises, and aggregate demand rises.

If the supply of money is increased, then the price of money − in effect, interest rates − will be reduced. Lower interest rates mean the cost of capital used in investment decisions will also be reduced, meaning that the net present value of investment projects will increase. This will lead to an increase in investment spending. Investments represent an injection into the economy, so a growth in investments will lead to an increase in aggregate demand.

Similarly, a fall in interest rates may make saving relatively less attractive. Saving is a withdrawal from the circular flow, so reducing the amount of saving could also be expected to lead to an increase in aggregate demand.

2   The correct answer is: 1 only.

The Government's intention to use a deflationary fiscal policy means that it wants to reduce inflation by reducing the level of aggregate demand in the economy. Taxes are a withdrawal from the circular flow of income, so increasing taxes will help to reduce the level of aggregate demand.

The budget deficit represents the excess of the Government's spending over its tax receipts. Government spending is an injection into the circular flow, but in this case, the Government is looking to reduce aggregate demand, not to increase it. Therefore in this scenario, the Government will be looking to reduce a budget deficit, not to increase it.

An interest rate rise is a potential measure which could be used to reduce the level of aggregate demand in an economy, but interest rate rises are an aspect of monetary policy, not fiscal policy.

3   The correct answers are:

- Increases in tax allowances for investment in capital equipment
- Increasing levels of government expenditure

Fiscal policy looks at levels of government expenditure and how they can be funded through tax revenues. An expansionary fiscal policy is one designed to promote growth in the economy, which could be achieved through reductions in taxation and/or increases in government spending.

Increases in tax allowances will have the same effect as a reduction in tax, and they would be used to encourage increased investment in capital equipment. Investment is an injection into the circular flow.

Although increases in tax rates relates to fiscal policy, increasing tax rates would be expected to reduce aggregate demand, rather than to increase it.

Interest rates and borrowing levels relate to monetary policy, rather than fiscal policy. Therefore, reducing interest rates could be a mechanism for promoting growth in an economy; we would not expect to see a reduction in interest rates specifically as a result of the Government's policy.

4   The correct answers are:

- Increasing direct taxes
- Applying more stringent controls over bank lending

Measures which can help to reduce the level of demand-pull inflation will be ones which reduce the level of aggregate demand in an economy.

Increasing direct taxes (taxes on income) will reduce the amount of disposable income households have available for buying goods and services – thereby reducing aggregate demand.

Making controls over bank lending more stringent will reduce the amount of money banks lend. If there is less credit available to consumers, this will in turn reduce the value of goods they can buy.

Changes to interest rates, budget deficits and the money supply could all be used as measures to try to stimulate an economy rather than to keep aggregate demand in check. Lowering interest rates would be expected to result in an increase in investment and other consumer borrowing, leading to even stronger demand-pull inflation. Increasing the money supply will also lead to a fall in interest rates.

Increasing government expenditure and/or reducing taxes (ie the budget deficit) will also provide an additional injection into the economy, thereby boosting aggregate demand rather than reducing it.

5   The correct answer is: Reduce the level of interest rates.

Lowering interest rates is a monetary policy designed to encourage more spending in the economy, thereby helping to reduce cyclical (demand-deficient) unemployment.

Making more training available for the unemployed is a supply side policy, and so will be less useful in reducing unemployment in this case, since the unemployment results from a lack of demand for labour rather than skill shortages amongst the workforce.

Increasing the exchange rate will make imports cheaper and exports more expensive. This could be expected to increase demand for imports into Ipland and reduce demand for exports from Ipland which would reduce aggregate demand overall, rather than increasing it.

6   The correct answer is: The bank will raise interest rates.

Inflation targeting is a policy in which the central bank uses interest rate changes and other monetary tools to control inflation towards a target rate.

Interest rates and the inflation rate tend to be inversely related so, as inflation appears to be above the target, the bank is likely to raise interest rates to reduce aggregate demand in the economy and help bring down inflation.

Increasing the money supply is likely to increase inflation and so will exacerbate the problem rather than help to fix it. Similarly, increasing the budget deficit will be expected to increase aggregate demand rather than helping to reduce it.

The presence of high inflation and high levels of aggregate demand suggests that there could be an inflationary gap in Bosland. Measures designed to reduce aggregate demand will be more likely to lead to an increase in unemployment than a fall. (As demand for products fall, if firms start to have spare capacity, this could lead to them reducing the size of their workforces.)

7   The correct answers are:

The level of investment Bizzi Co makes in new capital equipment will be expected to fall	True
The level of consumer demand for Bizzi Co's products will be expected to fall.	True

Interest rates are, in effect, the price of capital. Therefore a rise in interest rates represents a rise in the price of capital, which will mean that the level of investment would be expected to decrease.

Similarly, higher interest rates will typically cause a fall in consumer demand – particularly for relatively expensive goods such as Bizzi's, which consumers may buy on credit rather than paying for them in cash. (In turn, the reduced demand for Bizzi's products may further reduce the level of investment it makes.)

8   The correct answer is: To improve the ability of an economy to produce goods and services.

Supply side policy aims to increase the long-term productive capacity of an economy. This is based on the macroeconomic argument that economic growth can be most effectively created by lowering barriers for people to produce (supply) goods and services, such as lowering income tax and capital gains tax rates, and by allowing greater flexibility by reducing regulation. As a result, consumers will benefit from a greater supply of goods and services at lower prices.

A policy concerned with managing the money supply in an economy is a monetary policy rather than a supply side policy.

Although the labour supply is likely to be a key element of a supply side policy, the focus of the policy will typically be on increasing the supply of labour, not reducing it.

9   The correct answers are:

Income tax in Kayland is charged at 20% on a person's salary, regardless of what their salary is.

> Proportional

Income tax in Essland is charged at 25% on earnings of up to $50,000 and then at 40% on any excess over $50,000.

> Progressive

The price of petrol in Veeland includes a petrol duty of 30% of the net cost of the petrol.

> Regressive

A proportional tax takes the same proportion of income in tax from all levels of income (as is the case with the tax system in Kayland).

A progressive tax takes a higher proportion of income in tax as income rises. The different tax bands being used in Essland mean the tax is progressive.

A regressive tax takes a higher proportion of income from people with low incomes than those with high incomes. The cost of the petrol duty will represent a higher proportion of income for someone with a low salary than someone with a higher salary, meaning it is regressive.

10   The correct answer is: Country X and Country Z.

A progressive tax system means that the amount of tax paid (as a proportion of income) increases as income increases.

In Countries X and Z, the % of tax paid on salaries of $40,000 is higher than on salaries of $20,000 meaning their tax systems are progressive.

In Country Y the % of tax paid on a salary of $40,000 is lower than on a salary of $20,000, meaning that the tax system in Country Y is regressive.

	Income before tax $	Income after tax $	% tax paid on income
Country X	20,000	16,000	20
	40,000	30,000	25
Country Y	20,000	14,000	30
	40,000	29,000	27.5
Country Z	20,000	18,000	10
	40,000	34,000	15

11   The correct answer is: 1, 2 and 3.

Option 1. Although the theory of the multiplier effect suggests that the overall increase in national income following an injection into the economy will be greater than the initial economy, this may not necessarily be the case with government expenditure, because the rise in government expenditure might simply replace some private expenditure. For example, improvements in publicly funded health care may lead to fewer people paying for private treatment.

Option 2. describes the 'crowding out' effect. If the Government is competing against private sector firms to borrow money, it may have to offer higher interest rates in order to do so. But this will force private firms to also offer higher interest rates, which could discourage them from investing and higher interest rates could also discourage individuals from buying on credit. Therefore, government borrowing 'crowds out' private borrowing, with the result that aggregate demand rises less than expected.

Option 3. Interest rates (monetary policy) can be changed in a matter of hours, through intervention from a central bank. Fiscal policy can often take months to introduce, due to the need to pass legislation to change tax rates. These time lags can be problematic – for example, if economic growth slows down, meaning that a deflationary policy designed to control a boom actually gets implemented once the economy is already in recession.

12   The correct answer is: Sales will decrease; Net profit margin will decrease.

The increase in interest rates will be expected to lead to a reduction in consumer spending – either because people choose to save rather than spend, or because their disposable income is reduced as interest-based expenses such as mortgage payments increase. Therefore, an increase in interest rates will lead to a reduction in B Co's sales.

B Co will have to pay interest on the loans it took out to acquire its new premises, so the increase in interest rates will mean it incurs higher interest expenses. In turn, this will reduce the company's profit margin.

13   The correct answer is: Increasing government expenditure.

Fiscal policy looks at the way government expenditure and taxation are balanced. An increase in government expenditure will act as an injection to boost aggregate demand in the economy, so C is the correct answer.

An increase in corporation tax will reduce aggregate demand rather than increase it. Although lowering interest rates could boost aggregate demand in an economy (and is therefore expansionary), it is a monetary policy rather than a fiscal policy. Similarly, increasing the money supply, although expansionary, is a monetary policy rather than a fiscal policy.

14   The correct answer is: 1 and 3.

The purpose of the Government's policies will be to increase aggregate demand in the economy. A key component of that is consumer spending, and an increase in consumer spending should be reflected in increased sales for XXX Co (and all other companies in Beeland).

We would expect an expansionary monetary policy to lead to lower interest rates, and therefore a fall in interest charges rather than increased interest charges.

An expansionary fiscal policy would, typically, also lead to lower rates of taxation. So a combination of lower interest rates and lower tax rates should lead to increased profitability.

15   The correct answers are:

- Reduce income taxes in order to increase the incentives for people to work
- Increase flexibility in the labour market by reducing the power of trade unions

Two of the key propositions of supply side theory are:

- Rates of direct taxation can have a major influence on aggregate supply through their effects on the incentive to work. If people feel tax rates are too high, they will choose not to work.

- Inflexibility in the labour market (due to either the influence of trade unions or other restrictive practices) means that wages are held at competitively high levels. This creates unemployment and restricts aggregate supply – because potential employers are not prepared to pay the wages that are being demanded.

In addition, supply side policies seek to reduce the amount of government involvement in the economy, on the basis that free market forces will generate the highest level of national income and employment possible for an economy. Supply side economists argue that state-owned industries are likely to be uncompetitive, and accordingly will restrict aggregate supply below the level which could be achieved by the free market. Accordingly, supply side policies seek to increase competition through deregulation and privatisation (rather than supporting nationalisation).

Policies relating to money supply are part of monetary policy, not supply side policy. The purpose of increasing the money supply will be to increase aggregate demand (of which consumer spending is a key part), so this is a demand side policy, not a supply side one.

16   The correct answers are:

- Motorway tolls levied by the government.
- Tax on carbon emissions from firms.

A direct tax is a tax on income – this covers capital gains tax, corporation tax and inheritance tax.

Motorway tolls are a tax on spending and therefore represent an indirect tax.

Tax on carbon emissions is a tax on economic activity and will be passed to the consumer to 'indirectly' pay through higher prices.

17   The correct answers are:

- Borrowing money from the capital markets and spending it on capital goods.
- Reducing indirect taxation while maintaining public spending.

Fiscal policy is all about government tax (whether indirect or direct) and government spending.

Capital goods are investments in capital equipment such as schools / hospitals.

Notes on incorrect answers:

Stimulating private sector investment by cutting interest rates is part of monetary policy.

Manipulating exchange rates by buying and selling foreign currency reserves is part of exchange rate policy which is normally considered to be part of monetary policy.

11 International economics

1   The correct answer is: An expansionary fiscal policy.

An expansionary fiscal policy will stimulate aggregate demand in the country and lead to higher purchases of imports. (a rise in domestic saving would be expected to have the opposite effect.)

A devaluation will make imports more expensive (reducing demand for imports) and exports cheaper (increasing demand for exports). This should help to reduce a deficit on the balance of payments current account, rather than to make it worse.

Subsidies should help to increase the supply of domestic goods, and to lower their price, meaning that consumers buy more domestically produced goods rather than imported ones.

2   The correct answer is: £33.1 million.

The cost of the products, in $, is £32m × 1.5 = $48m.

At the new exchange rate, the cost in £ = 48m/1.45 = 33.1m

As the value of the £ has fallen against the $, the cost of goods imported into the UK from the US will increase. So the movement in the exchange rate will reduce BBB Co's profitability.

3   The correct answers are

A marked deterioration in the UK's balance of trade will lead to an increase in the value of £ sterling.	False
A deterioration in the balance of trade will lead to a reduction in demand for foreign currency to pay for imports.	False

A marked deterioration in the UK's balance of trade means there has been a significant increase in the value of imports relative to exports. This means that demand for foreign currency will increase relative to demand for sterling, because foreign currency will be needed to pay for the imports. This will lead to a decrease (rather than an increase) in the value of sterling.

4   The correct answer is: 1 and 2 only.

In a floating exchange rate, the rate is determined by the market forces of demand and supply for a given currency.

For example, if the UK's demand for imports falls, then the supply of the UK currency (£) will fall (so the price of £ will rise).

Conversely, a rise in foreign investment into a country increases demand for that country's currency – which again will lead to the price of that currency (the exchange rate) appreciating.

A fall in a country's interest rates (Option 3) will be expected to reduce the demand for that country's currency due to the low returns that investors can gain from depositing money in the country. Reduction in demand for the currency will reduce the exchange rate (depreciation).

5   The correct answer is: US customers will find Japanese goods cheaper and expenditure on goods imported from Japan will increase.

The movement in the exchange rate signifies that the US dollar has appreciated against the yen. This means that the price of Japanese imports, when translated into dollars, becomes cheaper.

Demand for Japanese imports is price elastic, therefore the fall in price will lead to a greater than proportional increase in demand, meaning that – overall – expenditure on Japanese imports will increase.

6   The correct answer is: An increase in the foreign exchange rate of Exland's currency.

The fall in the rate of inflation in Exland relative to the inflation rates in Exland's major trading partners will make Exland's exports more attractive, because the price of goods from Exland will be rising less quickly than goods from other countries. Demand for Exland's currency will rise because foreign customers will need the currency to pay for the exports. (This is likely to cause an increase in the supply of the currencies of Exland's trading partners, not a decrease.)

An increase in Exland's interest rate could help to explain why the rate of inflation has fallen (if it helps to control excess aggregate demand) but a fall in the rate of inflation would not be expected to lead to a rise in interest rates.

7   The correct answer is: 1 and 2 only.

A decision to reduce interest rates will normally be made in order to try to boost aggregate demand in a country. Lower interest rates will be expected to lead to an increase in consumer spending (Option 1) and lower interest expenses for business – a combination which usually means higher profits for businesses (Option 2).

However, lower interest rates will be expected to reduce the value of a currency relative to other currencies, leading to higher import costs.

8   The correct answer is: An increase in foreign tourism into the country.

The balance of payments (BoP) current account records inflows and outflows of funds into / out of a given economy, due to international trade of goods and services. If inflows exceed outflows, the account will be in surplus. It will be in deficit if there is a net outflow.

Foreign tourism is effectively an export for a country, so an increase in foreign tourism into a country will result in inflows of funds.

An increase in the volume of imports will typically lead the BoP current account towards a deficit, rather than a surplus.

Capital transactions between a given country and the rest of the world are recorded in the BoP financial account, not the BoP current account.

The level of government tax receipts compared to the level of government spending determines whether there is a budget deficit or surplus within a country. However, this is an internal deficit or surplus, rather than part of the balance of payments.

Increasing the tax rate (in the context of contractionary fiscal policy) might help to reduce imports as the level of aggregate demand in a country falls. However, the statement in the question only tells us that total tax receipts have increased, not that the tax rate has increased. For example, total tax receipts might have increased due to economic growth in the country, and this could lead to increased demand for imports.

9   The correct answer is: 1, 2 and 3.

A deterioration in the balance of payments current account could be caused by a reduction in exports, an increase in imports or a combination of both.

Reason 1. High levels of domestic inflation (particularly cost-push inflation) will mean that the price of goods produced in Country D increases more quickly than goods produced in other countries. This means Country D's goods become less competitive on the international market, and so will reduce the demand for them (ie Country D's exports fall).

Reason 2. The high price of domestically produced goods within Country D could increase demand for (substitute) imported goods, which will increase the volume of imports.

Reason 3. If inflation is caused by the level of aggregate demand in Country D (ie demand-pull inflation) domestic firms will not have sufficient capacity to produce goods for an export market as well as meeting domestic demand. In effect, the high levels of domestic demand mean that output has been 'diverted' from export markets to domestic markets, so the level of exports will fall.

10   The correct answers are:

Quantity of exports from Country B to its trading partners	Decrease
Quantity of imports into Country B from its trading partners	Increase
Balance of payments current account deficit	Increase

Exports: Currently, firms in Country B have spare capacity, and they can use this to produce goods and services to export. However, as domestic demand increases (as a result of the faster economic growth) firms will have less capacity available for exports, so the quantity of exports will fall.

Imports: Conversely, aggregate demand in Country B will increase as the economy grows, and this increased demand will include increased demand for imported goods as well as domestically produced goods. Therefore the quantity of imports into Country B will increase.

Balance of payments: A decrease in exports coupled with an increase in imports will lead to the existing deficit on the current account deficit becoming bigger.

11   The correct answers are:

A contractionary fiscal policy in Country DDD causing a reduction in the level of consumer spending in Country DDD

| Appreciation |

A reduction in the rate of inflation in Country DDD making exports from Country DDD more competitive in foreign countries

| Appreciation |

A reduction in the overall level of consumer spending in Country DDD will reduce the level of imports, because the reduction in spending will affect demand for imported goods in the same way as it would affect demand for domestically produced goods. The supply of Country DDD's currency coming on to the foreign exchange market will decrease as a result, meaning that there will be a shortage of DDD's currency which will lead to an appreciation in the exchange rate in order to restore equilibrium between supply and demand.

If Country DDD's exports become more competitive, demand for exports will increase, which in turn would be expected to increase the demand for Country DDD's currency. If demand for a currency exceeds supply then there will be an appreciation in its exchange rate in order to restore equilibrium.

12   The correct answers are:

The price, in £ sterling, of imported goods

| Increase |

Total spending by the UK on imported goods

| Decrease |

With a depreciation in the value of sterling, import prices rise. To take a simple example, if a product costs €120, then at an exchange rate of £1 : €1.20 that product costs £100 in the UK. However, if the £ exchange rate depreciates to £1 : €1, the price of the product in the UK would rise to £120.

Since demand for imports is elastic, the rise in the UK price of imported goods will lead to a greater than proportional fall in demand for imports. Therefore total spending on imports will fall.

13   The correct answer is: Demand for Company XXX's products will increase and Company YYY's profitability will decrease.

The fall in the exchange rate will make exports from Country B more competitive in other countries. For example, the price (in $) of a product costing 100B will fall from $112.5 to $110. Therefore demand for exports would be expected to increase.

Conversely, the fall in the exchange rate will increase the cost to Company YYY of the raw materials it has to import. For example, if the price of a unit of the raw material is $112.50, under the old exchange rate this would cost Company YYY 100B, but now it will cost 102.3B (112.50/110). Increasing Company YYY's costs in this way will decrease its profitability (because the change in the exchange rate will not alter its revenues).

14   The correct answer is: Increase by 6.82.

Under the old exchange rate, the cost to Company YYY of a unit of the raw materials was 300B ($337.50/1.125)

Under the new rate, the cost is now 306.82B ($337.5/1.1).

The cost (in Bs) has risen from 300 to 306.82, an increase of 6.82.

15   The correct answers are:

Demand for currency B

| Increase |

Value of currency B (exchange rate)

| Increase |

The increase in demand from foreign customers will increase demand for the B (in order that the customers can pay for these goods).

As the exchange rate for currency B is a floating exchange rate, it will be determined by the interaction of supply and demand for the currency. If demand for currency increases (at a rate of B = $1.10) then demand will exceed supply, meaning there is a shortage of the currency. This will lead to an appreciation in the currency, until a new equilibrium point is reached at a higher exchange rate.

16   The correct answer is: –$1,949 million

The balance of trade relates to imports and exports of tangible (or visible) goods only.

The country's balance of payments current account will include both goods and services, but the balance of trade includes only goods.

Therefore the country's balance of trade is $36,248 million – $38,197 million = –$1,949 million.

17   The correct answer is: Direct investment in a new factory in Zedland by a company based in Teeland

The financial account is made up of flows of capital in the non-government sector, such as direct investment in foreign facilities; portfolio investment (eg shares; bonds); and speculative flows of currency.

Public sector flows of capital, such as government loans to other countries form part of the capital account, not the financial account.

Insurance and foreign travel are both examples of trade in services, and so would be included within the current account. Insurance would, here, be an export of services, while foreign holidays would be an import of services.

18   The correct answer is: Decrease by $455.

New exchange rate will be 1A$ = 22 peso

Income (in pesos) falls from A$5,000 (100,000 / 20) to A$4,545.

This is a fall in income and therefore in profit of A$455.

The value of revenue in a foreign currency (here the peso) will be lower in local currency terms (here A$s) if the local exchange rate rises

Notes on incorrect answers:

If you convert the purchase cost to peso it becomes 6,000 x 20 = 120,000 peso.

Netting this against 100,000 peso income gives net costs of 20,000 peso.

Dividing this by 20 gives a net cost of A$1,000 and compared to dividing 20,000 by 22 (which gives a net cost of $909) there is an increase in profit of $91. This is incorrect because the purchase is due to be made in A$s and therefore is unaffected by exchange rate movements.

19   The correct answer is: C$40,000 lower.

The cost of the purchase at the current exchange rate = 100,000 x 1.2 = 120,000 euros or C$240,000 (120,000 / 0.5).

If the exchange rate changed to C$1 = 0.60 euros then the cost of the purchase will become 120,000 euros / 0.6 = C$200,000.

Costs have fallen by $40,000.

The cost of purchases in a foreign currency (here the euro) will be lower in local currency terms (here C$s) if the local exchange rate rises.

12 International trade

1   The correct answer is: It reduces the need for central banks to keep reserves of foreign exchange.

In a flexible exchange rate system, the exchange rate is determined by the free play of demand for and supply of a given currency, without government intervention.

Although the consequences of a government's monetary policy (eg increasing or decreasing interest rates) will affect the exchange rate, a key point about a flexible exchange rate system is that it leaves governments free to pursue domestic objectives (eg increasing or reducing aggregate demand) knowing that market forces will adjust exchange rates back to their equilibrium rates. So in this exchange rate system domestic monetary policy is not used to manage the exchange rate.

One of the main disadvantages of flexible exchange rates is that the inherent instability involved in them (as rates go up or down) creates uncertainty for organisations. Certainty is therefore created by a **fixed** exchange rate system, rather than a flexible one. Similarly, little currency speculation is normally an advantage of a fixed exchange rate system, not a flexible one – since there would normally be no point speculating on an exchange rate if it is fixed.

2   The correct answer is: Increasing the rate of direct tax in the country.

The expenditure to be reduced in this context is expenditure on imports. This can be achieved by deflating the economy, such that demand for imports is reduced (as well as demand for domestically produced goods and services).

All the other options aim to switch expenditure away from imported goods by making them more expensive or by restricting their availability – they are all expenditure switching policies.

3   The correct answers are:

- Import quotas
- Subsidies for local producers
- Tariffs

The underlying aim of protectionism is for a country to protect its own companies from international competition.

One way to do this is to reduce the threat from imported goods and services: for example by imposing a tariff on imported goods (which increases their price and therefore makes them less competitive), or by imposing import quotas which limit the quantities of imports.

An alternative way of protecting local firms is by subsidising them, thereby lowering the price of their goods and services, and making them more competitive in relation to imported products.

4   The correct answers are:

- Reduced transaction costs
- Elimination of exchange rate uncertainty
- Increased competition and efficiency

In the absence of a single currency, firms (and individuals) will incur transaction costs when converting their own currency into foreign currencies. The existence of a single currency, being used across a number of different countries, will remove these costs.

Having a single currency also removes the risk of unfavourable movements in exchange rates – for example, which could increase the price of exports and making them less competitive in foreign markets. Removing the **uncertainty** surrounding exchange rate movements should encourage trade within a single currency area.

A single currency enables greater transparency in price, because consumers no longer have to convert prices from one currency into another to compare them. This increased transparency should help to increase competition and efficiency, as firms need to ensure they are competitive against competitors in other countries (whose prices can now easily be compared against theirs).

In a single currency area, the member countries collectives decide the interest rate for all member countries, but there is no assurance that the interest rate will always be low. Similarly, the need for a single monetary policy could be a disadvantage if there is a disparity between the economic growth rates of countries within the currency area. For example, countries whose economies are booming could want a contractionary monetary policy, but if others are in a recession they might want an expansionary policy.

5   The correct answers are:

Demand in Country M for steel from Country X	Decrease
Expenditure in Country M on steel imported from Country X	Increase
Total revenue in Country X from steel exported to Country M	Decrease

Imposing a tariff on steel being imported into Country M will increase the price of this steel for consumers in Country M. Consequently, demand for imported steel will decline. However, because demand for steel is price inelastic, the fall in decline will be less than proportional to the increase in price, so total expenditure on the steel will increase.

However, although the price has increased, the amount received by producers in Country X does not increase because the tariff amount has to be paid to the Government of Country M. Consequently, the fall in demand for the steel (following the imposition of the tariff) will lead to a decline in the steel producers' revenue.

6   The correct answer is: 1, 2 and 4.

A customs union is a free trade area (Option 4) with common external tariffs and quotas (Option 1). The existence of these tariffs and quotas diverts consumption away from goods produced outside the union (and therefore subject to the tariff) towards goods produced within the union (and therefore tariff free).

The existence of a common system of taxation is a characteristic of a common market, rather than a customs union.

7   The correct answer is: The World Bank provides longer-term funding for developing and building economies whilst the IMF seeks to stabilise countries that are in crisis.

The World Bank's role is to encourage economic growth in developing countries, by providing them with loans and technical assistance.

The original role of the IMF was to provide a pool of foreign currencies from its member states that would be used to smooth out trade imbalances between countries, thereby promoting a structured growth in world trade and encouraging exchange rate stability. However, more recently, the IMF's focus has tended to switch towards international surveillance – helping to ensure the stability of the international monetary system, and monitoring the economic and fiscal policies of its member countries.

One of the IMF's core responsibilities is also to provide loans to member countries which are struggling with mounting debt or which are experiencing balance of payments problems.

8   The correct answer is: Developments in information and communication technologies

Improvements in the IT and communications technologies have helped to increase globalisation by reducing the significance of geographical distance as a barrier to trade. The internet is often seen as a significant driver for globalisation; for example, by enabling e-commerce and by enabling e-procurement or EDI across the supply chain.

Differences in consumer tastes in different national markets would encourage local specialisation, rather than globalisation.

One of the reasons firms might expand internationally is that entering new markets can provide them with new opportunities for growth and expansion. However, if firms already have the opportunity to grow in their existing domestic markets, there will be less need for them to expand internationally.

As barriers to international trade, tariffs and import quotas would be expected to restrict globalisation rather than to act as a driver for it.

9   The correct answer is: 1 only.

A free trade area is a trade bloc whose member countries have signed a free-trade agreement, which eliminates tariffs and quotas for goods and services traded between them. Therefore, firms in a free trade area will be able to import raw materials without paying tariffs from the member countries (Option 1).

Exchange rate stability occurs when two or more countries share a common currency or decide to peg their exchange rates (Option 2). However, membership of a free trade area does not require the adoption of a single currency.

Similarly, countries in a free trade area retain their own, pre-existing tariffs or restrictions; so joining a free trade area, in itself, will not lead to an increase in prices from outside the area (Option 3). The price will rise if the country increased its own tariffs (but it could do this regardless of whether it was in the free trade area).

The absence of a common external tariff is the key distinction between a free trade area and a customs union.

10   The correct answers are:

GDP in Erewhon	Decrease
Foreign direct investment in Keyland	Increase
Exports from Keyland	Increase

The relocation of the manufacturing process means that there will be a loss of jobs in Erewhon, and whereas XXX Co previously exported cars from Erewhon this will no longer be the case. As a result, the GDP of Erewhon will fall.

By contrast, exports from Keyland will rise, because the factory produces cars for the global market.

Establishing the manufacturing plant in Keyland constitutes foreign direct investment into the country.

11   The correct answer is: To liberalise trade by persuading countries to abolish tariffs and other barriers

The underlying aim of the WTO is to promote free trade in goods and services, by abolishing tariffs and other barriers (such as import quotas).

Encouraging economic growth loosely describes the function of the World Bank, although the World Bank's primary focus is on encouraging economic growth in developing countries.

Smoothing out trade imbalances describes a key purpose of the International Monetary Fund.

The internal market is part of the objectives of the European Union. The key phrase here is 'internal' – the EU's focus is on abolishing barriers within the single market, but it is still prepared to impose tariffs on imports from outside the EU market.

12   The correct answers are:

- A newly elected government intends to increase tariffs on imports.
- Interest rates are expected to increase soon.
- Changes in tastes and trends are increasing demand for a product.
- New technologies have led to the development of substitute products.

One of the key points about the PESTEL framework is that it looks at external factors.

Rising production costs and a highly skilled workforce relate to the company's internal weaknesses and strengths, rather than external opportunities or threats.

The other options relate to different aspects of the environment.

13   The correct answer is: 2 and 3 only.

Two of the main groups of drivers for international expansion can be seen as market drivers and cost drivers.

If growth opportunities in foreign markets (for example, due to rising per capita income) encourage firms to expand internationally, these would represent market drivers. However, in this case, the market growth is within Homeland, so Option 1 will not encourage LLL Co to expand internationally.

However, the relative costs in Homeland compared to other countries (Option 2) could provide a cost driver for LLL Co to relocate some of its operations outside Homeland.

Improved transport and communication links (Option 3) will make it easier to for LLL Co to interact with suppliers and/or customers in foreign countries, and so this should also support its expansion internationally.

14   The correct answer is: 1, 2 and 3.

As wage costs are more expensive in Homeland than other countries, if LLL Co's competitors move their production offshore (Option 1) they will be able to take advantage of the lower wage costs. More generally, this will help them to manufacture their products more cheaply, which in turn could help them reduce the price of their products relative to LLL Co.

New entrants joining the market (Option 2) will, by definition, lead to an increase in the level of competition in the market. Similarly, reducing the level of tariffs (Option 3) will make imports cheaper, and so will increase demand for imports at the expense of domestically produced goods (such as LLL Co's).

15   The correct answers are:

Consumer demand in Homeland is expected to fall following an increase in unemployment.

> Economic

There is a trend among consumers in Homeland to buy domestically produced goods in preference to imported ones.

> Social

The Government is expected to impose a quota on the volume of manufactured goods being imported into Homeland.

> Political

The 'Economic' category in a PESTEL analysis will typically include factors such as the economic growth rates, interest rates, inflation and levels of disposable income in a country.

The 'Social' category includes factors relating to tastes and trends, as well as wider demographic issues (such as population growth).

The 'Political' category relates to aspects of government policy, as well as the political stability in a country. Foreign trade regulations (such as tariffs and quotas) could be an important aspect of government policy, and should therefore be classified as political rather than economic. 'Economic' factors typically relate to the state of the economy as a whole, rather than the specific actions of a government.

16   The correct answer is: Common market.

A common market contains the features of a free trade area (free movement of goods and services), and a customs union (common external tariffs on goods and services). However, unlike a free trade area or a customs union, a common market also enables free movement of the factors of production (eg labour; capital) between member states.

In order for a common market to evolve further into an economic union, the countries would have to share a common currency and a common interest rate. But the countries have no plans to do this, meaning that the agreement between them constitutes a common market.

17   The correct answer is: An increase in the impact of the recession phase of the trade cycle.

In a recession, firms have the opportunity to export to more prosperous markets which should reduce the impact of the trade cycle's recession phase.

Notes on incorrect answers:

Countries can specialise in products or services in which they have a natural advantage and use the revenue from trade to purchase imported goods and services.
It may lead to the purchase of dangerous or unethical imported products (ivory for example).

The creation of external economies of scale is likely because international trade increase the potential size of the market and therefore will stimulate cost savings that result from an increase in the market size.

18   The correct answer is: A customs union.

A customs union contains the features of a free trade area (free movement of goods and services), and also has a common external tariffs on goods and services.

However, a common market also enables free movement of the factors of production (eg labour; capital) between member states, so does a single market and in addition has common regulatory framework.

19 The correct answer is: To support the stability of the international monetary system by providing support to countries with balance of payments problems.

The IMF's main purpose is to support the stability of the international monetary system by providing support to countries with balance of payments problems. Where a member is having difficulties overcoming balance of payments problems the IMF will either offer advice on economic policy or lend money, at subsidised rates to finance short-term exchange rate intervention.

Liberalising trade and settling trade disputes - describe some of the aims of the WTO.

Providing financial aid to developing countries - describes a key aim of the World Bank.

20 The correct answer is: Reduced economic divisions between countries.

Although many argue that globalisation has increased wealth across the world, there is considerable evidence that this has benefited wealthy nations far more greatly than poorer nations.

Notes on incorrect answers:

Multinationals, ie companies with production facilities in more than one country, are a key feature of globalisation.
Increased commonality of tastes across countries has been both a driver and a result of globalization (ie tastes are similar among consumers from many different countries).
Improved communications has facilitated the co-ordination of global businesses.

13 Functions of the financial system

1 The correct answer is: Maturity transformation.

When banks offer short-term savings and long-term lending (mortgages) they are providing maturity transformation.

The principle of maturity transformation means that financial intermediaries are prepared to lend money over longer periods of time than they borrow it. So the references to 'short-term' and 'long-term' are the key points in identifying that maturity transformation is the correct answer here.

Risk transformation relates to the way risk is spread among a large number of borrowers (for example, so that if one borrower defaults on a loan, a bank is able to absorb the loss from this due to the interest it has earned on all the other loans it has made).

Aggregation relates to the way that financial intermediaries can package up the amounts deposited by savers and lend them on to borrowers in bigger amounts.

2 The correct answer is: Share issue.

A long-term project should be financed with long-term finance, and issuing shares is a way of raising long-term finance. (If the company wanted to raise long-term debt finance instead of equity, then an alternative to a share issue would be to issue bonds.)

Bank overdrafts and bills of exchange are both short-term sources of finance, and a three year bank loan would be most suitable for a medium-term project (whose duration is approximately the same length as that of the loan).

3   The correct answers are: Mortgages, Bonds.

Long-term borrowing is usually in excess of 5 years.

Overdrafts are a form of short-term finance. Similarly, bills of exchange commonly have maturities of three months from the date of issue and so are also sources of short term finance. (As a guide, short-term sources of finance can be regarded as ones with a maturity of less than 1 year.)

Issuing shares can be a source of long-term finance, but constitutes equity finance, not debt finance.

4   The correct answers are:

- Channelling funds from depositors to borrowers
- Providing advice on alternative ways of obtaining finance

Financial intermediaries (eg banks) encourage savers to deposit funds by offering them interest on their savings, and giving them confidence that their savings are safe. The banks can then lend the money which has been deposited with them, meaning that funds have been channelled from depositors to borrowers.

Financial intermediaries can also advise their customers on the best way of investing funds or on alternative ways of obtaining finance.

By channelling funds from depositors to borrowers, financial intermediaries help to increase the level of liquidity in the economy, not to decrease it.

Financial intermediaries, in themselves, will not reduce the amount of debt which firms have. On the contrary, if firms need to borrow money (for example, to fund a capital expenditure project) doing so will actually increase, rather than decrease, the level of their debt.

5   The correct answer is: Risk transformation.

The process of risk transformation means that, typically, banks can spread the risks of lending by having a large number of borrowers. As such, if a few of these borrowers default on their loans, the bank can make good the shortfall from the interest they have earned on the remainder of the loans. However, in this case, the number of customers defaulting meant that the banks were unable to repay the money which had been invested with them by depositors.

Aggregation refers to the process where banks package up individual amounts invested by savers and lend them on to borrowers in larger amounts.

Maturity transformation refers to the fact that financial intermediaries typically lend for longer periods of time than they borrow. (In turn, this reflects the fact that savers typically want to invest funds for shorter periods of time than the periods over which borrowers want to borrow money.)

6   The correct answer is: To enable businesses and government to obtain liquidity.

The money market is the market for short-term loans and deposits.

Its focus on short-term financial instruments means the money market assists businesses and government to raise short-term capital in order to maintain their required levels of liquidity.

Markets whose main functions are the buying and selling of equity (shares) and long-term debt are capital markets, rather than money markets.

7   The correct answers are:

Short-term finance	Long-term finance
Commercial Paper	Convertible bonds
Bills of exchange	Shares
Overdraft	Debentures

Commercial Paper and bills of exchange are sources of short-term finance (ie maturing in less than 1 year), obtained through money markets.

Debentures (another name for 'bonds') and shares are long-term sources of finance, traded through capital markets.

Convertible bonds (also known as mezzanine finance) combine aspects of debt finance (bonds) and equity finance (shares), because the bond holder has the right to convert the bond into shares in the future.

8   The correct answer is: 4.2%

The bond holder will receive $4 in interest each year (4% of the nominal value of $100).

However, the yield is based on the current market price, which is $95. So the yield of the bond is $4/$95 = 4.2%.

9   The correct answer is: 1 and 3.

Financial intermediaries all have an underlying function of providing a link between people who wish to lend and those who wish to borrow (Option 1). In doing this, they act as the mechanism through which the supply of funds is matched to the demand for funds (Option 3).

Financial intermediaries are institutions which operate in the capital markets and money markets. As such, they will have to comply with the relevant regulations, but they themselves are not responsible for regulating the markets.

10   The correct answers are: Bank overdrafts, Bills of Exchange

Bank overdrafts are often used to ease pressure on working capital, or to provide a source of short-term finance for businesses that experience fluctuations in working capital.

Bills of exchange are, in effect, short-term loans, which are typically issued for a period of three to six months.

The periods over which finance leases and mortgages operate are much longer, and so these are more appropriate as sources of medium- and long-term finance respectively, not as sources of short-term finance.

A share issue would be more appropriate for a major capital project or strategic activity (eg funding an acquisition) rather than as a source of short-term finance.

11   The correct answer is: Sell bills of exchange

The scenario tells us that ZZZ's liquidity problems are being caused by weaknesses in its credit control function. Therefore the most appropriate solution will be one which allows it to collect cash from its customers more quickly and effectively.

Selling bills of exchange will specifically allow ZZZ do this, by 'selling' its receivables.

12   The correct answer is: Debentures

Ordinary shares constitute equity finance, not debt finance. Similarly, preference shares are a form of equity finance, not debt finance.

Commercial bills of exchange are a source of short-term debt finance, not a source of long-term finance, as required here.

Debentures are a form of long-term loan, which is what Zelda wants to use to finance its expansion.

13   The correct answer is: Maturity transformation and Aggregation

Highfly needs to borrow a large amount of money over a long period of time.

Aggregation refers to the fact that a bank can aggregate lots of small deposits from savers in order to make a large loan. Without this facility, Highfly itself would have to find a large enough number of individual savers, who were prepared to lend sufficient amounts of money to it, in order to raise the funds required to build the new terminal.

Maturity transformation supports Highfly's need to borrow for a longer period, because banks will lend money over longer time periods than individual savers would be prepared to do.

Liquidity and risk transformation are primarily benefits for the investor, not the company.

14   The correct answer is: Issuing new shares.

Since Highfly has a high level of gearing, equity finance will be more appropriate than debt finance as the source of funds for the new project.

Although debenture loans and mortgages are long-term sources of finance, they are both types of debt finance and so are unlikely to be appropriate here.

Certificates of deposit are sources of short-term finance, as well as being a type of debt finance, so they are not appropriate on either count.

15   The correct answer is: Retained earnings.

Debt finance involves borrowing money from an external source, and then subsequently repaying the amount borrowed plus interest on that amount.

If Highfly uses its own retained earnings as a source of finance, this is an internal source of finance, so it will not have to pay interest to a third party.

Trade credit is a form of debt financing, because if suppliers allow Highfly to delay payment products and services it has purchased then effectively the suppliers are giving Highfly a short-term loan for the amounts in question. In return, Highfly would be charged interest on purchases made on credit.

16   The correct answer is: Debentures.

The capital market is used to raise long-term finance.

Debentures are long-term bonds issued by companies.

Treasury Bonds (also called gilts) are long-term bonds issued by governments.

Treasury Bills are short-term IOUs issued by governments.

17   The correct answer is: Ordinary shares.

The money market is used to raise short-term finance. Ordinary shares are a source of long-term finances and are traded on the capital markets.

14 Commercial and central banks

1 The correct answer is: $16.8 million

The bank deposits multiplier is: 1/Liquidity ratio.

So in this case it is 1/0.125 = 8.

So the initial deposit leads to a total increase in bank deposits of $2.1 × 8 = $16.8 million.

2 The correct answer is: The relationship between the value of an initial increase in a bank's deposits and the total rise in deposits

The credit multiplier (or 'deposit multiplier') describes the relationship between an initial deposit and the total deposits resulting from that initial deposit.

Note that 'the multiplier' in the context of national income is completely separate from the credit multiplier used in the context of banking.

3 The correct answers are:

The rate of interest in Country S

Fall

Levels of borrowing and investment

Rise

In effect, interest rates are the price of money. Therefore, as with any situation of price equilibrium, an increase (outward shift) in supply will lead to a new equilibrium between supply and demand being reached at a lower price.

If interest rates fall (and therefore, in effect, borrowing has become cheaper) this will be expected to lead to a rise in investment and other forms of borrowing.

4 The correct answer is: 1, 3 and 4

The two most important roles a central bank plays in an economy are:

- To oversee the monetary system and ensure that banks and other financial institutions operate as stably and efficiently as possible (Option 1)

- To act as the Government's agent, which includes acting as its banker (Option 3)

Acting as the lender of last resort (Option 4) could be an important part of ensuring the stability of the banking system in a country.

Providing finance for capital investment (Option 2) is a function of a commercial bank, not a central bank.

5 The correct answer is: $75 million

The total increase in the money supply will be the initial deposit plus the additional $300 million.

So using the credit multiplier formula, we have:

$$\frac{C}{20\%} = 300 + C$$

$$C = 20\% \, (300 + C)$$

$$0.8C = 60$$

$$C = 75$$

If $75 million extra is deposited with banks, the total volume of deposits or cash (ie the money supply) will rise to $75 million ÷ 20% = $375 million. This includes the initial $75 million, and so the money supply will increase by $300 million.

A temptation might have been to give answer of $60m here; in this case, the total increase in the money supply would be $300 million, so the 'additional' amount following the initial deposit would only be $240 million (ie $300 million less the initial deposit).

6   The correct answers are:

- Setting interest rates at an appropriate level to meet the Government's inflation target
- Using open-market operations to influence interest rates and the size of the money supply
- Buying and selling currencies on the foreign exchange market in order to manage the exchange rate

One of the most important functions of a central bank is to maintain monetary stability in an economy. This includes setting interest rates at the level the bank considers appropriate in order to meet the Government's inflation target.

As part of its role in operating a country's monetary policy a central bank also uses open-market operations to manage interest rates. For example, if a central bank wants to raise interest rates, it will sell securities to banks, which reduces the money supply and thereby increases interest rates.

A central bank will also hold a country's foreign currency reserves and may use these to trade on the foreign exchange markets to stabilise a country's exchange rate.

Transforming customer deposits and packaging individual amounts, respectively, describe maturity transformation and aggregation which are two of the main functions of commercial banks.

7   The correct answer is: Liquidity, Profitability, Security.

Commercial banks have three main aims:

Liquidity – a bank must have sufficient liquid assets to be able to meet demands for withdrawals from depositors, and to settle its debts with other banks.

Profitability – a bank must make a profit for its shareholders, and it does this by earning interest on the funds that it lends. The level of risk a bank is prepared to accept can be important here. A bank will typically charge higher interest rates as the risk involved in a loan increases. The higher interest rates mean such loans are potentially more profitable to the bank than loans with lower rates, but if a borrower defaults on a loan and the bank has to write off the loan that will reduce profitability.

Security – customers deposit money with banks because they are regarded as stable and secure. If customers were worried that deposits with a bank were not secure, they would be unwilling to invest any money with that bank.

8   The correct answers are:

- Maintaining price stability
- Holder of the foreign exchange reserves
- Acting as lender of the last resort

A central bank will typically be involved in implementing and managing monetary policy and ensuring monetary stability in a country – for example, by using interest rates to control inflation levels.

However, a central bank will not be involved in managing fiscal policy. Fiscal policy is about government spending and taxation – neither of which are controlled by a central bank.

BPP
LEARNING
MEDIA

Similarly, the balance on a country's balance of payments current account depends on the relative demand for imports compared to exports, which again the bank cannot control. Changing the interest rate could affect a country's exchange rate, but in practice, the impact of interest rates on exchange rates and balance of payments is not something which a central bank could control or predict with any certainty.

Central banks typically hold a country's foreign currency reserves and can use these to trade on the foreign exchange markets to stabilise the exchange rate, but this, in itself, will not control the balance of payments current account.

9   The correct answer is: Decrease by $200 million.

$20 million × 1/0.1 = $200 million will be taken out of the money supply.

1/0.1 is the credit multiplier. This shows the process of credit 'creation' operating in reverse, meaning that the total reduction in money supply is 10 times greater (1/0.1) than the initial withdrawal required to buy the bonds.

10   The correct answers are:

Commercial banks' balances with the central bank

Decrease

Money supply

Decrease

Interest rates

Increase

A central bank will sell government securities if it wishes to reduce the money supply.

When people buy the securities, they pay for them with cheques drawn from the commercial banks, which means that those banks' balances with the central bank are reduced.

In turn, reducing the banks' balances – and assuming that their liquidity ratios remain unchanged – means the banks have to reduce the amount of money they can lend (ie reducing the money supply).

Reducing the supply of money (ie an inward shift in the supply curve) will lead to an increase in the price of money, which is the interest rate.

11   The correct answer is: Both of them.

Quantitative easing is a process by which the central bank attempts to increase the money supply by buying large quantities of securities through its open-market operations.

By increasing the money supply the bank hopes to stimulate aggregate demand in the economy.

One of the specific features of quantitative easing is that the way the central bank finances its purchases of government bonds (or other securities) is by creating new money electronically.

12   The correct answer is: $250

The nominal yield of the bond will be $5 (5% of $100).

In order to earn $5 of interest with a market interest rate of 2% an investor would have to invest $250 (2% of $250 = $5).

Therefore, the investor will be prepared to pay up to $250 for the bond.

13   The correct answer is: $11.5 million

The bank deposits multiplier is: 1/Liquidity ratio.

So in this case it is $1/0.08 = 12.5$.

So the initial deposit leads to a total increase in bank deposits of $1 \times 12.5 = \$12.5m$.

However, this $12.5 million includes the initial $1 million deposit, so the additional increase which results from the initial investment is $11.5 million ($12.5 million less the initial $1 million).

14   The correct answers are:

The level of the bank (or credit) multiplier	Decrease
The extent of the increase in total deposits resulting from an initial deposit	Decrease

The increase in the liquidity ratio (from 8% to 10%) means that the banks will be expected to increase the proportion of deposits they hold as liquid assets, and correspondingly to reduce the proportion they advance to customers.

The bank multiplier is the inverse of the liquidity ratio, so in this case the change in the liquidity ratio means that the bank multiplier will have reduced from 12.5 (1/0.08) to 10 (1/0.1).

The bank multiplier describes the relationship between the level of total deposits resulting from an initial deposit, and that initial deposit. The reduction in the multiplier from 12.5 to 10 means the value of the total deposits resulting from an initial deposit will fall as a result of the banks increasing their liquidity ratios.

15   The correct answer is: The bank should sell government securities in order to reduce the money supply and increase interest rates.

Because the central bank is concerned about the rapid growth of the economy, the primary purpose of its intervention via its open-market operations will be to reduce the money supply as a means of increasing the interest rate.

In order to reduce the money supply, the bank needs to sell government securities. People will need to withdraw money from the commercial banks in order to buy the government securities, which in turn will reduce the total value of the deposits the banks hold. The value of the loans a bank can make is dependent on the value of deposits it holds, so reducing the value of its deposits will reduce the amount of loans it can make (thereby reducing money supply).

15 Financial mathematical techniques

1   The correct answer is: $8,000

Interest = $5,000 \times 12\% \times 5$ years = $3,000

Total value of investment = $5,000 + 3,000 = \$8,000$

2   The correct answer is: $2,553

The value of the investment at the end of 5 years will be:

$2,000 \times (1 + 0.05)^5 = \$2,553$

3   The correct answer is: $18,785

$10,000 \times (1 + 0.08)^2 \times (1 + 0.1)^5 = \$18,785$

4   The correct answer is: $12,697

A nominal interest rate of 12% equates to a monthly rate of 1%.

The investment will have accrued 24 monthly interest payments over 2 years, so the value of the investment at the end of the second year is $10,000 \times (1 + 0.01)^{24} = \$12,697.35$.

5   The correct answer is: $375,000

$15,000 \times 1/0.04 = \$375,000$

6   The correct answer is: $6,697.50

$1,500 + (\$1,500 \times 3.465) = \$6,697.50$

3.465 is the annuity factor for Years 1–4 with an interest rate of 6%.

7   The correct answer is: $50,624

The initial payment is not discounted, so its present value is the full $8,000.

The present value of the remaining nine payments can be calculated using the cumulative discount factor for an interest rate of 12%, which is 5.328.

Therefore, the present value of the lease for Years 0–9 = $8,000 + (\$8,000 \times 5.328) = \$50,624$.

8   The correct answer is: $41,186

The annuity factor for 15 years @ 6% = 9.712.

Annuity = Present value / Annuity factor = $400,000 / 9.712 = \$41,186$

9   The correct answer is: $250,000

As Deeside expects the cash inflows to continue in perpetuity, the discount factor (based on its cost of capital of 8%) = 1/0.08 = 12.5

Therefore the present value of the inflows is: $20,000 \times 12.5 = \$250,000$.

This means the project will have a positive net present value of $50,000 ($250,000 – $200,000), but the question requirement only asked for the present value of the cash inflows, not the net present value of the project as a whole.

10   The correct answer is: Project B

	Year 1	Year 2	Year 3	Year 4	Cumulative	Present value
Discount factor @ 8%	0.926	0.857	0.794	0.735	3.312	
A	10,000	8,000	6,000	6,000		
Present value	9,260	6,856	4,764	4,410		25,290
B	8,000				3.312	**26,496**
C			16,000	14,000		
Present value			12,704	10,290		22,994
D				35,000		
Present value				25,725		25,725

BPP LEARNING MEDIA

11   The correct answer is: 15.6%

$$IRR = R_1 + (R_2 - R_1) \times \frac{NPV_1}{NPV_1 - NPV_2}$$

where R_1 = 10%
          R_2 = 17
          NPV_1 = $8,000
          NPV_2 = –$2,000

IRR = 10% + (17% – 10%) × (8,000/(8,000 – –2,000))
            = 10% + (7% × 0.8)
            = 10% + 5.6% = 15.6%

12   The correct answer is: $27,034.12

At the end of the first 3 years, the balance will be $40,000 × $(1.04)^3$ = $44,994.56

Balance	$44,994.56
Less withdrawal	$(20,000.00)
Remaining balance	$24,994.56

This balance then earns interest for a further two years, so the balance at the end of Year 5 will be:

$24,994.56 × $(1.04)^2$ = **$27,034.12**

13   The correct answer is: +$140,000

The discount factor for a perpetuity is 1/cost of capital.

So, the value of the cash inflows is $38,400/0.06 = $640,000.

Initial outflow:	$(500,000)
Discounted cash inflows	$640,000
Net present value	+$140,000

14   The correct answer is: Project B only.

Poch should only invest in a project if the discounted cash inflows from it are greater than $250,000 (the initial capital expenditure), and therefore it has a positive net present value.

	Year 1	Year 2	Year 3	Year 4	Total
Discount rate	0.926	0.857	0.794	0.735	
					($'000)
Project B	80	90	75	65	
	74.08	77.13	59.55	47.78	**258.54**
Project C	90	100	80		
	83.34	85.7	63.52		232.56
Project D	60	80	100	50	
	55.56	68.56	79.4	36.75	240.27

15 The correct answer is: 16%

The internal rate of return (IRR) of the investment can be calculated using the following formula.

$$IRR = R_1 + (R_2 - R_1) \times \frac{NPV_1}{NPV_1 - NPV_2}$$

Where R_1 = first interest rate = 10%
R_2 = second interest rate = 18%
NPV_1 = first NPV = $12,000
NPV_2 = second NPV = –$4,000

IRR = 10% + (18% –10%) × (12,000/(12,000 – –4,000))
  = 10 + (8% × 0.75)
  = 10% + 6%
  = 16%

14% is incorrect since this is simply the average of 18% and 10% = 14%.

22% is incorrect because no account has been taken of the fact that when –4,000 is subtracted from 12,000 the result is 12,000 – (–4,000) = 16,000 and not 8,000. Hence the IRR is incorrectly calculated as 10 +

$$\left(\frac{12,000}{8,000} \times 8\% \right) = 22\%$$

Moreover, the fact that the NPV is negative at a cost of capital of 18% should have been an indicator that the IRR has to be less than 18%.

16 The correct answer is: $52,360

	Now	Year 1	Year 2	Year 3	Year 4	Total
Outflows	-500,000					
Inflows – prod'n		140,000	170,000	160,000	150,000	
Inflows – scrap value					20,000	
Discount factor (at 6%)	1	0.943	0.89	0.84	0.792	
Present value	-500,000	132,020	151,300	134,400	134,640	**52,360**

If you selected $36,520, this suggests you omitted the scrap value at the end of the machine's life.

If you selected $56,520, this suggests you forgot to discount the proceeds received when the machine is scrapped at the end of its life (ie at the end of Year 4).

17 The correct answer is: $618,600

	$
S_3= 600,000(1.05)^3 =	694,575
Withdrawal	(100,000)
Balance at time 3	594,575

$S_5 = 594,575(1.02)^2$ = **618,596 or 618,600 to the nearest 100.**

18   The correct answer is: 1.47%

If compound interest is being charged every quarter, this can be converted from an annual equivalent, sometimes called an effective annual rate, using the following formula. (This formula is **NOT** given in the exam.)

$(1+R) = (1+r)^n$

R = effective annual rate

r = period rate

n = number of periods in a year.

Here **$(1.06) = (1+r)^4$**
       So the 4th root of 1.06 = (1 + r)
       So (1 + r) = 1.0147
       So r = 0.0147 or 1.47%

16 Impact of interest and exchange rate changes on business performance

1   The correct answer is: Depreciate by 1.57% against the US dollar over the next 3 months

One Euro will be able to buy fewer US dollars in three months than it could now (1.0977 compared to 1.1152 now) so this means the Euro is depreciating against the dollar.

(1.1152 – 1.0977)/1.1152 – 1 = 1.57%.

If you selected 'Depreciate by 1.59%...', this suggests you calculated the movement change as a percentage of the rate in three months' time, rather than as a percentage of the current rate.

2   The correct answer is: £425

If the £ price was £400 when €1 : £0.8, then the underlying price of the product, in Euros, is €500 (400/0.8).

After the change in exchange rate, the new price in the UK will now be 500 × 0.85 = £425.

This illustrates that a stronger exchange rate (for the Euro) results in an upward pressure on the price of exports (by a European company to the UK).

If you selected £376 you transposed the exchange rates (ie you started by calculating £1 : €0.8, rather than €1 : £0.8).

3   The correct answer is: $500 less

Henna Co will initially have recorded the amount receivable as $7,500 (5,000 × 1.5).

However, by the time the account was settled the exchange rate was £1 : $1.4 so the amount Edwards Ltd actually had to pay was $7,000 (5,000 × 1.4).

Therefore the movement in the exchange rate means Henna Co actually received $500 less than it originally expected to receive.

4   The correct answer is: £ | 22.22 | | loss ▾ |

At the initial exchange rate (£1 : 9.4 yuan) the company would have had to pay £500 per unit of the product (4,700/9.4).

At the new exchange rate (£1 : 9.0 yuan) the company would have to pay £522.22 per unit (4,700/9.0), meaning it has to pay an additional £22.22 per unit.

The movement in the exchange rate signifies that the UK £ has depreciated against the Chinese yuan, which in turn means that Chinese imports have become more expensive for UK customers.

5   The correct answers are:

Exporters who have made sales on credit but have not yet received payment for those sales | Worse off |

Importers who have made purchases on credit but have not yet paid for these purchases | Better off |

If a currency strengthens it gets more expensive (eg if the Euro strengthens against the $ it may move from $1 : €1 to $2 : €1).

We can illustrate the impact using a simple example, and assuming that the Euro vs $ exchange rate has moved from €1: $1 to €1: $2.

If the exporter sold goods which were purchased for $200, the exporter will originally have expected to receive €200 for this, but will now actually only receive €100.

If the importer bought goods costing $200 they will originally have expected to pay €200 to settle their account, but will now only have to pay €100.

6   The correct answer is: 1 and 2 only.

Statements 1 and 2 are true: As they are binding contracts, forward contracts fix the rate to that rate noted in the contract. By the same token therefore they are not flexible (so statement 3 is false). The contract contains named parties so the contracts cannot be sold on to someone else (statement 4 is false).

7   The correct answers are:

- They are only available in a small amount of currencies.
- They may be an imprecise match for the underlying transaction.

It is not possible to purchase futures contracts from every currency to every other currency – there are only limited combinations available.

Futures contracts are for standardised amounts so may not match the size of the transaction being hedged precisely.

Futures contracts are subject to a brokerage fee only (for example there is no spread on the rate) so they are relatively cheap.

Futures contracts can be 'closed out' so if, for example, customers pay early or late, the timing of the futures hedge can accommodate this, so they are seen as being relatively flexible.

8   The correct answer is: 2 or 3.

The Farland business will want to sell the US$ when it receives them, which implies either a US$ put (sell) option purchased in Farland, or a Splot call (buy) option purchased in the US. In this second alternative, payment would be in US$, effectively giving up US$ in return for Splots.

9   The correct answer is: Company Z will make an exchange gain of €18,584.07.

When the purchase was made – with an exchange rate of €1 : $1.1 – Company Z will have expected $770,000 to cost €700,000 (ie $770,000 / 1.1).

However, by the time payment was due, the value of the Euro had appreciated against the $, so Company Z now only had to pay €681,415.93 (ie $770,000/1.13).

Therefore, Company Z will make an exchange gain of €18,584.07 (€700,000 − €681,415.93).

10   The correct answers are:

Consumer spending	Increase
Borrowing	Increase
Saving	Decrease
Business investment	Increase

Lower interest rates will be expected to lead to an increase in spending and investment.

Lower interest rates mean the cost of borrowing decreases, so consumers and businesses will be willing and able to borrow more. In turn, this means that spending will increase and business investment will increase.

Lower interest rates will also be expected to reduce firms' cost of capital, which again should help to increase business investment.

Conversely, though, lower interest rates will lead to a fall in saving. Interest represents the return people get from saving, so as interest rates fall saving becomes relatively less attractive compared to alternative uses for money (such as spending).

11   The correct answers are:

Expected revenues from the new product	Decrease
Cost of capital used to discount future revenues	Increase
Net present value of the investment in the new product	Decrease

An increase in interest rates will lead to an increase in Sunrise Co's borrowing costs (for example, it would incur higher interest payments on any loans it takes out). To account for this, Sunrise would be expected to increase the cost of capital it uses to evaluate the project.

Sunrise's products are considered to be luxury products, so consumer spending on them could be seen as discretionary expenditure. An increase in interest rates will therefore be expected to lead to a reduction in consumer demand for the product, and consequently a decrease in the expected revenue from the product.

A combination of lower revenue coupled with an increased cost of capital will to lead to a reduction in the net present value of a potential investment.

BPP
LEARNING
MEDIA

12   The correct answers are:

- The amount of capital expenditure by businesses in Country Y will decrease.
- The demand for exports from Country Y will decrease.

An increase in interest rates will be expected to lead to a fall in capital spending and borrowing, because they become more expensive.

However, the corollary of this is that saving becomes more attractive so the level of saving will be expected to increase rather than decrease.

The combination of reduced consumption and investment, and increased saving, prompted by an increase in interest rates will be expected to lead to a fall in aggregate demand, not an increase.

An increase in interest rates will also be expected to lead to a rise in Country Y's exchange rate, which will increase the price of exports and make them less competitive. Therefore the demand for exports will be expected to decrease.

Governments have to pay interest on their national debt just as individuals or businesses have to pay interest on loans. Therefore an increase in interest rates will increase the amount of interest the Government in Country Y has to pay on its national debt, so this will encourage the Government to reduce the amount it borrows rather than to increase it.

13   The correct answer is: The value of the M$ weakens (depreciates) against the Euro but strengthens (appreciates) against the Chinese yuan.

Since the demand for its product from European customers is price sensitive, Multon Co will want the price of its product (in Euros) to be as low as possible. As such, it will benefit if the value of the M$ depreciates against the Euro.

At the same time, Multon Co will want the cost of the goods it imports from China to be as low as possible. If the M$ appreciates against the Chinese yuan, this will help Multon to achieve this.

14   The correct answer is: $606.06

If the M$ is strengthening against the Euro, this means that each M$ is worth a greater number of Euros.

The 10% increase means that each M$ will now be worth €1.65 (1.5 × 1.1).

The M$ receipt will therefore be €1,000 / 1.65 = M$606.06

15   The correct answer is: Enter into a forward contract to buy 10 million Chinese yuan in 3 months

Multon Co has to pay 10 million Chinese yuan, so the uncertainty it faces relates to the price at which it will be able to buy Chinese yuan in three months' time.

Entering into a forward contract to buy Chinese yuan will enable Multon to fix the price at which it buys the yuan, thereby removing the uncertainty which it is concerned about.

A call option in $ is not suitable because a call option in dollars is not needed. (A call option allows dollars to be bought but, in this case, Multon will need to sell dollars and buy yuan, so the call option will need to be in yuan, not $.)

A forward contract to buy M$1 million would not help to remove the risk, because it relates to buying M$ rather than Chinese yuan.

A put option in yan relates to the wrong type of option. Multon needs to buy Chinese yuan, so the appropriate action here would be to arrange a call option in Chinese yuan conferring the right to buy 10 milllion yuan in three months' time.

16   The correct answer is: An increase in the price of imported goods.

A higher exchange rate is likely to result from the interest rate increase. This will **reduce** the price of imported goods.

Investment will be more expensive and so is likely to fall whether this is private sector or public sector.

Consumer saving may rise if interest rates are higher because savers are getting a better return on their savings.

17 Data and information

1   The correct answer is: Information is data that has been processed.

Data are the raw materials for processing. Information is data that has been processed.

Data can be either quantitative or qualitative, as can information. The distinction between quantitative and qualitative relates to whether something can be measured or not. If data can be measured, it is quantitative (eg value of sales per week); if it cannot be measured, then it is qualitative.

2   The correct answer is: Completeness.

The notion of completeness relates to the fact that incomplete information could lead to the users of that information making bad decisions. In this case, the stores which have only been open for half of the year will show much lower revenues than stores which have been open for a full year (and so could therefore be targeted for closure). However, if the figures were adjusted (for example to show weekly averages) then the managers may find that some of these new stores performed better than stores which had been open for the whole year.

The notion of relevance relates to the fact that information must be relevant to the manager who the information is being communicated to. This is the case here.

The figures in the report have been summarised from the operational records in the store. There is no suggestion that the figures have been wrongly prepared (which would be the case if they are inaccurate) and the decision to use an annual summary is appropriate for the level of decision being made.

3   The correct answer is: Component bar chart.

Component bar charts illustrate the way in which one or more totals are broken down into their components.

The key phrase in the question requirement is 'the relative sizes' and this is what a component bar chart would help to show. The size of each 'segment' within the bar will show the level of costs incurred by that cost category compared to the costs incurred by each of the other categories.

4   The correct answer is: A simple bar chart

The most appropriate diagram to draw to highlight the differences in average salary between the regions is a simple bar chart.

A simple bar chart is a chart consisting of one or more bars, in which the length of each bar indicates the magnitude of the corresponding data items. In this case, the differences in the height of the bars will give a clear indication of the difference in the average salaries between the regions.

BPP
LEARNING
MEDIA

We are not interested in showing the breakdown of the total salary, therefore a component bar chart and a percentage component bar chart are not really appropriate.

A multiple bar chart is a bar chart in which two or more separate bars are used to present subdivisions of data. However, the data available relating to salaries is not subdivided, so this type of chart is therefore not appropriate here.

5   The correct answer is: Diagram C.

Diagram A shows strong negative relationship (correlation) ie unemployment falls as national income rises, B shows weak positive correlation and D shows weak negative correlation.

In diagram C, however, there is no discernible pattern between the level of unemployment and the level of national income.

6   The correct answer is: 8

The target is achieved when the inflation figure is less than or equal to 2.0%. This means the target had been achieved in January, February, July, August, September, October, November and December.

The inflation rate in February was exactly 2.0% which means it had not exceeded the target figure.

7   The correct answer is: Point D

A competitor launching a rival product would be expected to lead to an inward shift in the demand curve for Delph Co's product – which is, in effect, what is being illustrated by point D.

Points B and C, in effect, suggest an outward shift in the demand curve, which might be the case if a product which was a complement to Delph Co's product had been introduced, but not for a rival product.

8   The correct answers are:

Total operating costs

    Increase

Marketing costs as a percentage of total operating costs

    Decrease

Although the chart doesn't show total operating costs as such, the fact that production costs and logistics costs have both increased over the 5 years will mean that total operating costs will have also increased.

The absolute value of the marketing costs has remained constant over the 5 years. However, as total operating costs have increased, this means that marketing costs as a percentage of total operating costs have decreased.

9   The correct answer is: 22 weeks

The ogive chart shows that for 30 weeks of the year, the number of mortgage offers made was less than or equal to 60.

Based on a 52 week year, this means that for the remaining 22 weeks the building society made more than 60 mortgage offers.

10   The correct answer is: Graph B.

Since the class intervals are different, adjusted frequencies need to be calculated. The adjusted frequencies are calculated as follows. (Standard class width is taken as 2.)

Class interval	Size of interval	Frequency	Adjustment	Height of bar
0–6	6	18	× 2/6	6
6–8	2	30	× 2/2	30
8–10	2	18	× 2/2	18
10–14	4	12	× 2/4	6

The histogram which represents the above bar heights correctly is Graph B.

The other graphs are incorrect because the class intervals need to be adjusted to take account of unequal class widths (as shown above).

11   The correct answer is: 1 and 3 only.

Big data is collected from diverse sources and much of the resulting data is unstructured; for example, one significant source of big data can be the opinions and preferences that people express via social media. So Option 2 is incorrect.

Big data analytics is a recent development and enhances an organisation's ability to analyse and reveal insights in data which had previously been too difficult or costly to analyse – due to the volume and variability of the data involved. Option 1 correctly identifies this point.

One of the key features of big data is the speed with which data flows into an organisation (with much data being available in real time, or almost in real time). If an organisation can then also process this data quickly, this can improve its ability to respond effectively to customer requirements or market conditions. Option 3 identifies this point.

12   The correct answers are:

- Online video clips of clothes being shared by customers
- Keywords from conversations about fashion on social media

Although the data obtained from daily transaction records, inventory records and discounts could all be valuable to Seon Co's managers in analysing the company's performance, they are all data sets which we would expect to be available from 'traditional' database software within the company.

One of the key benefits big data can provide for a business is the insights it can give in terms of identifying trends and patterns, and gaining a deeper understanding of customer requirements. Social media (video clips, social media posts) can be a key source of such data – for example, by identifying what sorts of designs customers are commenting on favourably and which are receiving less favourable feedback.

13   The correct answer is: 15 weeks

The vertical axis on the graph ('Cumulative frequency') shows that for 15 weeks of the year the value of weekly sales was less than or equal to $40,000.

14 The correct answer is: $45,000–$50,000

One way to answer this question would be to assign values to the vertical axis of the graph (corresponding to each level of sales) and then work out the frequency with which each level of sales was achieved. Alternatively, you could look at the gradient of the graph – the level of sales which occurs most frequently will have the steepest gradient.

In this case, sales in the range of $45,000 – $50,000 were achieved 9 times in the year (cumulative frequency 22–31).

15 The correct answer is: Year 3.

Over the 5 years as a whole, there is an upward trend in sales and operating profits (ie they are increasing over time).

However, in Year 3 there is a decline in both sales and operating profit figures, which can be explained by the store being closed for a week and therefore not being able to earn any revenue for that week.

16 The correct answer is: Rory.

The sales for December are shown by the upper segment of each of the stacked bar charts.

Although Dylan achieved the highest sales over the three month period as a whole (and therefore had the highest column overall), Rory achieved the highest sales in December.

17 The correct answer is: 3 cm.

In a histogram, the width of each bar on the chart reflects the size of the class interval.

The height of each bar is determined by the frequency of a class multiplied by (standard class width ÷ actual class width).

In this case, the standard class width = 100, but the class width for 500-700 = 200, so the 'height' of the rectangle for this class is half (100/200) of those with standard width.

So the height of the rectangle for wages between 500-700 = 6 (frequency) × 100/200 = 3.

18 Forecasting

1 The correct answer is: +44.5

Average x = 60/10 = 6
Average y = 1,048 / 10 = 104.8b
a = y − bx
a = 104.8 − (10.05 × 6)
   = 44.5

2 The correct answer is: +0.98

Correlation coefficient $= \dfrac{n\Sigma xy - \Sigma x\Sigma y}{\sqrt{\left[n\Sigma x^2 - (\Sigma x)^2\right]\left[n\Sigma y^2 - (\Sigma y)^2\right]}}$

$= \dfrac{10 \times 4,208 - 210 \times 187}{\sqrt{\left[10 \times 4,634 - 210^2\right]\left[10 \times 3,865 - 187^2\right]}}$

$= \dfrac{2,810}{\sqrt{2,240 \times 3,681}}$

$= \dfrac{2,810}{2,871.49} = 0.98$

3   The correct answer is: –0.95

Demand is high when prices are low (and vice versa) which means that there is a negative correlation between the two variables.

The closer the correlation is to 1 (or –1 for a negative correlation), the stronger the relationship between the two variables.

In this case, although the individual points do not fall exactly on the trend line, there is nonetheless a strong clustering around the trend line, which indicates the correlation coefficient must still be close to –1.

4   The correct answer is: –0.6

The formula for calculating rank correlation (R) is:

$$R = 1 - \left[\frac{6\Sigma d^2}{n\left(n^2 - 1\right)} \right]$$

Where n = numbers of pairs of data
       d = difference between the rankings in each set of data

Product	Country A – rank	Country B – rank	d	d^2
Alpha	1	4	3	9
Beta	3	1	2	4
Camma	4	3	1	1
Delta	5	2	3	9
Epsilon	2	5	3	9
				32

$$R = 1 - \left[\frac{6 \times 32}{5 \times (25 - 1)} \right] = -0.6$$

5   The correct answer is: 2 and 3 only.

Statement 1. High levels of correlation do not prove that there is cause and effect.

Statement 2. A correlation coefficient of 0.83 is generally regarded as indicating a strong linear relationship between the variables.

Statement 3. The coefficient of determination indicates the extent to which variations in one variable can be explained by variations in another. This information given by squaring the correlation coefficient, resulting in 69% in this case.

Statement 4. The coefficient of determination, not the correlation coefficient, indicates the extent to which variations in one variable can be explained by variations in another. Remember that you must square the correlation coefficient in order to obtain the coefficient of determination.

Statements 2 and 3 are therefore valid.

6   The correct answer is: 25.36

$$a = \frac{\Sigma y}{n} - b\frac{\Sigma x}{n}$$

where   b   = 17.14
Σx = 5.75
Σy = 200
n   = 4

$$a = \frac{200}{4} - 17.14 \times \frac{5.75}{4}$$
= 50 − (17.14 × 1.4375)
= 50 − 24.64
= 25.36 (to 2 decimal places)

7   The correct answer is: 92

The equation of the trend line is: y = 7.112 + 3.949x

If x = 19, trend in sales for month 19 = 7.112 + (3.949 × 19) = 82.143

Seasonally adjusted trend value = 82.143 × 1.12 = 92

8   The correct answer is: 91

If   t = 1 in the first quarter of 20X5
         t = 8 in the fourth quarter of 20X6

         Trend (Y)   = 65 + (7 × 8)
                      = 121

         Forecast   = trend + seasonal component
                      = 121 + (−30)
                      = 121 − 30
                      = 91

If you selected 63, you calculated your answer based on t = 4 rather than t = 8. $63,000 would have been the forecast profit in the fourth quarter of 20X5, not 20X6.

9   The correct answer is: $46.48 million

Actual sales = trend × seasonal variation. The seasonally adjusted figures represent the 'trend' figures, so:

Actual sales = $47.92 million × 0.97 = $46.48 million.

If you selected $49.40 million, this suggests you divided the 'trend' figure by the seasonal variation, whereas you should have multiplied the 'trend' figure by the seasonal variation.

10   The correct answer is: The impact on sales of a fire which destroyed part of a company's warehouse and the inventory in it

The residual is the difference between the actual results and the figure predicted by time series analysis. It is the unexplained element in the actual figure.

The fire is a one-off event, and so could not have been predicted by the time series forecast.

Although the recession is a factor which is causing the level of unemployment to increase above its long-term trend, the fact that there has been a recession for two years means that unemployment forecasts could have been adjusted to take account of this. There would not be any such opportunity for a company to predict a fire in its warehouse, meaning that the impact of a fire is a better example of a residual component than the impact of a recession.

A long-term increase in costs could be predicted by forecasting a rise in cost of 2% per year.

Seasonal visitor numbers can be adjusted for by including a seasonal factor in the time series.

11   The correct answer is: 2 and 4 only.

    Option 1.   Provided the multiplicative model is used, it does not matter if the trend is increasing or decreasing, therefore Option 1 is not necessarily correct.

    Option 2.   Forecasts are made on the assumption that the previous trend will continue. This is one of the inherent weaknesses in forecasting.

    Option 3.   In general, extrapolation does not produce reliable estimates, but in forecasting the future using time series analysis we have no option but to extrapolate.

    Option 4.   Forecasts are made on the assumption that previous seasonal variations will continue. If the pattern of seasonal variations changes, then any seasonal adjustments to a forecast will no longer be reliable.

Options 2 and 4 are therefore necessary for a forecast to be reliable.

12   The correct answer is: –114

The actual volume of cars sold in the second quarter of 20X4 was 124. However, the trend line predicted that 238 cars should have been sold.

Therefore, the actual number of sales is 114 less than the trend line would have predicted so the variation is –114.

13   The correct answer is: –0.968

$$r = \frac{n\Sigma xy - \Sigma x\Sigma y}{\sqrt{\left[n\Sigma x^2 - (\Sigma x)^2\right]\left[n\Sigma x^2 - (\Sigma y)^2\right]}}$$

$$= \frac{(12 \times 1,674) - (137.6 \times 211.5)}{\sqrt{\left[(12 \times 2,101.1) - 137.6^2\right]\left[(12 \times 4,879.59) - 211.5^2\right]}}$$

$$= \frac{20,088 - 29,102.4}{\sqrt{(25,213.2 - 18,933.76)(58,555.08 - 44,732.25)}}$$

$$= \frac{-9,014.4}{\sqrt{6,279.44 \times 13,822.83}}$$

$$= \frac{-9,014.4}{9,316.63}$$

$$= -0.968$$

14   The correct answer is: 10million kWh.

The expected gas consumption when the temperature is 17°C can be seen by highlighting the relevant point on the graph, as below.

At a temperature of 17°C, expected gas consumption is 10 million kWh.

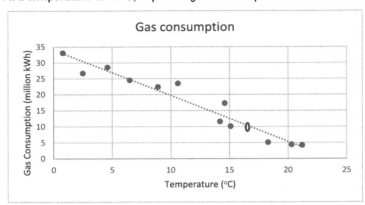

15   The correct answer is: $106.06 million

First we need to adjust the Quarter 2 actual revenue figure for the seasonal variation to find the 'underlying' quarterly revenue:

= $350 million × 100 / 165 = $212.12 million

Then we need to adjust this trend for the expected seasonal variation in Quarter 3:

= $212.12 million − 50% = $106.06 million

16   The correct answer is: 29,858

The equation of the regression line is y = a + bx

First, we need to find 'a':

$$a = \frac{\Sigma y}{n} - b\frac{\Sigma x}{n}$$

where b   = 5,400
         Σx = 21 (the total number of adverts placed)
         Σy = 208,690 (the total number of products sold)
         n   = 5 (the number of months)

a = 208,690/5 − (5,400 × 21/5)
  = 41,738 − (5,400 × 4.2)
  = 41,738 − 22,680
  = 19,058

Having found 'a', we can now complete the equation for the regression line, to find 'y'.

If there are two adverts placed in the month ('x'), the expected level of products sold in the month ('y') will be:

19,058 + (5,400 × 2) = 29,858

BPP
LEARNING
MEDIA

17   The correct answer is: $85,057

Seasonally adjusted revenue = Actual revenue / Seasonal factor

$$= \$74,000/0.87 = \$85,057$$

If you selected $64,380 you multiplied actual revenue by the seasonal factor, rather than dividing by it.

If you selected either of the other alternative answers this suggests you adjusted the underlying trend number by the seasonal factor, rather than adjusting the actual revenue.

Note that the de-seasonalised figure is close to, but not identical to, the trend. The difference may be due to one-off events, for example residual factors that affect the actual data but are not seasonal in nature.

18   The correct answer is: 116.

If the indexed is rebased to 100 in 20X5 (when it previously stood at 132), then the revised index figure in 20X7 will be $153/132 \times 100 = 115.9$, which rounds to 116 as the nearest whole number.

19   The correct answer is: +0.31.

The formula for calculating rank correlation (R) is:

$$R = 1 - \left[\frac{6\Sigma d^2}{n(n^2 - 1)} \right]$$

Where n = numbers of pairs of data
       d = difference between the rankings in each set of data

$$R = 1 - \left[\frac{6 \times 196}{12 \times (144 - 1)} \right]$$

R = 1 − (1,176/1,716)   = 0.31

20   The correct answer is: 330

Quarter	y = 15x + 7,230	Trend	Seasonal factor	Predicted admissions
1	(15 × 21) + 7230	7545	× 1.1	8,299.5
2	(15 × 22) + 7230	7560	× 0.95	7,182.0
3	(15 × 23) + 7230	7575	× 0.9	6,817.5
4	(15 × 24) + 7230	7590	× 1.05	7,969.5

The difference between Quarter 1 and Quarter 4 = 8299 − 7969 = 330

If you selected, 369 this suggests you divided by the seasonal factor, rather than multiplying by it.

21   The correct answers are:

- Values of y increase as values of x increase
- 81% of the variation in y can be explained by the corresponding variation in x

The correlation coefficient is positive, which means the value of y will be expected to increase when the value of x increases. Because the correlation coefficient (0.9) is close to 1, we would expect there to be a strong relationship between the two variables (not a weak one). However, correlation does not imply causality – even when the correlation coefficient is high.

If the correlation coefficient (r) is 0.9, then the coefficient of determination (r^2) will be 0.81. This means that 81% of the variation in y can be explained by the corresponding variation in x.

The correlation coefficient does not provide any information about the gradient of a line connecting two variables.

22   The correct answer is:–0.1

		Difference	
Restaurant		(d)	d^2
Holly		2	4
Ivy		1	1
Juniper		0	0
Kirsch		1	1
Lemon		-4	16
		0	22

The differences are calculated by subtracting the two ranks provided eg for Lemon the difference = 1 – 5 = -4.

The formula for calculating rank correlation (R) is:

$$R = 1 - \left[\frac{6\Sigma d^2}{n\left(n^2 - 1\right)} \right]$$

Where n = numbers of pairs of data
        d = difference between the rankings in each set of data

$$R = 1 - \left[\frac{6 \times 22}{5 \times (25 - 1)} \right]$$

R = 1 – (132/120)
R = 1 – 1.1   = – 0.1

Rank correlations can range from +1 to – 1 just as correlation coefficients can, and in this case the correct answer is – 0.1 not +0.1.

23   The correct answer is: 22,750

$$\text{Seasonally adjusted data} = \frac{\text{Actual results}}{\text{Seasonal factor}} = \frac{18,200}{0.8} = 22,750$$

If you selected 14,560 you multiplied by the seasonal factor, rather than dividing by it.

If you selected 28,000 you adjusted the underlying trend number by the seasonal factor, rather than adjusting the actual revenue.

Note that the deseasonalised figure is close to the trend – but it is not the same as the trend because there may be one-off events, for example residual factors that affect the actual data (such as the sudden closure of a local employer) that are not seasonal in nature.

24   The correct answer is: Total cost is expected to be $700,000.

If x = 2 (in thousands) then total costs will be 225 x 2 + 250 = 700 (in $000s)

At this level of output total variable costs ($450,000) exceed total fixed costs ($250,000).

Variable costs are $225 (in 000s) per 000 units so this is $225 per unit.

Fixed costs are $250,000 not $250 per unit, in fact at the suggested output level fixed costs per unit will be $250,000 / 2,000 = $125.

25   The correct answer is: 0.4

Division	Profits ($m)	Rank	Average customer satisfaction score	Rank	Difference (profits rank – satisfaction rank)
A	3.6	2	3.6	1	1
B	2.5	3	2.5	2	1
C	1.8	4	0.8	4	0
D	4.0	1	2.0	3	-2

	D	D^2
A	1	1
B	1	1
C	0	0
D	-2	4
		6

The formula for calculating rank correlation (R) is:

$$R = 1 - \left[\frac{6\Sigma d^2}{n(n^2 - 1)} \right]$$

Where n = numbers of pairs of data
d = difference between the rankings in each set of data

R = 1 − (6 × 6)/ (4 × (16-1))
R = 1 − (36/60)
R = 1 − 0.6   = 0.4

Remember to rank the data before using the formula.

Practice mock questions

ALL questions are compulsory and MUST be attempted

1   **Which TWO of the following are most accurately classified as private sector AND profit seeking?**

☐   A listed company that sells pharmaceutical drugs.

☐   A co-operative retailer owned by its members.

☐   A hospital operated by a private medical insurance company.

☐   A professional accountancy institute that organises the development and training of accountants (eg CIMA).

☐   A charity that raises funds from the public to support medical research.

---

2   **Which one of the following is NOT a characteristic of not-for-profit organisations?**

○   They have a wide range of stakeholders.
○   They make financial surpluses or deficits.
○   They only occur within the public sector.
○   Their primary objectives are often non-financial.

---

3   **Which of the following objectives is an appropriate objective for a public sector organisation?**

Select all that apply:

☐   Achieving economy and efficiency.
☐   Acting in the public interest.
☐   Maximising financial surpluses.
☐   Achieving high quality output.

---

4   The following figures have been extracted from a company's most recent financial statements:

Profit before interest and tax	$52,000
Interest payments	$2,000
Ordinary shares ($0.50 nominal value)	$10,000
Dividends	$20,000

The rate of tax on corporate profits is 20%

The earnings per share for this company is:

$ ☐ %

(insert your answer in $s to 1 decimal place)

5   The figures below have been taken from a company's financial statements for the year ending 31 December 20X7.

	$
Gross profit	192,500
Operating costs	104,750
Operating profit	87,750
Interest payable	10,000
Profit before tax	77,750
Tax charges	15,550
Profit after tax	62,200
Capital employed at 1.1.20X7	1,300,000
Capital employed at 31.12.20X7	1,400,000

What is the company's return on capital employed (ROCE) for 20X7?

(Give your answer to 1 decimal place.) [   ]%

---

6   Klobe Co is a manufacturing company, based in Essland. Klobe Co only makes sales within Essland, but a significant amount of its supplies are imported.

Which of the following is most likely to lead to a fall in a Klobe Co's share price?

○   An announcement that a major multinational company is interested in acquiring Klobe Co.

○   An increase in the value of the Essland currency.

○   Recent economic data which shows that an expected slowdown in growth in the manufacturing sector in Essland is not as bad as was expected.

○   An increase in interest rates in Essland.

---

7   Demand and supply for a good are currently in equilibrium.

Which of the following will lead to a decrease in the price of the good and an increase in the quantity of it sold?

○   An increase in demand for the good.
○   An increase in supply of the good.
○   A decrease in demand for the good.
○   A decrease in supply of the good.

---

8   **Which of the following would lead to an outward shift in the demand curve for Good A?**

Select all that apply:

☐   A fall in the price of a complementary good (Good B).
☐   An increase in efficiency allowing the price of Good A to be cut.
☐   A decrease in direct taxes.
☐   A rise in the price of a substitute good (Good C).

---

9   Goods X and Y are substitutes in production.

    Which TWO of the following will shift the supply curve for Good X to the right?

    ☐   An decrease in labour productivity in the production of Good X.
    ☐   An increase in labour productivity in the production of Good Y.
    ☐   An increase in the price of Good X.
    ☐   An increase in the price of Good Y.
    ☐   The introduction of a government subsidy for producing Good X.
    ☐   A decrease in the price of materials used to produce Good X.

10 In an attempt to boost sales for its product, and to increase its market share, a company has reduced the price of the product from \$425 to \$400.

    Following the price reduction, demand for the product has increased from 350 to 370 units per day.

    What is the price elasticity of the company's product, calculated using the average arc (midpoint) method?

    O   -0.97
    O   -1.09
    O   -0.92
    O   -1.03

11 **What will happen to the market price of a fixed rate bond if the market rate of interest increases?**

    O   Fall.
    O   Can't say without further information.
    O   Stay the same.
    O   Rise.

12 The overall price elasticity of demand for exports from Teeland is -1.7.

    Which of the following is most likely to result from a devaluation of Teeland's currency?

    O   The quantity of goods and services exported from Teeland will fall.
    O   Products and services from Teeland will become more expensive in other countries.
    O   Foreign expenditure on products and services from Teeland will increase.
    O   The price of products and services imported into Teeland will fall.

13 **If a firm finds that its revenue rises by 5% when it increases the price of its product by 5%, then this shows that the price elasticity of demand for this product is:**

    O   Unitary.
    O   Elastic.
    O   Perfectly elastic.
    O   Perfectly inelastic.

14 A firm currently sells 15,000 units of a product per month, at a price of $20 each. The product has a price elasticity of demand of -0.6.

In response to rising costs, the firm has decided to raise the unit price of the product to $21.

What will be the effect of this change on the firm's total monthly revenue from selling the product?

○ Revenue will decrease by $11,250.
○ Revenue will increase by $5,550.
○ Revenue will increase by $5,780.
○ Revenue will increase by $24,450.

15 **If the government imposes a minimum price for a good above the equilibrium price, the resulting market surplus will be greatest when which TWO of the following are true?**

☐ Demand is price elastic.
☐ Supply is price elastic.
☐ Demand is price inelastic.
☐ Supply is price inelastic.

16 **Which of the following would be LEAST likely to act as barrier to entry?**

○ Financial economies of scale.
○ Vertical integration.
○ Economies of scope.
○ Government assistance to support growing industries.

17 **Which of the following is an example of forward vertical integration?**

○ The takeover of a fashion clothes store by a manufacturer of clothes.
○ The takeover of a mobile phone manufacturer by a computer manufacturer.
○ The takeover of a grocery retailer by an e-commerce retailer (eg Amazon).
○ The takeover of a battery maker by a car manufacturer specialising in electric cars.

18 **Which TWO of the following are external economies of scale for high-tech electronics companies?**

☐ A locally available, skilled labour force.
☐ Larger electronics companies are able to secure cheaper bank loans.
☐ A merger between two electronics companies leading to increased profitability.
☐ Specialist suppliers providing electrical components.
☐ Increasing demand for skilled labour leading to an increase in staff costs.

19 **Which of the following courses of action is likely to occur as a result of the production of a good creating significant social costs as well as private costs?**

○ A subsidy paid to the consumers of the product to compensate for the social costs.
○ A cut in supply of the good by the producer of that good.
○ The imposition of an indirect tax on the good.
○ The imposition of a minimum price below the equilibrium price.

BPP LEARNING MEDIA

20 Which TWO of the following are characteristics which are unique to public goods?

☐ They can only be provided by a natural monopoly.

☐ They are provided by a 'not for profit' organisation.

☐ The benefit can be enjoyed by consumers who have not paid for the good.

☐ Positive externalities result from the provision of the good or service.

☐ There is no less of the good available after it is used by consumers.

21 Which of the following will cause the value of the multiplier to increase?

○ A reduction in direct tax rates.

○ An increase in the level of national income.

○ A rise in the level of exports.

○ A fall in the marginal propensity to consume.

22 Using the circular flow model of the economy, identify whether the following will cause an increase or a decrease in the level of national income, assuming that - in each case - all other factors remain unchanged.

Increase in imports
[▼]
(i) Increase in the level of national income
(ii) Decrease in the level of national income

Increase in government expenditure
[▼]
(i) Increase in the level of national income
(ii) Decrease in the level of national income

Increase in investment spending
[▼]
(i) Increase in the level of national income
(ii) Decrease in the level of national income

23 Country A is experiencing near-full employment and an increasing growth in national income.

Which of the following would be likely to create cost-push inflationary pressures in the economy of Country A?

○ A reduction in direct taxes.

○ An appreciation in the value of Country A's currency.

○ An expansion of Country A's quantitative easing program.

○ A shift in taxation towards indirect taxes and away from direct taxes.

24 Which of the following is NOT a typical feature of the recovery phase of the trade cycle?

○ A fall in frictional unemployment.

○ A worsening of the balance of payments current account.

○ A rise in inflation.

○ A move towards a budget surplus

25 Inflation in Essland is monitored by calculating a weighted average index for three different types of product.

The price indices for these products, compared to a base of 100 in the previous year, were 104, 107, and 103 respectively.

The weightings for the index are based on quantities sold. Last year, sales of the three types of product were in the ratio 1:4:5 respectively.

This year, sales of the three types of product were in the ratio 2:5:3 respectively.

What is the current year's inflation figure in Essland using a current weighted price index approach?

(Give your answer as a percentage, to one decimal place). [   ]%

---

26   A company's revenues for the last four years are show below, in nominal terms, along with the inflation index in the company's country.

Year	20X1	20X2	20X3	20X4
Revenue ($m)	95	99	104	107
Inflation index	100	102	103	105

How much have the company's revenues increased, in real terms, between 20X2 and 20X4?

- ○   8.1%
- ○   5.0%
- ○   7.3%
- ○   2.9%

---

27   **Which one of the following is most likely to reduce unemployment - according to supply-side economics?**

- ○   Increasing the pay of workers supplying public sector services.
- ○   Increasing the money supply.
- ○   Switching the burden of taxation from direct taxation to indirect taxation.
- ○   Increasing the fiscal deficit

---

28   A government has stated that it intends to pursue an expansionary monetary policy to stimulate aggregate demand in its economy.

Which TWO of the following initiatives are most appropriate in relation to the government's policy?

- ☐   Reduce corporation tax rates.
- ☐   Reduce interest rates.
- ☐   Increase public spending.
- ☐   Increase competition through privatising state-owned industries.
- ☐   Increase the money supply.

---

29   Which of the following economic policies could be described as expenditure reducing policies designed to improve the current account balance in a country's balance of payments?

- ○   Raising the level of income tax.
- ○   Depreciation of the currency.
- ○   Import quotas.
- ○   Increased taxes on imported goods.

30   The exchange rate for Kayland's currency, which is determined through a freely floating exchange rate system, has fallen recently.

Which of the following is the most likely to explain the movement in the exchange rate?

   ◦   Central banks in other countries buying Kayland's currency on the foreign exchange markets.

   ◦   An increase in interest rates in Kayland.

   ◦   Kayland's balance of payments current account balance has moved from a surplus to a deficit.

   ◦   The rate of inflation in Kayland has fallen and is now lower than the rates in Kayland's main trading partners.

31   **Which of the following are in the PESTEL analytical framework?**

Select all that apply:

☐   Political.
☐   Enterprise.
☐   Supplier power.
☐   Threat from substitutes.
☐   Ecological.
☐   Legal.

32   **Which of the following does NOT represent a potential benefit of globalisation to a multinational company?**

   ◦   Increased economies of scale.
   ◦   Reduced transport costs.
   ◦   Cheaper sources of supply.
   ◦   Improved communications infrastructure facilitating e-commerce.

33   **Lending money to assist a country in dealing with balance of payments problems is a main function of which of the following?**

   ◦   A country's Central Bank.
   ◦   The WTO.
   ◦   The World Bank.
   ◦   The IMF.

34   The three countries of Ayeland, Beeland and Ceeland have entered into a trade agreement which means there are no restrictions on the movement of goods and services between the countries, but each of them applies a common external tariffs to goods and services imported from countries which are not members of the trade agreement.

Although there are no restrictions on the movement of goods and services between Ayeland, Beeland and Ceeland, there remain restrictions which prevent workers from one of countries being able to move freely to jobs in one of the other countries. Similarly, banking restrictions in the countries limit the flow of capital between them.

BPP
LEARNING
MEDIA

What type of trade agreement do the three countries have?

- ○ Common market.
- ○ Free Trade area.
- ○ Customs union.
- ○ Economic union.

---

35 **Which of the following is the major disadvantage to an individual country of joining a single currency zone (like the euro zone)?**

- ○ Higher transaction costs.
- ○ Loss of control of monetary policy.
- ○ Increased price transparency.
- ○ Loss of control of fiscal policy.

---

36 A 6% bond is trading for 120% of its nominal value of $1,000.

The running yield of this bond is: ☐ %

(insert your answer as % to 1 decimal place)

---

37 **Which TWO of the following are sources of funds for capital investment for a private limited company?**

- ☐ The central bank.
- ☐ Commercial banks.
- ☐ Retained earnings.
- ☐ The stock market.

---

38 **Which THREE of the following are sources of long-term finance?**

- ☐ Debentures.
- ☐ Preference shares.
- ☐ Commercial paper.
- ☐ Convertible bonds.
- ☐ Bills of exchange.
- ☐ Overdraft

---

39 **Which TWO of the following are money market instruments?**

- ☐ Bills of exchange.
- ☐ Corporate bonds.
- ☐ Ordinary shares.
- ☐ Overdrafts.
- ☐ Treasury bills.

40 **If financial intermediaries parcel up short-term deposits and lend them to companies as long-term loans, which of the following functions of a financial intermediary is being fulfilled?**

    ○   Risk transformation.
    ○   Maturity transformation.
    ○   Aggregation of funds.
    ○   Pooling.

41 **Which of the following are functions of a Central Bank?**

i   Holding reserves of foreign currency.
ii   Supervision of a country's banking system.
iii   Conducting government fiscal policy.
iv   Issuing notes and coins.

    ○   (i), (ii) and (iv) only.
    ○   (i), (ii) and (iii) only.
    ○   (ii), (iii) and (iv) only.
    ○   (i), (ii), (iii) and (iv).

42 A firm is considering entering into a 5 year lease. Lease payments of $10,000 are to be made every 6 months, with payments made in advance.

What is the total present value of the lease payments assuming an effective annual interest rate of 4.04% (to the nearest $)?

$ ⬚

43 A company is considering investing in a new machine, which will cost $165,000.

The machine will increase productivity, leading to increased revenues of $70,000 per year. The machine is expected to have a three year life.

At a cost of capital of 10%, the net present value (NPV) of investing in the machine is $9,090, but at a cost of capital of 15%, the NPV is -$5,190.

What is the expected internal rate of return (IRR) of the decision to invest in the machine?

    ○   9.6%
    ○   11.8%
    ○   13.2%
    ○   21.7%

44 Consider the following data for a proposed investment project, which is expected to have a useful economic life of three years.

Initial capital cost of the project	$120,000
Income generated by the project	
Year 1	$20,000
Year 2	$70,000
Year 3	$50,000

What is the net present value for the project, assuming a discount rate of 8%?

(Use present value tables, and give your answer in $s, to the nearest $. Use the pull down box to indicate whether the net present value is positive or negative.)

[_____ ▼]

---

45   A bank pays monthly interest at a nominal compound annual rate of 3%.

An investor deposits $20,000 on 1 June 20X1.

How much interest will have been earned by 31 December 20X1 (to the nearest $)?

$ [_____]

---

46   Ananas Co is based in a European country whose home currency is the Euro (€).

Ananas Co buys fruit from suppliers in a number of different countries, and manufactures juice drinks which it also sells to a number of different countries.

Ananas Co has to pay €150,000 to one of its major suppliers in South America one month's time, and is due to receive £250,000 from a major supermarket customer in the UK in two months' time.

What type (or types) of foreign exchange risk exposure is Ananas Co exposed to in relation to the payment to its South American supplier?

- ○   Transaction risk only.
- ○   Translation risk only.
- ○   Transaction risk and translation risk.
- ○   Neither transaction risk nor translation risk.

---

47   Rosen Co (based in the UK) makes the majority of its sales to customers in countries within the European Union, whose currency is the euro.

Last month, Rosen Co completed a major order for one of its European customers, and raised an invoice for €580,000. The exchange rate at the time was £1 : €1.16.

Rosen Co allows customers 30 day credit terms, and the customer has now paid the invoice. The current exchange rate is £1 : €1.145.

Assuming Rosen Co does not use any hedging techniques to cover its exchange rate risk, which of the following is correct, to the nearest £, in relation to the recent order?

- ○   Rosen Co will make an exchange loss of £8,700.
- ○   Rosen Co will make an exchange loss of £6,550.
- ○   Rosen Co will make an exchange gain of £6,550.
- ○   Rosen Co will make an exchange gain of £8,700.

---

48   Jiri GmBH is a German company that imports electrical equipment from a supplier in China and sells it throughout Europe. Jiri has just received a shipment of equipment, invoiced in Chinese yuan. Jiri will settle the invoice in one month's time, in line with the supplier's payment terms.

Neither Jiri nor the Chinese supplier use any hedging techniques to cover their exchange risk.

Using the pull down options below, identify the foreign exchange gain or loss effects on Jiri and the Chinese supplier if the euro (Jiri's home currency) weakens substantially against the Chinese yuan during the next month.

Jiri GmBH   [▼]

(i)   Foreign exchange gain
(ii)   Foreign exchange loss
(ii)   No effect

Chinese supplier   [▼]

(i)   Foreign exchange gain
(ii)   Foreign exchange loss
(ii)   No effect

---

49   A hairdressing company has plotted recent historic data on average hours worked per member of staff and customers' assessment of service quality (maximum score = 10) on a scatter diagram.

This is shown below:

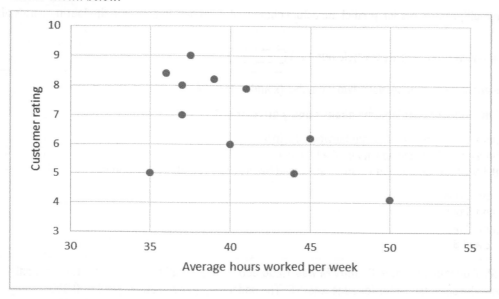

Which of the following can be concluded from an analysis of this diagram?

○   There is a positive correlation between customer service ratings and working hours.
○   Hours worked can be considered to be the independent variable.
○   Higher customer service levels require longer hours to be worked.
○   Customer service levels are determined by hours worked.

---

50   The following table shows how average house prices vary in the six different regions of a country

Region	Average house price ($)
South east	400,000
East	325,000
North east	275,000
North west	250,000
West	300,000
South west	350,000

What would be the most appropriate type of chart or diagram to highlight the differences between the regions?

- ○ Scatter graph.
- ○ Simple bar chart.
- ○ Component bar chart.
- ○ Ogive.

---

51 The trend (Y) in the number of unemployed people in a region is given by the regression equation Y = 3,000 + 0.25t where 't' denotes the quarters of the year, with the first quarter of 20X1 being given as t = 1.

However, the region experiences significant seasonal variations in the unemployment, and the average seasonal variations are as follows:

Quarter	Q1	Q2	Q3	Q4
Variation	+10%	0	-25%	+15%

Using the multiplicative model, predict the actual number of unemployed people in the fourth quarter of 20X5.

(Give your answer to the nearest whole number) [   ]

---

52 The correlation coefficient between two variables (x and y) is –0.94.

Which of the following statements about x and y are correct?

1 There is a strong relationship between x and y
2 Values of y decrease as values of x increase
3 88.4% of the variation in y can be explained by the corresponding variation in x

- ○ 1 and 2 only
- ○ 1 and 3 only
- ○ 2 and 3 only
- ○ 1, 2 and 3

---

53 In June 20X7 unemployment in Country M was 1,200,000. Using a multiplicative model for seasonal adjustment, the seasonal factor for June was 1.2. The underlying trend in June was 1,100,000.

Which of the following represents seasonally adjusted unemployment for June 20X7?

- ○ 1,320,000
- ○ 1,000,000
- ○ 1,100,000
- ○ 1,440,000

---

54 **In the multiplicative model Actual = Trend (T) x Seasonal variation (S) x Residual variation (R), which of the following is NOT correct?**

- ○ S is estimated by using an average calculation based on A-T.
- ○ T may be estimated using a centred moving average approach.
- ○ T may be estimated from a line of regression
- ○ R represents residual factors

---

55   Company A is trying to forecast how its costs are likely to behave over the next year by analysing the cost of its operations over the last year and extrapolating them using a regression equation of the type Y = a + bX (where b may be positive or negative).

A year ago Company A invested heavily in automating a significant part of its production processes.

Which of the following will make a forecast based on a line of regression more reliable for Company A?

○   A larger sample size by expanding the time period for the cost analysis.
○   Negative correlation.
○   Extrapolation further into the future.
○   A linear relationship between costs and the factors causing cost to be incurred.

56   A bank has analysed the relationship between the number of mortgage advisors it has in its branches across the country (X) and the number of mortgage applications it receives per year (Y).

The bank estimates the following least squares line of regression:

Y = 125.2 + 23.8 X

Which of the following statements is a correct interpretation of this regression line?

○   An additional 23.8 mortgage applications are expected per mortgage advisor employed.
○   The cost of a new mortgage application is $23.8
○   No branch will have fewer than 125 mortgage applications.
○   An additional 23.8 staff are needed to process new mortgage applications.

57   The relationship between units of output (X) and cost (Y) in $000s is as follows: Y = 1,250 + 4.5X

Which of the following correctly uses this regression equation to calculate total costs when output is 2,000 units?

○ $10,250
○ $1,259,000
○ $9,001,250
○ $10,250,000

58   There has been lots of debate among football supporters in Kayland about the extent to which the teams which perform best are the ones which spend the most on buying players.

Kayland's football season has just finished. The final table for its top league (which contains eight teams) is shown below, along with the amount each team spent on players.

League position	Team	Spending on players ($m)	Spending on players - Rank
1	Ayville	150	3
2	Beeton	145	4
3	Ceebury	160	2
4	Deeford	130	5
5	Easbridge	175	1
6	Fetton	60	8
7	Geechester	110	6
8	Harcastle	85	7

What is the coefficient of rank correlation between league position and spending on players?

(Give your answer to 2 decimal places, and use the pull down box to indicate if the correlation is positive or negative.)

[▼]

59 An analysis has been completed of the relationship between meeting held with potential customers (X) and sales (Y) in each month over the course of the last year, and the results are as follows:

$\sum XY$ = 3,751
$\sum X$ = 176
$\sum Y$ = 220
$\sum X^2$ = 3,022
$\sum Y^2$ = 4,794

What is the value of the correlation coefficient (to 2 decimal places)? [   ]

60 An estimate has been made that the coefficient of determination between the level of staff training (X) and staff morale (Y) is 0.62.

Which of the following statements about the relationship between staff training and staff morale is correct?

○ 62% of the variation in X can be explained by changes in Y.
○ 38% of the variation in Y can be explained by changes in X.
○ 62% of the variation in Y can be explained by changes in X.
○ 38% of the variation in X can be explained by changes in Y.

Practice mock answers

1   The correct answers are:

- A listed company that sells pharmaceutical drugs.
- A hospital operated by a private medical insurance company.

Both of these are private sector organisations which have a primary objective to seek profits for their owners - eg the shareholders of the listed company, or the shareholders of the private company.

The hospital is specifically identified as being operated by a private company, and so it will be a 'for profit' organisation, as opposed to a hospital operated by a local health authority, which would be a public sector, not-for-profit organisation.

Notes on incorrect answers:

Co-operatives and charities are private sector organisations. However, although they may make profits in the course of their activities, their primary objective is not to seek a profit. (The co-operative retailer's primary objective is likely to relate to delivering good value to its customers; while the medical charity's primary objective is likely to be linked to the level of research it can fund.)

An accountancy institute will have some financial objectives, but its primary objective will be to support its members rather than to generate profits, so it will not be a profit-seeking organisation.

2   The correct answer is: They only occur within the public sector.

Public sector organisations (such as schools, police forces, hospitals) are not-for-profit organisations, but there are also not-for-profit organisations (such as charities) within the private sector.

Notes on incorrect answers:

Although their primary objectives tend to be non-financial (eg quality of education in a school), they can still make financial surpluses or deficits. For example, if a school spends more than the budget it has been allocated by the local education authority, this will result in a financial deficit.

Similarly, although not-for-profit organisations do not have shareholders, they have a wide range of stakeholders. For example, the stakeholders in a hospital could be: patients (and their families); doctors and surgeons (who work in the hospital); pharmaceutical companies (who supply medical drugs and equipment) and the health authority which provides funding.

3   The correct answers are:

- Achieving economy and efficiency.
- Acting in the public interest.
- Achieving high quality output.

Maximising financial surpluses is more appropriate for a 'for-profit' organisation.

Achieving economy and efficiency is not a complete set of objectives, but they are valid if used as part of a broader value for money framework

Equally, achieving high quality is not a sufficient objective, but it is valid if used as part of a broader value for money framework

Acting in the public interest is not commonly listed as an objective, but it is difficult to think of an example where not acting in the public interest would be appropriate!

BPP
LEARNING
MEDIA

4   The correct answer is: 2.0.

Earnings = profits after interest and tax = (52,000 – 2000) – 20% tax = $40,000

The number of shares = 10,000 / 0.5 = 20,000

EPS = 40,000 / 20,000 = 2.0

5   The correct answer is: 6.5%.

Return on capital (ROCE) is calculated as: Profit before interest and tax / Capital employed. Where opening capital employed figures are provided as well as closing capital employed figures, the figure to use in the ROCE calculation is the average of the two; in this case, 1,350,000.

Therefore, ROCE = 87,750/1,350,000 = 6.5%.

6   The correct answer is: An increase in interest rates in Essland.

An increase in interest rates (and therefore in the cost of capital) would be expected to reduce profits and future investments. As share values reflect a company's expected future cash flows, these consequences of an increase in interest rates would be expected to lead to a fall in share prices.

Notes on incorrect answers:

An increase in the value of the Essland currency will decrease the cost of imported supplies which should boost Klobe's cash flows and share price.

Share prices typically respond negatively to bad news, but confirmation of an expected slowdown is only confirming existing expectations which would already be built into the share price and in fact the slowdown is not as bad as expected so the share price may even rise. The share prices of potential acquisition targets typically increase (rather than fall) when news of a possible takeover emerges.

7   The correct answer is: An increase in supply of the good.

If demand and supply are currently equilibrium, then an increase in supply will lead to a surplus of the good. In response to the surplus, the price will fall and the quantity demanded will rise.

Notes on incorrect answers:

An increase in demand for the good would have created a shortage of the good, and therefore would have resulted in an increase in price (not a decrease in price.)

Decreases in demand or supply would lead to a decrease in the quantity sold (not an increase).

8   The correct answers are:

- A fall in the price of a complementary good (Good B).
- A decrease in direct taxes.
- A rise in the price of a substitute good (Good C).

A fall in the price of a complement will lead to an increase in demand for Good B and therefore an increase in demand for Good A as well.

A decrease in INDIRECT taxation would affect the supply curve but a decrease in DIRECT taxation means that consumers would have a higher discretionary income and would normally lead to an increase in demand at any given price (and therefore an outward shift in the demand curve).

A rise in the price of a substitute will lead to a fall in demand for Good C and therefore an increase in demand for Good A.

Notes on incorrect answer:

An increase in efficiency will shift the supply curve to the right. Lower prices will mean that demand extends along the demand curve (more will be demanded at a lower price) but this will not shift the demand curve.

9   The correct answers are:

- The introduction of a government subsidy for producing Good X.
- A decrease in the price of materials used to produce Good X.

The introduction of a government subsidy, and a decrease in the price of materials used to produce Good X, will both increase the profitability of producing Good X even if its price remains unchanged. Therefore both of these scenarios will lead to an outward (rightward) shift in the supply curve for Good X.

Notes on incorrect answers:

A decrease in labour productivity in the production of Good X would lead to an increase in costs per unit and would be expected to lead to an inward (leftward) shift in the supply curve for Good X.

An increase in labour productivity in the production of Good Y would lead to an increase in the relative profitability of Good Y which is a substitute in production. This would be expected to lead to an inward (leftward) shift in the supply curve for Good X.

A shift in the supply curve for Good X will result from changes in the conditions of supply of Good X, not a change in the price of the good itself. An increase in the price of Good X will result in a movement along the supply curve, not a shift in it.

If it becomes relatively more profitable to produce Good Y rather than Good X, then the supplier will divert resources away from Good X and onto Good Y. This will lead to an inward (leftward) shift in the supply curve for Good X.

10   The correct answer is: -0.92.

Price elasticity of demand = % change in quantity demanded / % change in price

Using the average arc method, % changes are calculated in relation to the average quantity [(350+370)/2 = 360] and the average price [(425+400)/2 = $412.5].

% change in quantity demanded = (20 / 360) × 100 = 5.56%

% change in price demanded = (-25 / 412.5) × 100 = -6.06%

Price elasticity of demand = 5.56% / -6.06% = -0.92

Notes on incorrect answers:

0.97 is calculated using the simple arc method which is based on the percent change in price and quantity versus the starting price and the starting quantity. The remaining values are possible if the formula is incorrectly calculated with quantity demanded as the denominator (ie the bottom of the formula) and the percent change in price as the numerator (ie the top of the formula).

11   The correct answer is: Fall.

The price of a bond will be calculated as the discounted rate of its future cash flows. If interest rates rise the future cash flows are discounted more heavily and so the present value of the cash inflows (and therefore the market price of the bond) will fall.

12   The correct answer is: Foreign expenditure on products and services from Teeland will increase.

A devaluation of Teeland's currency means that exports from Teeland become cheaper in other countries, and therefore quantity demanded for them will be expected to increase.

Price elasticity of -1.7 indicates that the exports are price elastic. Therefore, a fall in price will lead to a greater than proportional increase in demand, meaning that total revenue from exports will increase.

13   The correct answer is: Perfectly inelastic.

Revenue = price per unit × volume sold. If the price has risen by 5% then volume sold must be unchanged for revenue to rise by 5%. In this case demand is perfectly inelastic.

Notes on incorrect answers:

If demand responded (downwards) at all then revenue would not rise by as much as 5%, so demand is not price elastic.

If elasticity is unitary this means that price elasticity of demand has a value of 1. In this case the 5% price rise would lead to a 5% fall in volume and revenue would therefore be unchanged.

14   The correct answer is: Revenue will increase by $5,550.

Where a question does not specify the method of elasticity to be applied, CIMA have said that you should apply the simple arc (non-average) method. That is the case in this question.

The rise in price from $20 to $21 represents an increase of 5%.

Price elasticity of demand of -0.6 means that this will result in a fall in demand of 3% (5% × -0.6) 3% of 15,000 = 450, so demand for the product after the price increase will be 14,550 (15,000 - 450).

Total monthly revenue will now be 14,550 x $21 = $305,550

The original monthly revenue was $300,000 (14,000 × $20), so the increase in price results in an increase in total revenue of $5,550 ($305,550 – $300,000)

A price elasticity of -0.6 means that demand is inelastic, and therefore an increase in price will lead to an increase in total revenue.

Notes on incorrect answers:

$5,780 is obtained if the average arc method is used.

$24,550 if the percent change in demand is treated as an increase in demand.

$11,250 can be obtained if the change in quantity is mistakenly calculated as percent change in price divided by 0.6

15   The correct answers are:

- Demand is price elastic.
- Supply is price elastic.

The surplus will be higher when supply increases at a fast rate as price rises, and demand falls at a fast rate if price rises. In both cases supply and demand are responsive (or elastic) as price changes.

16   The correct answer is: Government assistance to support growing industries.

This is an example of an external economy of scale and would be available to any firm entering the industry.

Notes on incorrect answers:

Financial economies of scale are available to large firms, and this would then give these firms a cost advantage over smaller firms trying to enter the industry.

Vertical integration can tie in suppliers or distribution outlets, making it harder for firms to enter the industry.

Economies of scope are cost savings from selling a wider variety of products and again this would then give existing firms which already do this a cost advantage over smaller firms trying to enter the industry.

17   The correct answer is: The takeover of a fashion clothes store by a manufacturer of clothes.

This is an example of a company moving forwards towards the final customer. The manufacturer currently sells its clothes to the store, and the store then sells them to the final customer.

Notes on incorrect answers:

The takeover of a mobile phone manufacturer by a computer manufacturer is an example of conglomerate integration.

The takeover of a grocery retailer by an e-commerce retailer (eg Amazon) is a move outside the core market of the e-commerce retailer, and therefore also illustrates conglomerate integration.

The takeover of a battery maker by a car manufacturer specialising in electric cars is an example of a company securing its supply base and is an example of backward (not forward) vertical integration.

18   The correct answers are:

- A locally available, skilled labour force.
- Specialist suppliers providing electrical components.

External economies of scale reflect cost reductions which result from the growth of an industry as a whole, rather than the growth of an individual firm. In this case, the presence of a skilled labour force, and the availability of specialist suppliers providing electrical components will benefit all the high-tech electronics companies in a region, and so they are external economies of scale.

Notes on incorrect answers:

The ability of larger companies to secure cheaper bank loans is an internal (financial) economy of scale, because it depends on the size of the individual company.

Similarly, economies of scale (leading to increased profitability) as a result of the merger are internal, because they are restricted to the two firms who have merger.

Rising staff costs as a result of increasing demand for skilled labour are an external diseconomy of scale, because costs are rising (rather than falling) as a result of the industry's growth.

19   The correct answer is: The imposition of an indirect tax on the good.

This will either deter production of the good or raise revenue which can be used to pay for the social costs.

Notes on incorrect answers:

A subsidy would encourage demand for and therefore production of the good, whereas the desired outcome in this case is to reduce production (and consumption) of the good.

A cut in supply of the good by the producer of that good is unlikely because they will care about the private, not the social costs.

The imposition of a minimum price below the equilibrium price would have no impact.

20   The correct answers are:

- The benefit can be enjoyed by consumers who have not paid for the good.
- There is no less of the good available after it is used by consumers.

These are the characteristics of non-exclusivity (the benefit can be enjoyed by consumers who have not paid for the good, creating a free rider problem) and non-diminishability (there is no less of the good available after it is used by consumers) which together describe the unique characteristics of a public good.

Note on incorrect answers:

They are provided by a 'not for profit' organisation.

Benefits enjoyed by consumers who have not paid for the good and positive externalities resulting from the provision of the good or service are characteristics that may be displayed by some public goods, but are not unique to public goods.

A natural monopoly is one where fixed costs are so high that there is only room for 1 supplier in the market, this is not connected with the concept of public goods.

21   The correct answer is: A reduction in direct tax rates.

The multiplier can be calculated either as 1(1–MPC) or as 1/MPW, and the second of these formulae (1/MPW) shows that the multiplier will increase as the marginal propensity to withdraw falls.

The types of withdrawals from the circular flow are savings, taxation and imports. Therefore, a reduction in direct tax rates (ie taxes on income) will contribute to a reduction in MPW, which, in turn, will cause the multiplier to increase.

Notes on incorrect answers:

The level of national income might increase as a result of an increase in the multiplier, but it will not cause a change in the value of the multiplier.

Exports (along with government expenditure and investment) are injections into the circular flow, and may increase the multiplier **effect** (ie injections x the multiplier) but do not directly increase the value of the **multiplier** itself.

The multiplier is calculated as 1/(1–MPC), so as the marginal propensity to consumer falls, the multiplier will also fall.

22   The correct answers are:

- Increase in demand for imports - Decrease
- Increase in government expenditure -Increase
- Increase in investment spending - Increase

The equilibrium level of national income is achieved when the level of injections equals the level of withdrawals.

If injections are greater than withdrawals, national income will increase, but if withdrawals are greater than injections, national income will decrease.

Imports are a withdrawal from the circular flow of income; therefore an increase in imports (and an increase in withdrawals) will result in a decrease in the level of national income.

Government expenditure, and investment spending (remember this is spending on the creation of new assets) are both injections into the circular flow, and so increases in them will result in an increase in the level of national income.

23   The correct answer is: A shift in taxation towards indirect taxes and away from direct taxes.

Indirect taxes are paid by firms, who will look to increase prices and pass these on to the consumer (which they are likely to be able to do as the economy is growing strongly).

Notes on incorrect answers:

Reducing direct taxation and quantitative easing will boost demand-pull inflation. An appreciation of the currency will reduce the cost of imports and make cost push inflation less likely.

24   The correct answer is: A fall in frictional unemployment.

Frictional unemployment is short-term unemployment (for example due to seasonal factors) and is not affected by the trade cycle (it is cyclical unemployment that would reduce).

Note on incorrect answers:

As national incomes rise more imports are purchased (so the balance of payments will worsen), more tax is paid (so there is a move towards a budget surplus) and prices rise (so inflation rises).

25   The correct answer is: 5.2%.

The inflation figure is calculated from the weighted average index for the three types of products using the latest year's sales (ie the current year's sales) as the basis for the weightings.

$(104 \times 2) + (107 \times 5) + (103 \times 3) = 1,052$

Weighting: $3 + 5 + 2 = 10$

Weighted average index = 1,052 / 10 = 105.2

Therefore the % increase (compared to the base of 100 in the previous year) is 5.2%

$((105.2 - 100)/100)$

26   The correct answer is: 5.0%.

The revenue figures shown are nominal figures, so they need to be adjusted for the inflation index in order to find the real revenue growth.

	20X2	20X4
Nominal revenue ($m)	99	107
Index	102	105
Real revenue ($m)	97.06	101.90

Therefore the growth in real revenue is $4.84m ($101.9m - $97.06m), which expressed as a percentage of $97.06m = 4.99% (rounded up to 5.0%).

Notes on incorrect answers

7.3% is the growth in real revenue from 20X1-20X4, which is the incorrect time period.

8.1% is the growth in nominal revenue between 20X2 and 20X4, so the figures have not been adjusted to take account of inflation.

If you selected 2.9%, this suggests you correctly calculated the growth in real revenue in 20X4, but you calculated the % increase based on nominal revenue in 20X2.

27   The correct answer is: Switching the burden of taxation from direct taxation to indirect taxation.

Supply side economists argue that lower direct taxation creates higher incentives to invest and to work.

Notes on incorrect answers:

Increasing the pay of workers supplying public sector services will not increase efficiency or motivation (which are key supply-side policies for improving employment levels).

Increasing the money supply and increasing the fiscal deficit affect unemployment caused by low demand levels, however supply side economists do not believe that such policies are effective.

28   The correct answers are:

- Reduce interest rates.
- Increase the money supply.

The main elements of monetary policy are interest rates, money supply, and exchange rates. Lowering interest rates and increasing the money supply will would both be expected to increase aggregate demand, and so would support an expansionary monetary policy.

Reducing corporation tax rates and increasing public spending are examples of possible components of an expansionary fiscal policy, rather than a monetary policy.

Increasing competition through privatising state-owned industries is a potential example of a supply side policy (rather than a demand-side policy).

29   The correct answer is: Raising the level of income tax.

This will reduce the demand for imported goods (without affecting reducing demand for exports).

Note on incorrect answers:

All of the other policies are expenditure switching policies designed to reduce expenditure on imported goods without reducing expenditure as a whole.

30   The correct answer is: Kayland's balance of payments current account balance has moved from a surplus to a deficit.

In a freely floating exchange rate system, exchange rates are determined by supply and demand for a currency. If Kayland's exchange rate is falling this would suggest that supply of its currency is greater than demand for it, which would be the case if Kayland is experiencing a deficit on its balance of payments current account. The current account deficit would indicate that imports are greater than exports, and consequently supply of Kayland's currency (from buying imports) is greater than demand for Kayland's currency (to pay for the exports).

Notes on incorrect answers:

Central banks in other countries buying Kayland's currency will increase demand for it, and will therefore be expected to lead to an increase in the exchange rate, not a fall.

Similarly, an increase in interest rates would be expected to encourage investors to deposit more money in Kayland, which should increase (rather than decrease) demand for its currency.

If the inflation rate in a country is higher than that of its trading partners, this means that the country's products are likely to become relatively more expensive than those produced by its trading partners, and therefore demand for its exports will fall. In this case though, Kayland's inflation rate is lower than its trading partners, which should help increase demand for its exports, and - in turn - demand for its currency.

31   The correct answers are

- Political.
- Ecological.
- Legal.

Ecological is also referred to as environmental.

The complete list is

Political, Economic, Social, Technological, Ecological (or environmental) and Legal.

32   The correct answer is: Improved communications infrastructure facilitating e-commerce.

This is a factor that has helped to facilitate globalisation, but is not a specific benefit to a multinational company.

Note on incorrect answers:

Increased economies of scale will result from serving a wider market and will drive down costs per unit.

Reduced transport costs may result from locating more production facilities closer to overseas customers.

Cheaper sources of supply may result from accessing cheaper foreign suppliers.

33   The correct answer is: The IMF.

The IMF exists to promote stability in the international monetary system.

Notes on incorrect answers:

A country's Central Bank may need to borrow to deal with balance of payments problems.

The WTO exists to promote free trade.

The World Bank will lend, but for the purpose of financing infrastructure projects and alleviating poverty - rather than for addressing balance of payments problems.

BPP
LEARNING
MEDIA

34   The correct answer is: Customs union.

A customs union contains the features of a free trade area (free movement of goods and services) plus the application of common external tariffs to imports from non-member countries.

In order for the countries to develop their trade agreement further - from a customs union into a common market - they would need to enable the free movement of the factors of production (ie labour and capital) in addition to the free movement of goods and services. However, the current restrictions, preventing the free movement of workers, or capital, signify that the agreement is a customs union rather than a common market.

35   The correct answer is: Loss of control of monetary policy.

The major disadvantage to an individual country of joining a single currency is loss of monetary control. If the country has its own currency, with a floating exchange rate, the country can use interest rates to manage its exchange rate. However, by definition, if the country adopts a single currency, it can no longer influence its own exchange rate.

Notes on incorrect answers:

Joining a single currency does not, in itself, affect fiscal control, because the country's government will still have control over taxation and public spending. A single currency zone may have restrictions on the fiscal policy of its members (to control inflation) but this does not amount to a loss of control.

Joining a single currency reduces (rather than increases) transaction costs, because entities will not incur any foreign exchange costs when doing business in other countries within the single currency zone.

Increased price transparency (and consumers' ability to compare prices in different countries more easily) is typically seen as an advantage of joining a single currency, not a disadvantage.

36   The correct answer is: 5.0%.

Interest earned = $1,000 \times 0.06 = $60

Running yield = interest earned / market price of bond = $60 / $1,200 \times 100 = 5.0\%

37   The correct answers are:

- Commercial banks.
- Retained earnings.

The central bank acts on behalf of the government, and regulates the banking sector, rather than lending to businesses in the way that commercial banks do.

The key difference between private and public limited companies is that shares in a public limited company may be offered to the public (through the stock market) whereas shares in a private limited company may not be offered to the public. Therefore the stock market is not a potential source of funds for a private limited company.

38   The correct answers are:

- Debentures.
- Preference shares.
- Convertible bonds.

Shares and bonds are both sources of long-term finance. A debenture is a type of bond. A convertible bond offers the bond holder the right to convert the bond into shares in the future, so it combines aspects of both debt and equity finance.

Notes on incorrect answers:

Commercial paper and bills of exchange are sources of short-term finance, available through the money markets. Bills of exchange are typically settled within 180 days, and commercial paper within 270 days.

Overdrafts are sources of short-term finance available through financial intermediaries (such as banks).

39   The correct answers are:

- Bills of exchange.
- Treasury bills.

Money markets are markets for short-term finance, by contrast to capital markets which focus on long-term finance. Corporate bonds and shares are long-term sources of finance and so are capital market instruments (rather than money market instruments).

Overdrafts are sources of short-term finance, but are obtained from financial intermediaries (eg banks) rather than directly through the financial markets.

Bills of exchange and treasury bills are short-term sources of finance, obtained through the financial markets, meaning they are money market instruments.

40   The correct answer is: Maturity transformation.

Depositors will still have access to their funds so short-term deposits have become a source of long-term finance for companies.

Notes on incorrect answers:

The other options are all functions of a financial intermediary but are not being demonstrated in the wording of this scenario.

Risk transformation (or Pooling losses) refers to a bank's ability to absorb losses from a single bad debt without them impacting savers (because the bank has earned enough interest from its other loans to cover the loss).

Aggregation of funds occurs when a bank can aggregate lots of small amounts of money from different savers into a large loan.

41   The correct answer is: (i), (ii) and (iv) only.

Notes on incorrect answers:

Government finance will be organised by a Central Bank, but government spending will not, so fiscal policy is not controlled by the Central Bank.

42   The correct answer is: 91,620.

An effective annual rate of 4.04% equates to a 6 monthly rate of = 1.02 ie 2% Payments are made in advance, 10 payments will be made in total starting at time 0.

Time	0	1 to 9
	10000	10000
df 2%	1	8.162
PV	10000	81620 **91620**

43   The correct answer is: 13.2%.

The internal rate of return (IRR) of the investment is calculated using the formula:

$$IRR = R_1 + (R_2 - R_1) \times \frac{NPV_1}{NPV_1 - NPV_2}$$

Where: $R1$ = lower interest rate = 10%

      $R2$ = higher interest rate = 15%

      $NPV1$ = NPV at lower rate = $9,090

      $NPV2$ = NPV at higher rate = –$5,190

      IRR = 10% + (15% –10%) x (9,090/(9,090 – –5,190))

          = 10 + (5% × 0.64)

            = 10% + 3.2%

Notes on incorrect answers:

If you selected 21.7% this suggests you used 9,090 - 5,190 in your calculation, rather than 9,090—5,190 (in effect 9,090 + 5,190). However, the fact that the NPV was positive at a cost of capital of 10%, and negative at a cost of capital of 15%, should have indicated that the IRR had to be somewhere between 10% and 15%.

44   The correct answer is: - $1,790.

	Year 0	Year 1	Year 2	Year 3	Net present value
Cash outflow	-120,000				
Cash inflows		20,000	70,000	50,000	
Discount factor (8%)		0.926	0.857	0.794	
Present value	-120,000	18,520	59,990	39,700	- 1,790

45   The correct answer is: 353.

A nominal rate of 3% per year is a monthly rate 3% × 1/12 = 0.25%

Interest will be earned on a compound basis for 7 months so the value of the investment at the end of December is $20,000 × = $20,353 (to the nearest £).

So the interest earned (to the nearest $) is $20,353 – $20,000 = $353

46   The correct answer is: Neither transaction risk nor translation risk.

Because the amount it has to pay is denominated in its home currency (Euro), Ananas does not face either transaction risk or translation risk.

Transaction risk is the risk that the exchange rate moves after a transaction has been agreed, so the amount a company has to pay for imported goods (or receives from exported goods) differs from what it expected when the transaction was agreed. Ananas is exposed to transaction risk on the money it is due to receive from the UK supermarket customer (because the supermarket pays in £), but it is not exposed to transaction risk on the payment to the South American supplier, because it was originally quoted in euros.

Translation risk relates to the way movements in exchange rates can affect the value of foreign assets and foreign liabilities when they are converted ('translated') into a company's domestic currency. Although the amount owing to the supplier is a liability, there is not risk of its value changing, because it is stated in euros.

47   The correct answer is: Rosen Co will make an exchange gain of £6,550.

When the order was raised, Rosen would have expected the £ value of the payment it receives to be £500,000. (580,000 / 1.16 = 500,000).

However, the movement in exchange rate means that the £ value of the payment will actually be £506,550 (580,000 / 1.145 = 506,550).

The fall in the value of the £ relative to € means that Rosen makes an exchange gain, not an exchange loss.

Notes on incorrect answers:

Note that 8,700 can be obtained if the euro amount is incorrectly multiplied by the exchange rate to convert into £s.

48   The correct answers are:

- Jiri GmBH - Foreign exchange loss
- Chinese supplier - No effect

The Chinese supplier is not affected by any movements in the exchange rate because it has invoiced in its local currency (Chinese yuan). The supplier will receive the amount of yuan shown on the invoice, regardless of any movements in the value of the yuan against the euro.

However, the fall in the value of the euro means that Jiri will have to pay more euros to purchase the number of yuan required to settle the invoice. Therefore, Jiri suffers a foreign exchange loss.

We can demonstrate this using an example: suppose the invoice is for 1 million yuan and the exchange rate is initially 1 euro : 10 yuan; therefore, Jiri would initially expect to have to pay 100,000 euros to settle the invoice.

However, if the exchange rate falls to 1 euro : 8 yuan, then 1 million yuan will cost Jiri 125,000 euros, meaning it has incurred a foreign exchange loss of 25,000 euros (125,000 - 100,000).

49   The correct answer is: Hours worked can be considered to be the independent variable.

In the context of a hairdressing company it seems likely that service levels will fall if staff are overworked therefore service levels are the dependent variable and hours worked are the independent variable.

Notes on incorrect answers:

There is a NEGATIVE correlation between customer service ratings and working hours because as one falls the other rises.

Higher customer service levels may require longer hours to be worked in some businesses but this does not seem likely for a hairdresser (especially given the negative correlation between longer hours and customer ratings).

Customer service levels are not only determined by hours worked as shown by the scatter of data which indicates less than perfect negative correlation. Also, a scatter diagram does not prove causality ie even if long hours are associated with poor customer ratings it does not prove that long hours cause poor customer service ratings.

50   The correct answer is: Simple bar chart.

A simple bar chart would show six bars (one for each region), with the length of each bar illustrating the average house price in the different regions.

Notes on incorrect answers:

There is no requirement to show how the figures from each region combine, so a simple bar chart is all that is required here, not a component bar chart.

A scatter graph illustrates the relationship between two variables, but only one 'variable' (price) is given in the data, so it would not be possible, or appropriate, to construct a scatter graph here.

An ogive would illustrate cumulative frequencies, but again, there are no frequencies given in the data so it would be possible to construct an ogive here.

51   The correct answer is: 3,456.

For the first quarter of 20X5 t = 20.

Therefore the trend line Y = 3,000 + (0.25 × 20) = 3,005.

Actual prediction (time series) = trend × seasonal variation

Therefore, the predicted number = 3,005 × 1.15 = 3,455.75 (rounded to the nearest whole number: 3,456.)

52   The correct answer is: 1, 2 and 3.

The correlation is negative (−0.94), which means the value of y will be expected to decrease when the value of x increases (Statement 2).

Because the correlation coefficient is close to−1, we would expect there to be strong relationship between the two variables (Statement 1). Correlation coefficients close to−1 signify a strong negative relationship between the two variables, while coefficients close to +1 indicate a strong positive relationship.

If the correlation coefficient (r) is−0.94, then the coefficient of determination ($r2$) will be 0.884 (ie -0.94 x - 0.94). This means that 88.4% of the variation in y can be explained by the corresponding variation in x (Statement 3).

53   The correct answer is: 1,000,000.

This is actual of 1,200,000 divided by the seasonal factor of 1.2. You divide to reflect that June has above average unemployment (the seasonality factor is above 1) so we need to strip this effect out of the actual figures. The answer is close to the trend and presumably differs because of residual factors.

Note on incorrect answers:

1,440,000 has multiplied the actual figure by the seasonal factor, rather than dividing by it.

1,320,000 has multiplied the underlying trend by the seasonal factor, so includes two errors: using the trend figure rather than the actual; and multiplying by the seasonal factor rather than dividing by it.

54   The correct answer is: S is estimated by using an average calculation based on A-T.

This should be A / T not A-T because a multiplicative model is being used.

55 The correct answer is: A linear relationship between costs and the factors causing cost to be incurred.

A formula of the type Y = a + bX assumes a linear (ie straight-line) relationship.

Note on incorrect answers:

A larger sample size by expanding the time period for the cost analysis will introduce historic data that is not relevant because it pre-dates the automation of A's production processes. This will make the forecast less reliable.

Negative correlation does not make forecasting less reliable, it simple means that an increase in a variable X) will cause a fall in cost (Y).

Extrapolation further into the future makes it harder to forecast costs

56 The correct answer is: An additional 23.8 mortgage applications are expected per mortgage advisor employed.

Notes on incorrect answers:

This analysis is not looking at the costs of mortgage applications.

This is looking at average information so we cannot say that NO branch will have fewer than 125 mortgage applications, just that on average we would not expect a smaller number than this.

57 The correct answer is: $10,250,000.

Costs are in $000s, so variable costs are 4,500 × 2,000 = 9,000,000 plus fixed costs of 1,250,000 = total costs of $10,250,000.

Note on incorrect answers:

$10,250 ignores that costs are in 000s

$1,259,000 ignores that variable costs are in 000s as well as fixed costs.

$9,001,250 ignores that fixed costs are in 000s as well as variable costs.

58 The correct answer is: + 0.62.

League position (x)	Team	Spending on players – Rank (y)	Difference (D)	D2
1	Ayville	3	-2	4
2	Beeton	4	-2	4
3	Ceebury	2	1	1
4	Deeford	5	-1	1
5	Easbridge	1	4	16
6	Fetton	8	-2	4
7	Geechester	6	1	1
8	Harcastle	7	1	1
			0	**32**

The formula for calculating rank correlation (R) is:

$$R = 1 - \left[\frac{6\sum d^2}{n(n^2 - 1)} \right]$$

n = numbers of pairs of data

d = difference between the rankings in each set of data

$R = 1 - [(6 \times 32) / (8 \times (64 - 1))]$

$R = 1 - (192 / 504)$

$R = 1 - 0.38$

$R = + 0.62$

59   The correct answer is: 0.91.

n=12

$$r = \frac{n \sum XY - \sum X \sum Y}{\sqrt{[n \sum X^2 - (\sum X)^2][n \sum Y^2 - (\sum Y)^2]}}$$

$$r = \frac{12 \times 3751 - 176 \times 220}{\sqrt{[12 \times 3022 - 176^2][12 \times 4794 - 220^2]}} = 0.91$$

60   The correct answer is: 62% of the variation in Y can be explained by changes in X.

The level of staff training is the independent variable.

Notes on incorrect answers:

0.38 is 0.62 squared. This adjustment would be needed if we were adjusting a correlation coefficient to calculate a coefficient of determination, however here the coefficient of determination is given so no further adjustment is needed.

Tell us what you think

Got comments or feedback on this book? Let us know.
Use your QR code reader:

Or, visit:
https://www.smartsurvey.co.uk/s/VN5OFD/